PASSAGES: KEY MOMENTS IN HISTORY

The End of the Ottoman Empire and the Forging of the Modern Middle East

A Short History with Documents

PASSAGES: KEY MOMENTS IN HISTORY

The End of the Ottoman Empire and the Forging of the Modern Middle East

A Short History with Documents

Martin Bunton and Andrew Wender

Hackett Publishing Company, Inc.
Indianapolis/Cambridge

Copyright © 2025 by Hackett Publishing Company, Inc.

All rights reserved
Printed in the United States of America

28 27 26 25   1 2 3 4 5 6 7

For further information, please address
    Hackett Publishing Company, Inc.
    P.O. Box 44937
    Indianapolis, Indiana 46244-0937

    www.hackettpublishing.com

Cover design by Rick Todhunter
Interior design by Laura Clark
Composition by Aptara, Inc.

Library of Congress Control Number: 2024943505

ISBN-13: 978-1-64792-207-8 (pbk.)
ISBN-13: 978-1-64792-208-5 (PDF ebook)
ISBN-13: 978-1-64792-209-2 (epub)

The paper used in this publication meets the minimum requirements of American National Standard for Information Sciences—Permanence of Paper for Printed Library Materials, ANSI Z39.48–1984.

∞

TABLE OF CONTENTS

Acknowledgments   vii
Chronology   ix
List of Major Figures   xi
Glossary   xv
List of Illustrations   xxiii
List of Maps   xxiv
Preface: Salonica on the Eve of World War I   xxv

Introduction: Reflecting on the End of the Ottoman Empire and the Forging of the Modern Middle East, One Century Later   1

Chapter One: 1798–1914   11

Chapter Two: 1914–1918   54

Chapter Three: 1918 Onward   86

Conclusion: Transformations, Directions, and Entanglements   121

Documents
1. Abd al-Rahman Al-Jabartī's 1798 Condemnation of Egypt's French Occupiers   128
2. 1839 Edict of Gülhane   130
3. 1856 Reform Edict   132
4. 1876 Ottoman Constitution   134
5. 1901 D'Arcy Concession   136
6. Iran's 1906 Constitution and Supplementary Fundamental Laws of 1907   138
7. Jamāl ad-Dīn Al-Afghānī's circa Late-1870s Letter to Abdülhamid II   143
8. Theodor Herzl's 1896 Pamphlet "The Jewish State"   145

Table of Contents

9. Halide Edib's 1908 Recounting of the Young Turk Revolution — 148
10. 1913 Resolution of the Arab-Syrian Congress — 150
11. Mehmed V's 1914 Call to *Jihād* — 151
12. John Buchan's 1916 Novel *Greenmantle* — 153
13. Britain's 1914 Establishment of a Protectorate over Egypt — 155
14. Henry Morgenthau on the "Murder of a Nation," 1918 — 157
15. 1915 Constantinople Agreement — 161
16. 1915–1916 Husayn-McMahon Correspondence — 163
17. Ihsan Turjman's Diary, 1915–1916 — 167
18. Leaflets Thrown from British Airplanes during the Arab Revolt — 170
19. George Antonius, *The Arab Awakening*, 1939 — 171
20. 1915 British Treaty with Ibn Saud — 173
21. 1918 Anglo-French Declaration — 175
22. 1921 Editorial from *The Times* — 176
23. League of Nations Covenant, Article 22, including 1924 Amendments — 177
24. 1919 King-Crane Commission — 179
25. Burning of Smyrna, 1922 — 182
26. Atatürk Declaration, 1927 — 184
27. Reza Shah Pahlavi Coronation, 1926 — 186
28. 1919 Zaghlul Telegram — 188
29. Hudá Sha'rāwi's Memoir of the 1919 Egyptian Revolution — 190
30. 1922 Churchill White Paper — 192
31. 1922 Mandate for Palestine — 195
32. Sāti' al-Husrī on the 1920 Battle of Maysalūn — 199
33. 1920 Muhammad Habib al-'Ubaydi Poem — 202
34. Gertrude Bell, "[W]e've Got Our King Crowned," 1921 — 203

Further Reading — 206
Index — 210

ACKNOWLEDGMENTS

We would like to express sincere thanks to Rick Todhunter for extending the opportunity to undertake this rewarding, challenging project. Rick's kindness and patience have been invaluable through delays owing to the COVID-19 pandemic, family emergencies, and the complexities both of life generally and, more specifically, the history with which this book deals. If we have been at all able to make the latter more digestible for readers, this is due in no small measure to the expertise of Rick and the Hackett team, especially Laura Clark. We also share special gratitude for the invaluable research support from Laurence Claussen, Julianna Nielsen, Samantha Olson, Erin Spence, Hannah-Mariah West, and Darren Reid (who helped draw the maps), and we are pleased to recognize the helpful assistance given by Sophia Anderson, Maya Christensen, Alec Lazenby, and Rowan Salverda.

Andrew: I would like to thank my colleague and friend of twenty-five years, Martin, for the pleasure of collaborating on this book. It has been deeply enriching to work on translating and distilling our conversations, and reciprocal research and teaching interests, into the following pages. My wife, Arezoo Zamany, has been generously steadfast through the peaks and valleys marking the considerable time spent on this project, and she inspires key aspects of Chapter 1, in particular, with all that she teaches me. My daughter Sophia, to evoke her late grandfather Stephen, is truly the spark plug who ignites every day with verve and joy. My brother Jonathan strives to fill with caring the gaps that loss has opened in our family, and this is appreciated with love. As for those gaps and Sophia's above-mentioned paternal grandfather, anything that I might know, and any question that I might think to explore, exists only in concert with my brilliant, wonderful father, whose daily presence I miss profoundly, and whose wisdom and friendship are always with me. My mother, Harriet, and sister Regina, whose daily expressions of love, encouragement, and fortitude also were taken away by historical contingencies during the writing of this book, are always in my heart and mind. The gratitude that I hold for you is without end.

Martin: I need first to thank Andrew for all I have learned from him, his formidable command of the literature and his inspiring resilience in difficult times. It has been a real pleasure to build this project together. To my family, I offer heartfelt thanks for the years of support. My wonderful children, Eila, Peter, and Seth, have curiously followed me through museums and ruins, and (with Cleo) cheerfully stayed with me throughout COVID. My wife, Saija, has, as always, made the world of difference.

Andrew Wender and Martin Bunton
University of Victoria

CHRONOLOGY

1798–1801	Napoleon's campaign in Egypt
1821–1832	Greek War of Independence
1838	Anglo-Ottoman Convention
1839	Gülhane Edict
1856	The Hatt-ı Hümayan (Reform Edict)
1853–1856	Crimean War
1869	Opening of the Suez Canal
1876–1909	Reign of Sultan Abdülhamid II
1876	Ottoman Constitution
1877–1878	Russo-Ottoman War
1882	British occupation of Egypt
1896	Publication of Herzl's *Der Judenstaat*
1898	Kaiser Wilhelm II's visit to Jerusalem
1901	D'Arcy Concession
1908–1909	Young Turk Revolution
1905–1911	Iranian Constitutional Revolution
1911	Italo-Turkish War
1912–1913	Balkan Wars
1913	Arab Congress of Paris
1914	Assassination of Archduke Franz Ferdinand
1914–1918	World War I
1914–1922	British formal protectorate of Egypt
1915–1916	Gallipoli campaign
1915	Arrest and execution of Armenian intellectuals (April 24)
1915	British Treaty with Ibn Saud
1915–1916	Siege of Kut
1915–1916	Husayn-McMahon correspondence
1916	Sykes-Picot Agreement
1916	Arab Revolt begins

Chronology

1917	Balfour Declaration
1917	British capture of Jerusalem
1918	President Woodrow Wilson's Fourteen Points
1918	Mudros Armistice
1918	Anglo-French Declaration
1918–1920	Arab Kingdom of Syria
1918–1920	Flu pandemic
1919	Treaty of Versailles
1919	King-Crane Commission
1919–1920	Paris Peace Conferences
1919–1922	Greco-Turkish War/Turkish War of Independence
1919	French General Gouraud lands at Beirut
1919	Formation of the Wafd Party
1920	San Remo Conference
1920	Treaty of Sèvres
1920	Iraq revolt
1920	Battle of Maysalūn
1921	Winston Churchill's Cairo Conference
1921	Russo-Turkish Treaty March
1921	Faysal crowned king of Iraq
1922	Chanak Crisis
1922	Abolition of the Ottoman Sultanate
1922	Egypt's "Unilateral Declaration of Independence"
1923	Treaty of Lausanne
1924	Abolition of the Ottoman Caliphate
1925–1927	Syrian Great Revolt
1926	Reza Khan crowned shah of Iran
1926	Ibn Saud proclaimed king of Hejaz and Nejd
1932	Iraq's nominal independence
1939	Palestine White Paper

LIST OF MAJOR FIGURES

Abdülhamid II (1842–1918, r. 1876–1909): Sultan and supreme caliph of the Ottoman Empire who attempted to reinvigorate Ottoman Islamic identity, as well as claim broader pan-Islamic leadership, in the face of territorial losses to European rivals. Favored autocratic governance but also sought to modernize and advance Ottoman imperial power.

Abdullah I (1882–1951, r. 1946–1951): Son of Sharif Husayn and brother to Faysal. Presided over emergence of the new state of Transjordan in the post–World War I years.

Abdülmecid (1823–1861, r. 1839–1861): Ottoman sultan who presided over much of the *Tanzimat* era (1839–1876) of administrative reforms.

al-Afghāni, Jamāl ad-Dīn (1838–1897): Iranian-born Shi'i Muslim who advocated for pan-Islamism to combat encroachments of European imperialism across the Muslim world.

Ahmad, Muhammad (1844–1885): Sudanese religious leader and self-proclaimed Mahdi (Islamic messianic figure) who advocated a reinvigoration of purified Islam to combat British occupying forces in Sudan during the 1880s.

Allenby, Edmund (1861–1936): British officer leading the Egyptian Expeditionary Force (EEF) that occupied Jerusalem in 1917. Following the conquest of Ottoman territory in 1918, Allenby divided areas under his control into administrative zones (OETAs) that inaugurated the process by which European powers imposed new state borders onto the Middle East.

Atatürk, Mustafa Kemal (1881–1938): Given the honorific Atatürk, or "Father of the Turks," in 1934, Mustafa Kemal rose to prominence first for his role in defending Gallipoli and then for founding the modern Republic of Turkey. He served as Turkey's first president, and engaged in forcible nation-building, until his death in 1938.

al-ʿAyn, Qurrat (d. 1852): Women's rights activist, poet, scholar who was emblematic of the progressivism and modernist propensities of the Babi movement. Venerated as a martyr in the Bahaʾi faith following her execution in 1852.

Bāb, Sayyed Ali Mohammed (1819–1850): Founder of the Babi movement and subsequent worldwide Bahaʾi faith during the Persian Qajar dynasty. Self-proclaimed "gate" (*bāb*) to the truth who would prepare for the messianic Mahdi's return at the end of time.

al-Banna, Hassan (1906–1949): Egyptian founder in 1928 of the Muslim Brotherhood, which advocated a reinvigoration of Muslim doctrine and practice to overcome Western colonial encroachments.

Churchill, Winston (1874–1965): While serving as Britain's first lord of the admiralty, he helped orchestrate the disastrous 1915–1916 Gallipoli campaign, following which he was demoted. In 1921, having been newly appointed colonial secretary, he convened the Cairo Conference where he boasted his creation of Transjordan "with the stroke of the pen, one Sunday afternoon."

Clemenceau, Georges (1841–1929): Prime minister of France (1906–1909, 1917–1920) who played a crucial role in the negotiations of the Treaty of Versailles after World War I.

Cromer, Lord (1841–1917): British consul general in Egypt who readministered Egyptian finances to European advantage and solidified British dominance in Cairo.

Faysal I (1885–1933): Son of Sharif Husayn and brother to Abdullah. Presided over the Kingdom of Syria, prior to the impositions of the French mandate, and then over the Hashemite Kingdom of Iraq.

Gökalp, Mehmed Ziya (1876–1924): Turkish writer whose ideas of Turkish nationalism manifested in Mustafa Kemal's founding of a Turkish state.

Herzl, Theodor (1860–1904): Vienna-based journalist and early proponent of Zionism who advocated that the founding of a Jewish state was the only solution to continued Jewish persecution.

List of Major Figures

Husayn, Sharif (1854–1931): Custodian of the Muslim holy sites at Mecca and Medina whose negotiations with British high commissioner in Cairo, Sir Henry McMahon, spurred the Arab Revolt of 1916. The Arab Revolt attempted to destabilize the Ottoman Empire during World War I in exchange for British support in the creation of an independent Arab state.

Ibn Saud (1875–1953): Founder and king of Saudi Arabia whose political and territorial expansion from his base in Riyadh was aided by Wahhabi fighters and later by British weapons and subsidies.

al-Jabartī, Abd al-Rahman (1754–1825): Egyptian scholar and cleric critical of the presence of Napoleon's 1798 occupation of Egypt and France's devastating "divide-and-rule" tactics.

Kemal, Mustafa (1881–1938): See Atatürk.

Lawrence, T. E. (1888–1935): Also known as Lawrence of Arabia, his involvement in the Arab Revolt as adviser to Faysal I became legendary with the publication of his memoirs, in which he wrote that "we were quit of the wartime Eastern adventure with clean hands."

Lloyd George, David (1863–1945): Liberal British prime minister (1916–1922) of a coalition government during World War I, who was instrumental in negotiations at the Paris Peace Conferences.

McMahon, Sir Henry (1862–1949): British high commissioner in Cairo whose negotiations with Sharif Husayn and his son Abdullah spurred the 1916 initiation of the Arab Revolt, but whose perceived promises to Husayn conflicted with other pledges.

Muhammad Ali (1769–1849): Ottoman military officer and founder of modern Egypt who modernized the Egyptian military and centralized political control.

Pahlavi, Reza Khan (1878–1944): Later Reza Shah Pahlavi, the first shah of the Pahlavi dynasty after overthrowing the Qajar monarch in 1925. Succeeded by son Mohammad Reza Pahlavi in 1941.

Sykes, Sir Mark (1879–1919): Negotiated 1916 Sykes-Picot Agreement dividing the Middle East between Britain and France along an imaginary line that ran "from the E in Acre to the last K in Kirkuk."

al-Tahtawi, Rifa'a Rafi' (1801–1873): Egyptian translator, scholar, and intellectual sponsored by Muhammad Ali in the 1820s to travel to France for the purposes of acquiring European technical knowledge.

Townshend, Charles (1861–1924): British commander of Allied forces (including many from India) in southern Mesopotamia. Forced to endure a terrible siege at Kut before surrendering; the siege was one of Britain's worst defeats of World War I, but also one of the most forgotten.

Weizmann, Chaim (1874–1952): Biochemist and advocate of Zionism who was instrumental in securing Britain's support as embodied in the 1917 Balfour Declaration.

Wilhelm II (1859–1941): German emperor (kaiser) whose 1890s *weltpolitik* declared Germany as a worldwide defender of Muslims and forged a relationship with Ottoman sultan Abdülhamid II.

Wilson, Woodrow (1856–1924): President of the United States (1913–1921) who advocated self-determination for some (but notably, or perhaps notoriously, not all) colonized peoples at the Paris Peace Conferences following World War I.

Zaghlul, Saad (1859–1927): Sought to lead a delegation to advocate for Egyptian self-determination at the Paris Peace Conferences, but which was rejected by Britain. Went on to lead the Wafd (meaning "delegation" in Arabic) Party and was elected prime minister of Egypt in 1924.

GLOSSARY

Alexandretta: Former Ottoman province, located between Lebanon, Syria, and Turkey, which became part of the French mandate for Syria following World War I, before being ceded to Turkey in 1939 in return for that country's neutrality in World War II.

Anatolia: Historically contested geographical land mass on which the Ottoman Empire was founded and in which present-day Turkey is located.

Anglo-Afghan Wars (1839–1842; 1878–1880; 1919): The first two of these wars, in particular, were conflicts in Britain and Russia's so-called Great Game whereby the two powers vied for influence in Central Asia.

Anglo-French Declaration (1918): Jointly issued by Britain and France immediately following World War I, promising that imperial powers would respect the desires of indigenous populations.

Anglo-Iraqi Treaty (1930): Gradual move toward independence for British-Mandate Iraq (Kingdom of Iraq), while still allowing British military presence and economic privileges.

Anglo-Ottoman Convention (1838): Also known as the Treaty of Balta Limanı, the convention abolished all monopolies in Ottoman territories and granted foreign goods to be imported at low tariff rates.

ANZAC forces: Australian and New Zealand Army Corps; deployed at Gallipoli in 1915.

Arab Revolt (1916): Led by Sharif Husayn's son Faysal, the Arab Revolt played a key role in securing the right flank of the British-led invasion of Ottoman Palestine and Syria. In return, Sharif Husayn was promised a vaguely defined independent Arab kingdom.

Armenian genocide: Committed in 1915 by Ottoman forces, resulting in hundreds of thousands of Armenians being murdered or deported to the Syrian and Iraqi deserts in what proved to be death marches. Turkey still does not recognize the genocide and instead regards the events as a tragic by-product of war.

Armistice of Mudanya (1922): Brought an end to the Chanak Crisis and provided recognition for the Turkish Grand National Assembly as the sole authority in Anatolia.

Babi Revolt: Religious movement and mass uprising led by Sayyed Ali Mohammed (the Bab) in nineteenth-century Qajar Persia. Though violently put down by the Qajar administration and Shi'i clerical class, the Babi Revolt spawned the worldwide Baha'i faith.

Balfour Declaration (1917): Diplomatic statement pledging British support for Zionism and for establishing "a national home for the Jewish people," though without explicit mention of creating a state. This pledge conflicted with other promises made during World War I.

Balkan Wars (1912–1913): Conflicts between the Ottoman Empire and Balkan League (Greece, Bulgaria, Serbia, and Montenegro) that resulted in Ottoman defeat, costing the empire the majority of its European territory and populations.

Berlin Conference (1884–1885): Also known as the Scramble for Africa, the conference regulated European colonial claims in Africa in the second half of the nineteenth century.

Bosporus: Strategic waterway connecting the Black Sea with the Sea of Marmara.

Caliphate: Islamic state under the political and religious leadership of the "caliph," a Muslim religious leader. The term indicates leadership succession from the Prophet Muhammad.

Central Powers: World War I alliance of the Ottoman Empire, Austria-Hungary, Germany, and Bulgaria.

Chanak Crisis (1922): Unsuccessful attempt by Britain to rally imperial troops for another war with Turkish forces led by Mustafa Kemal (see Atatürk). Resulted in the Armistice of Mudanya.

"Civilizing Mission": Imperial rationale employed to justify military, political, and cultural presence in colonial territories while purporting to modernize, Westernize, or civilize indigenous populations.

Committee of Union and Progress (CUP): Group of secularism-minded activists who opposed Sultan Abdülhamid II's autocracy from exile in Paris during the 1890s through the early 1900s.

Cossack Brigade: Cavalry founded in 1879 for the Persian Qajar dynasty but commanded by Russian officers.

Crimean War (1853–1856): Conflict between French, British, and Ottoman forces united against those of Romanov Russia. Spurred by the imperial powers' backing of Ottoman Christian minorities, the war resulted in decisive Russian losses as well as accelerated Ottoman claims to reform.

D'Arcy Concession (1901): Oil agreement between British financier William Knox D'Arcy and Persian Qajar monarch Mozaffar ad-Dīn Shah granting D'Arcy a monopoly on southern reserves.

Eastern Question: Emerging from the 1815 Congress of Vienna, connotes European powers' concern with preserving the balance of power in Europe amid the relative weakness of the Ottoman Empire.

Gallipoli campaign (1915): British and French–planned amphibious landing in the Dardanelles strait. Resulted in a devastating Allied defeat.

"Great Game": Term coined amid the 1839–1842 Anglo-Afghan War, referring to the British-Russian contest to hold sway over a large swath of Central and South Asia.

"Great Revolt" (Syria, 1925–1927): Nationwide uprisings against French rule, beginning with the Jabal Druze rebellion in 1925. Brutally suppressed by the French but resulted in notable political concessions.

"Great Revolt" (Palestine, 1936–1939): Palestinian nationalist rebellion against British colonial rule, put down by harsh counterinsurgency methods but also forcing a reevaluation of British policy (see White Paper).

Greco-Turkish War (1919–1922): Conflict emerging from Greek claims to former Byzantine lands in western Anatolia and culminating with Turkish victory and the forcible population exchange of Christians and Muslims.

Greek War of Independence (1821–1832): Nationalist revolt against Ottoman control, with British, French, and Russian support, that culminated in Greek independence.

Gülhane Edict (1839): Inaugurated Abdülmecid I's *Tanzimat* era of reforms, including promises of personal security for all Ottoman citizens, Muslim as well as non-Muslim.

Hashemites: Clan descended from the Prophet Muhammad's Quraysh tribe, notable members of which include Sharif Husayn and his sons Faysal and Abdullah.

Hatt-ı Hümayan (Reform Edict) (1856): *Tanzimat*-era reform that eliminated religious distinctions and abolished the collection of the *jizya* tax paid by non-Muslims. Referred to in modern Turkish as Islahat Fermanı.

Hejaz Railway: Connecting Aleppo with Mecca and Medina, a railway built to transfer pilgrims (and military forces) as part of an effort to better integrate distant Arabian provinces.

Husayn-McMahon Correspondence (1915–1916): Negotiations between the British government and the family of Sharif Husayn, by which Britain purported to support Arab independence in exchange for Sharif Husayn's launching of the Arab Revolt (1916).

"Iron Wall": Concept promoted by revisionist Zionist Vladimir Jabotinsky advocating for the use of military might to secure the borders of a Jewish state (see Zionism).

Irridentism: Doctrine advocating, often on the basis of shared history, language, or race, the restoration of any territory formerly belonging to a nation-state. The idea was born from the formative nineteenth-century era of Italian nationalism.

Italo-Turkish War (1911–1912): Conflict between Italy and the Ottoman Empire over Italian claims to Libya, resulting in Italian victory.

Jihād: Arabic word meaning to strive or struggle in God's path.

King-Crane Commission (1919): Inter-Allied commission appointed by US president Wilson to survey public opinion in Palestine, Syria, Anatolia, and Lebanon.

League of Nations: Founded in 1920 with the aim of preserving world peace, the League was officially responsible through the Permanent Mandates Commission (PMC) for the oversight of mandated territories.

Majles: Persian legislative body emerging from the 1905–1911 Constitutional Revolution.

Mandate/Mandatory: Legally, the status conferred by the League of Nations to describe the administrative control of a particular territory by a foreign power following World War I; in practical terms, a fig leaf for colonialism.

Maronites: Christian denomination residing primarily in Lebanon.

Millet system: Refers to the limited ability of recognized religious denominations to regulate their own affairs under Ottoman rule.

Mudros Armistice (1918): Specified the unconditional surrender of the Ottoman Empire and set the stage for European expansion in former Ottoman lands.

Muslim Brotherhood: Activist organization founded in 1928 by Egyptian schoolteacher Hassan al-Banna that, along with chapters in neighboring Arab countries, advocated a reinvigoration of Muslim doctrine and practice to overcome Western colonial encroachments and corruption.

Nahda: Meaning "awakening" or "renaissance," a *Tanzimat*-era Arab literary flowering that brought about thriving cosmopolitan intellectual, literary, and political cultures throughout the empire.

OETA [Occupied Enemy Territory Administration] (1918–1920): Various zones of military occupation, set up by Lord Allenby following his victory over Ottoman forces.

Orientalism: As characterized during the 1970s by Palestinian-American scholar Edward Said, a Western mindset in which Western colonial powers justify their self-perception as rightfully dominant over the supposedly underdeveloped and uncivilized East ("Orient").

Ottoman Constitution (1876): Capstone of the *Tanzimat* era of reforms, provided for an elected chamber of representatives and reaffirmed equality for all citizens of the Ottoman Empire.

Paris Peace Conferences (1919–1920): International meetings of Allied powers following World War I with the aim of negotiating the terms of peace.

Peel Commission Report (1937): British inquiry, following from 1936 Palestinian uprising, which recommended the Palestine mandate be terminated in favor of a hurried plan of partition.

Qajar dynasty (1789–1925): Persian dynasty overthrown by Reza Khan in 1925.

Russo-Ottoman War (1877–1878): Military conflict between Romanov Russia and the Ottoman Empire resulting in Russian victory, official recognition of the independence of the Balkan states, and Ottoman cessation of three provinces (Kars, Batum, and Ardahan).

San Remo Conference (1920): Post–World War I Allied conference allotting Arab mandates to the British and French Empires.

Sectarian(ism): Indicates strict delineation between and contentious division among religious denominations, often stemming from or exacerbated by manipulative European imperial tactics of "divide and rule."

Seferberlik: Devastating general mobilization of Ottoman society in August 1914, including mass conscription and the centralization of trade and agriculture.

Shi'i Islam: Second largest branch of Islam after Sunnism. Refers to Muslims who believe the Prophet Muhammad's rightful successor was his son-in-law, Ali ibn Abi Talib (see also Sunni Islam).

Siege of Kut (1915–1916): Mass starvation of British colonial troops under siege at Kut, leading to unconditional British surrender in April 1916.

Suez Canal: Egyptian waterway completed in 1869 connecting the Mediterranean and Red Seas and facilitating trade with India. Became known as the "jugular vein" of Britain's empire.

Sunni Islam: Largest branch of Islam. Refers to Muslims who believe Abu Bakr, the first caliph, to be the Prophet Muhammad's rightful successor.

Sykes-Picot Agreement (1916): Clandestine agreement between Britain and France to partition former Ottoman lands following the end of World War I. Came into direct conflict with other vague wartime promises.

Tanzimat **(1839–1876):** Meaning "reordering," refers to an 1839–1876 period of wide-ranging administrative reforms within the Ottoman Empire, affecting institutions like the military, law, and education. Motivated by the Ottomans' perceived need to keep pace with European rivals (see also Gülhane Edict; Hatt-ı Hümayan [Reform Edict]; and Ottoman Constitution).

"Three Lost Provinces": The Ottoman provinces of Kars, Batum, and Ardahan, located on the Black Sea, which were annexed by Russia in the Treaty of San Stefano in 1878 and whose recapture was a major irredentist Ottoman military objective during World War I.

Treaty of Balta Limanı (1838): See Anglo-Ottoman Convention.

Treaty of Constantinople (1913): Concluded the Second Balkan War, which facilitated the Ottoman Empire's regaining the European territory of Edirne.

Treaty of Lausanne (1923): Negotiated following the Greco-Turkish War, it abrogated the Treaty of Sèvres and established the borders of the Republic of Turkey.

Treaty of Sèvres (1920): Signed between the Allied powers and defeated Ottoman Empire following World War I, the treaty initiated the partition of former Ottoman lands between the victorious powers.

Triple Entente: Describes the pre–World War I alignment of Britain, France, and Russia that served as a countering force to the Central Alliance.

Triumvirate: The dictatorial "Three Pashas" of the late Ottoman Empire who came to power following the 1913 Ottoman coup (Enver Pasha, Cemal Pasha, and Talat Pasha).

'Urabi Revolt (1879–1882): Egyptian uprising led by Ahmad 'Urabi who challenged the rule of Tawfiq, the European-backed ruler of Egypt. The revolt resulted in Britain invasion and occupation of Egypt.

Wafd Party: From the Arabic term for "delegation," an Egyptian political party founded by Saad Zaghlul from the delegation of Egyptian public figures who were prevented by Britain from arguing their case for Egyptian self-determination at the Paris Peace Conferences.

Wahhabi(sm): Conservative form of Sunni Islamic revivalism that emerged in the eighteenth century and in the nineteenth and twentieth centuries effectively allied with Ibn Saud to found present-day Saudi Arabia.

White Paper (1939): Policy issued by the British government following the Palestinian revolt (1936–1939), which placed limits on Jewish immigration and land purchase and called for an independent Palestinian state within ten years.

Young Turk Revolution (1908–1909): Uprising against Abdülhamid II's rule, led by the Committee for Union and Progress. Culminated in the 1909 exiling of Abdülhamid to Salonica and the CUP's dominance of Ottoman governance (see Committee of Union and Progress).

Zionism: Form of Jewish nationalism, classically articulated by Theodor Herzl, in which shared traits of religion, culture, ethnicity, and language are deemed to legitimate the reestablishment of a political community situated in the biblical land of Israel.

LIST OF ILLUSTRATIONS

Unless otherwise noted, all illustrations are in the public domain.

1.	Salonica	xxviii
2.	Egyptian workers on the Suez Canal	29
3.	The Eastern Question cartoon	35
4.	Comparative entries into Jerusalem: Kaiser Wilhelm II in 1898 and General Edmund Allenby in 1917	37
5.	Celebrating the Ottoman constitutional regime	47
6.	The Ottoman Camel Corps at Beersheba, 1915	62
7.	The Last Crusade cartoon	64
8.	Balfour Declaration, 1917	65
9.	Armenians who escaped from the Turkish starvation zone approach British lines	70
10.	A pictorial cotton map of the Gallipoli campaign	72
11.	Sykes-Picot Agreement of 1916	75
12.	Hanging of Arab nationalists in Damascus, 1916	76
13.	Sharif Husayn, guardian of the holy places	78
14.	"British Maurice Farman Attacked by a German Fokker While Dropping Sacks of Corn on Kut"	80
15.	Liberated prisoners, Kut al-Amara	81
16.	Occupied Enemy Territory Administrations	84
17.	Allied Supreme Council at San Remo, 1920	94
18.	Mustafa Kemal, 1919	96
19.	Henri Gouraud with the Maronite patriarch and the Sunni mufti	104
20.	Arab forces enter Damascus, 1918	110
21.	Coronation of King Faysal in Baghdad, 1921	115
22.	Screenshot that was originally posted to social media by ISIS, when declaring an end to Sykes-Picot	126

LIST OF MAPS

1. Middle East 1914 53
2. World War I battlefronts in the Middle East 61
3. Treaty of Sèvres 95
4. Middle East mandates post–World War I 103

PREFACE
Salonica on the Eve of World War I

An Empire in Decline?

After enduring for longer than six centuries (c. 1300–1922), the Ottoman Empire dissolved approximately 100 years ago. One of the longest-lived empires in world history, it was defeated at the end of World War I (1914–1918) alongside the German and Austro-Hungarian Empires. Prior to the war, a typical presumption was that the Ottomans' demise was imminent. Its perceived decline was captured by the popular expression, the "sick man of Europe" (a phrase coined within the context of 1850s diplomacy between Romanov Russia and Britain, over how the sick man's remains might be divided between rival European powers). The Ottomans' death was suggested to be foreordained by their presumed inability to keep pace with modern progress. The Ottoman decline thesis, as this reading of history might be termed, is the product of many voices, beginning with early-modern-era (1500s and 1600s) European Christians. At that point, the Ottomans' territorial holdings extended deep into eastern and central Europe, North Africa, and southwestern Asia. Accordingly, disparaging notions of Ottoman despotism belied a deeper concern with countering, as well as fearful admiration for, an expansionist Islamic empire at the peak of its dominance. Then, after more than a century of Ottoman territorial rollback beginning in the late 1600s, European diplomats at the 1815 Congress of Vienna brought to the fore the watershed "Eastern Question": namely, how the Ottomans' increasingly vulnerable hold over valuable and strategic territory might ultimately upset Europe's balance of power. Even after the Ottomans' defeat in WWI, the rulers of its successor states continued to benefit from perpetuating this view of the ancien régime as an exhausted and disreputable anachronism. No voice was as emblematic as the 1920s declarations of Mustafa Kemal (Atatürk, or "Father of the

Turks," 1881–1938): though he had just served the Islamic empire heroically as an Ottoman military officer, he now insisted that it belonged to a "bygone era" and demanded replacement by the new foundations of a Turkish nation-state.

However, a decidedly different historical reading has reached prominence in recent decades. The self-congratulatory idea of enlightened European progress inexorably triumphing over inherent Ottoman backwardness has come under sharp critique. Ironically, the revised interpretation is neatly exemplified by a glimpse of Atatürk's own birthplace, the Aegean Sea port city of Salonica, shortly prior to the outbreak of WWI. (Salonica became known as Thessaloniki, once the city was claimed by Greece after the 1912–1913 Balkan Wars.) One of the Ottoman Empire's main port cities, Salonica was in fact a conduit among cultures surrounding the Mediterranean basin. It thus captured a singular cosmopolitanism that had been fostered by Ottoman governance from the 1800s onward.[1] The origins of Salonica's cultural and religious mosaic reached as far back as the expulsion of Jews from Iberia after the 1492 Reconquista. With the Reconquista, Christian kingdoms completed the displacement of Islamic rule in Iberia, which had reached its peak with the storied Cordoba caliphate (c. tenth–eleventh centuries) that epitomized learning across religious, cultural, and linguistic lines. Iberia's loss was the Ottomans' gain, as a large proportion of expelled Jews resettled throughout the empire's lands. By the nineteenth century, as much as half of Salonica's population was Jewish, living alongside Muslims and Christians.[2] Salonica's multireligious demography also underscores how the Ottoman Empire had been built atop Greek Christian (and thereby the Eastern Roman Empire or Byzantium's) roots absorbed through the Ottomans' 1453 conquest of Constantinople. As viewed in this light, the Ottomans straddled cultural as well as geographic continental divides, presiding over an empire that was simultaneously European, Asian, and African. The Ottomans' own seat

---

1. Mark Mazower, *Salonica, City of Ghosts: Christians, Muslims and Jews, 1430–1950* (New York: Vintage, 2006).

2. Sarah Abrevaya Stein, *Family Papers: A Sephardic Journey Through the Twentieth Century* (New York: Farrar, Straus and Giroux, 2019). On the legacies of Jewish life in Salonica, see also Devin E. Naar, *Jewish Salonica: Between the Ottoman Empire and Modern Greece* (Stanford, CA: Stanford University Press, 2016).

of power in Istanbul lay atop and integrated Eastern Christian motifs like the Church of Hagia Sophia (which was converted to a mosque following the 1453 conquest of Constantinople). In fact, Istanbul had been home to more Christian than Muslim residents for a brief time during the mid-1800s. (Interestingly, the Ottomans alternately referred to both Kostantiniyye, the Turkish rendition for the "city's Byzantine name," and the Greek-derived Istanbul, which would become "the ... official name [only] in 1930.")[3]

Over centuries, the Ottomans had practiced the classical Islamic *dhimmi* principle. The *dhimmi* principle extended legal protection to "people of the Book" (specifically, Jews and Christians, inasmuch as their genealogy stemming from the biblical prophet Abraham was shared with Islam), as well as Zoroastrians, in exchange for the payment of a poll tax called *jizya*. However, nineteenth-century Ottoman reforms significantly enhanced the status of non-Muslims. During the 1839–1876 *Tanzimat*, or "reordering" era, fully equal rights were extended to all Ottoman citizens, irrespective of their religion. Salonica became an avatar for the Ottomans' innovative policies, at least insofar as these policies worked to the benefit of non-Muslims in urban areas (e.g., conditions for peasants might have remained much less advantageous). Relative prosperity flourished across differing strata of religion and class. By the first decade of the twentieth century, Salonica emerged as a base for activists who wanted to strengthen the empire by bolstering its stalled movement toward constitutionalism.

So consider a few of the personal perspectives that might have been in play in this bustling port. First, let us not lose sight of a British or French banker or industrialist—with his own stake in, and predetermined perceptions of, Ottoman affairs—picking up a European newspaper that could only affirm his expatriate community's anxiety about a declining Ottoman Empire and a foreboding summation to the Eastern Question. However, were a Jewish civil servant in Ottoman employ to be seated in a nearby Salonica coffeehouse, while reading from among a multilingual variety of newspapers, listening to the city's polyglot music, and surrounded by excited preparations for Sultan Mehmet V's (1844–1918, r. 1909–1918) visit in 1911, he might well have reflected more on a

---

3. Caroline Finkel, *Osman's Dream: The History of the Ottoman Empire* (New York: Basic Books, 2007), 57.

Postcard image of the bustling seaport at the late Ottoman-era, multicultural and commercially significant city Salonica.

halcyon world than one whose ending was nigh. But let us also accept that this relatively content member of Salonica's Jewish community, committed to what we will come to see as the Ottoman Empire's emerging, proto-nationalist and multicultural identity of Ottomanism, likely would have perceived matters quite differently than a much less privileged person. One of the nearby port workers might well have in his hand a pamphlet deploring the plight of profound inequality published by the burgeoning Salonica workers' movement that ended up auguring, so to speak, the storm to come after the calm.[4]

The endpoints that are superimposed onto the direction of history, by way of interpretation undertaken after the fact, are not necessarily those toward which history was headed, if indeed history is ever headed anywhere in particular. History may be rather more like that contented Salonica coffeehouse patron, or for that matter the discontented port laborer, lacking any foresight of what events might prove to radically transform the surrounding world, springing right around the bend. The positions we each occupy inevitably shape our after-the-fact interpretations of history. This includes our sense of whether a past era might

---

4. Mazower, *Salonica: City of Ghosts*, 265, 267.

be regarded with fond nostalgia or as a time whose passage was long overdue.

In considering such contending perspectives on history, we would encourage you to reflect on how today's news concerning the Middle East might impact your own perceptions of the region (including its past and future). What presuppositions and preconceptions might you as a reader bring to bear on this book's historical narrative and primary documents?

INTRODUCTION

Reflecting on the End of the Ottoman Empire and the Forging of the Modern Middle East, One Century Later

Why This Book and Why Now? The World War I Centenary and the Present-Day Middle East

Coinciding in recent years with the unfolding centenaries of World War I and its aftermath, there has been a proliferation of literature and public reflection on the significances of this unprecedented, modern global conflict. WWI left both a cataclysmic trail of devastation, and transformative influences for countless dimensions of life and society—from gender roles, to rapid technological developments in communication, transportation, and weaponry, to changes of consciousness in the arts, learning, and scientific inquiry, to remaking of the world map and international legal order through the collapse and expansion of empires, as well as multiple revolutions. These consequences continually remind us why WWI was known as the Great War, before the Second World War had ensued. The futile carnage of the Western Front within Europe (crucial though it was) continues to dominate historical perceptions of the war. But a pivotal theme emphasized throughout centenary commemorations has been WWI's truly global nature. The conflict was fought among, across the terrain, and by the diverse subjects of numerous globe-spanning empires: Britain, France, Germany, Romanov Russia, Austria-Hungary, Italy, the United States (US), Japan, and the Ottomans.[1] The fate of the last of these is the focus of this book.

---

1. Jörn Leonhard, *Pandora's Box: A History of the First World War*, trans. Patrick Camiller (Cambridge, MA: Harvard University Press, 2018).

This heightened awareness of WWI as a war that reshaped the entire world has also drawn attention to its ongoing implications for twenty-first-century global affairs. In this regard, there has been distinct concern with the question of how the Ottoman Empire's dissolution, together with the folding of much Ottoman heritage into the post-WWI expansion of British and French Empires, connects to turmoil reverberating across today's Middle East. Here lies, in the most direct sense, the inspiration for this book: the end of the Ottoman Empire is germinal to the formation of a geographic area that has come to be thought of and referred to as the "Middle East," the term itself being largely unknown prior to the war. Indeed, it is difficult to think of any present turbulent scenario throughout the Middle East whose underlying history is not in some way linked with the end of the Ottoman Empire. A non-exhaustive accounting highlights the following manifestations of outside interference in WWI's aftermath.

The long-festering Israel/Palestine conflict, most recently re-exploded in the devastating 2023– war between Israel and the Gaza-based Islamic organization Hamas, can be traced back to Britain's wartime decision to throw support behind the emergent Zionist, or Jewish nationalist, movement just as Britain moved to conquer Palestine from the Ottomans in late 1917. Iraq's descent into devastating intercommunal violence, following from the US's 2003 overthrow of the Saddam Hussein regime, points to Iraq's origins; namely, the early-1920s assemblage of three Ottoman *vilayets* (provinces) into a highly centralized and hierarchical British colony. Similarly, Syria's still-smoldering civil war, one of the most destructive such conflicts in modern history, as well as an inordinately complex proxy war drawing in both Middle East and global powers, traces to French colonial tactics of sectarian divide and rule. Lebanon's continuing struggle with the legacies of intercommunal civil strife is also closely interconnected with the post-WWI history of Syria, from which France, on behalf of their Maronite Christian allies, carved out Greater Lebanon as a separate mandate. In each of these situations, the imposition of authoritarian colonial systems of governance was structured around the demarcation and patronage of minority religious and ethnic communities.

As for Turkey, the present government led by a self-styled sultan, Recep Tayyip Erdoğan (1954–, leader since 2003), is characterized by geopolitically assertive nostalgia for the Ottomans' Islamic-based legitimacy. In sharp divergence from the nationalist republic created from

Ottoman ruins under Mustafa Kemal's (Atatürk; 1881–1938) stridently secularist leadership in 1923, Erdoğan's posturing has supported Turkish intervention in the post-2011 Syrian and Libyan civil conflicts. Libya, for its part, also factors into this book's broader story, in that the country's foundation was shaped by Italian colonial conquest from the Ottomans during the 1911–1912 Italo-Turkish War.

Further beyond the Arab world, the neo-Ottoman policies of early twenty-first-century Turkey see it embroiled within other conflict situations echoing the end of the Ottoman Empire. These include contestation with Greece over natural resources in the eastern Mediterranean, as well as opposition to unrealized Kurdish nationalist aspirations that had surged with the Ottomans' WWI defeat. Moreover, there is Turkey's intervention on behalf of Azerbaijan in its ongoing fight against Armenia over the latter's redoubt of Nagorno-Karabakh. Russian-backed Armenia is a resolute foe of Turkey's, due to the Ottomans' violent repression of Armenians from the late nineteenth century through the widely recognized (but Turkish-denied) Armenian genocide undertaken by Ottoman forces during WWI. Salient, too, is the Russia-Ukraine war sparked by Vladimir Putin's 2022 invasion of what he declares to be a nonexistent country lying at the historical heart of Russian imperial culture once presided over by the Ottomans' Romanov rivals. The ambivalence with which Erdoğan has positioned himself in relation to the Russian assault, notwithstanding Turkey's membership since 1952 in the North Atlantic Treaty Organization (NATO) opposing Putin, attests to a tense mixture of historical and contemporary factors. On the one hand, Erdoğan was forced to come to terms with his fellow, neo-imperial autocrat Putin over conflicting interests in Syria, when Russia intervened during 2015 to prop up Damascus's Bashar al-Assad (1965–, leader since 2000) regime. Then there is Ukraine's Crimean Peninsula—a center of gravity amid Russian-Ukrainian hostilities, jutting into the Black Sea basin that was fought over by the Ottomans and Russians during WWI and that remains a fault line between Ankara and Moscow today. Under the Treaty of Küçük Kaynarca, the Romanovs took Crimea from the Ottomans in the 1770s, and the region's Tatar Muslims were expelled into Ottoman territory. Moreover, Russia's subsequent attack on the Ottomans in the 1853–1856 Crimean War is pivotal to the story told in this book.

In all events, we wish to underscore that the study of history cannot be reduced to the high-level deliberation of power brokers over the disposition of resources and territory. The fact that history entails the narration of all people's lived experiences, the agony and the ecstasy, as it were, is poignantly made by the eminent Russian writer, spiritual seeker, and critic of war-making, Leo Tolstoy (1828–1910). While chronicling the Siege of Sevastopol during the Crimean War, Tolstoy wrote:

> Yes, there are white flags on the bastions and the trenches but the flowery valley is covered with dead bodies. The glorious sun is sinking towards the blue sea, and the undulating blue sea glitters in the golden light. Thousands of people crowd together, look at, speak to, and smile at one another. And these people—Christians professing the one great law of love and self-sacrifice—on seeing what they have done do not at once fall repentant on their knees before Him who has given them life and laid in the soul of each a fear of death and a love of the good and the beautiful and do not embrace like brothers with tears of joy and gladness.
>
> The white flags are lowered, the engines of death and suffering are sounding again, innocent blood is flowing, and the air is filled with moans and curses.
>
> There, I have said what I wished to say this time. But I am seized by an oppressive doubt. Perhaps I ought to have left it unsaid. What I have said perhaps belongs to that class of evil truths that lie unconsciously hidden in the soul of each man and should not be uttered lest they become harmful, as the dregs in a bottle must not be disturbed for fear of spoiling the wine....
>
> Where in this tale is the evil that should be avoided, and where the good that should be imitated? Who is the villain and who the hero of the story? All are good and all are bad....
>
> The hero of my tale—whom I love with all the power of my soul, whom I have tried to portray in all his beauty, who has been, is, and will be beautiful—is Truth.[2]

Nor is it only the status of former Ottoman lands that are relevant to the book's broader narrative. Most prominently, Persia (today's Iran), a historical rival of the Ottomans that was ruled by the Qajar dynasty

---

2. Leo Tolstoy, *Sevastopol*, in John Bayley, ed., *The Portable Tolstoy* (Harmondsworth, UK: Penguin, 1978), 293.

from the 1790s to the 1920s, saw a post-WWI transition to the authoritarian Pahlavi dynasty. The Pahlavis' secularizing, Westernizing paradigm of modern nation-state building, modeled in part on that of Atatürk, roused to action the 1979 revolutionaries. Their establishment of the Islamic Republic of Iran has profoundly affected regional and global affairs ever since. Moreover, Afghanistan's age-old reputation as the "graveyard of empires" was most recently underscored by the US's chaotic 2021 withdrawal, after two decades of military intervention following the September 11, 2001, al-Qaeda attacks. In the Third Anglo-Afghan War of 1919, Afghanistan took advantage of post-WWI opportunities to wrestle away from Britain's India-based sphere of dominance.

Striving to better understand how the present-day world came to be, including how claims to territories and expressions of peoplehood have been (re-)articulated and (re-)asserted, offers an important reason to study history. Notwithstanding, it is extremely difficult for historians not to import current conditions and perceptions into their assessments of history.[3] Still, one must beware the "presentist" hazard of distorting the past by viewing it through a present-day lens. The Ottoman decline thesis critiqued in the preface underscores the characteristically modern tendency of imagining that all history has been "progressing" toward a self-ascribed, high point of enlightenment. We are not seeking to make it seem as if the end of the Ottoman Empire and forging of the modern Middle East were following any sort of fated path leading toward early twenty-first-century conflicts. Quite the contrary: emphasis is often placed on contingencies. Chance events acted as pivotal factors helping to make events turn out in one way rather than another—for instance, the Ottomans' non-predetermined 1914 decision to join the war on the side of Germany.

We are fortunate to be able to draw on a fast-growing body of literature foregrounding WWI as a turning point—a historical "passage," to invoke the series title in which this book appears. There has of course been long historical memory within Middle East states and societies recognizing the role that imperial power, and resistance to it, played before, during, and after WWI. Within English-language literature, there appeared by the late 1980s a more wide-scale engagement with the

---

3. For a compelling discussion of this premise, see James M. Banner, Jr., *The Ever-Changing Past: Why All History Is Revisionist History* (New Haven, CT: Yale University Press, 2021).

question of how WWI, and the resulting Ottoman defeat, prompted the emergence of new Middle East states and societies.[4] This literature has vastly expanded over the past decade or so, as the WWI centenary coincided with early twenty-first-century Middle East turmoil, demonstrating the extent to which such turmoil was bound together with events surrounding the war.[5] Within some Anglophone societies, there has been for decades especial awareness of the Ottoman theater's centrality to WWI. A key example would be how the evolution of national identities in Australia and New Zealand have been entwined with formative experiences of the Australian and New Zealand Army Corps (ANZAC) in the 1915–1916 Gallipoli campaign. Although some within those two countries regard Gallipoli as a moment that forged their new nations, the protracted campaign saw well dug-in Ottoman forces successfully defend the Dardanelles waterway from an Anglo-French amphibious assault (which also included South Asian colonial troops and Canadian Newfoundlanders). Though devastating for all sides, the Ottoman victory impressed upon Britain the formidable military capabilities of their Ottoman foe (this, after British military planners had been dismissing the Ottoman Empire as a "sick man" and the Ottoman battlefront as a mere "sideshow").

---

4. Starting, most notably, with David Fromkin, *A Peace to End All Peace: The Fall of the Ottoman Empire and the Creation of the Modern Middle East* (New York: Henry Holt, 2009 [1989]).

5. For example, see the following: James Barr, *A Line in the Sand: Britain, France and the Struggle That Shaped the Middle East* (London: Simon & Schuster, 2011); Scott Anderson, *Lawrence in Arabia: War, Deceit, Imperial Folly and the Making of the Modern Middle East* (New York: Doubleday, 2013); Ali A. Allawi, *Faisal I of Iraq* (New Haven, CT: Yale University Press, 2014); Ian Rutledge, *Enemy on the Euphrates* (London: Saqi, 2014); Kristian Coates Ulrichsen, *The First World War in the Middle East* (London: Hurst, Ulrichsen, 2014); Eugene Rogan, *The Fall of the Ottomans: The Great War in the Middle East* (New York: Basic Books, 2015); Sean McMeekin, *The Ottoman Endgame: War, Revolution, and the Making of the Modern Middle East, 1908–1923* (New York: Penguin, 2016); Rob Johnson, *The Great War and the Middle East* (Oxford: Oxford University Press, 2016); M. E. McMillan, *From the First World War to the Arab Spring: What's Really Going On in the Middle East?* (New York: Palgrave Macmillan, 2016); and Laila Parsons, *The Commander: Fawzi Al-Qawuqji and the Fight for Arab Independence, 1914–1948* (New York: Farrar, Strauss and Giroux, 2016).

Introduction: Reflecting on the End of the Ottoman Empire 7

Defining the "Middle East"

Central to this book's narrative is that the idea of a geographic area constituting the "Middle East" is distinctly modern. The idea is largely the product of Western geopolitical interests and intellectual as well as civilizational perceptions. This is revealed in the Western colonial origins of the term itself: "Middle East" is often regarded as having been coined in 1902 by the US Navy officer and professor Captain Alfred T. Mahan (1840–1914) who, according to Huseyin Yilmaz,

> [g]ave ... [it] a strategic and geopolitical cast by defining it in relation to maritime routes essential for military control of the area. Although he was an American naval officer, Mahan's region was an exclusively British definition of the area constructed in response to the objectives and capabilities of sea power.[6]

This is not to say that all aspects of the idea remain invalid alien representations of the region. Millions of people with diverse national, ethnic, and religious identities now reflexively refer to themselves as coming from the Middle East, the term's underlying Western colonial implications notwithstanding. Moreover, the complexities of world history being what they are, artificial binary constructs like "West" and "East" necessarily signify interpenetrating sets of influences. Thus, for instance, the great Arab historian and sometimes-asserted, proto-modern social scientist Ibn Khaldun (1332–1406) differentiated between *maghrib* (west) and *mashriq* (east) in speaking about geographic settings for Arab history. Related to the manner in which Ibn Khaldun linked the two terms with North Africa, Maghreb today generally refers to Morocco, Algeria, and Tunisia, countries which some regard as located neither within "Africa nor the Middle East."[7] Yet, exemplifying the ambiguity of geographic signifiers, others

---

6. Huseyin Yilmaz, "The Eastern Question and the Ottoman Empire: The Genesis of the Near and Middle East in the Nineteenth Century," in Michael E. Bonine, Abbas Amanat, and Michael Ezekiel Gasper, eds., *Is There a Middle East?: The Evolution of a Geopolitical Concept* (Stanford, CA: Stanford University Press, 2012), 24–25.

7. Abdelmajid Hannoum, *The Invention of the Maghreb: Between Africa and the Middle East* (Cambridge: Cambridge University Press, 2021), 6.

today perceive these countries as part of a broader Middle East and North Africa (MENA) region.

The specific genealogy underlying the Anglo-American–framed Middle East idea is revealing. As far back as the early 1800s, the seminal German Romantic poet Johann Wolfgang von Goethe (1749–1832), who held a singular fascination for Persian Islam, "used the term *Mittler Orient* . . . in reference to Persia and her neighbors."[8] This usage informed widespread, nineteenth-century European applications of the notion to Persia and India, including by some British commentators—not least, George Curzon (best known as Lord Curzon, 1859–1925), while serving as viceroy of the British Raj in India. Throughout the 1800s, European writers and policymakers consumed with the Ottoman-focused "Eastern Question" often tended to use "Near East" or "Nearer East." They also referenced the "Levant," a French-originating term indicating the direction from which the sun rises (that is, eastern Mediterranean lands like present-day Lebanon, Syria, Israel, and Palestine), and more broadly "ancient civilizations between Mesopotamia and the Nile, including the Aegean."[9]

Thus, by the time Mahan entered the picture, the Persian Gulf was central to unfolding understandings of the Middle East. The Gulf and "South Persia" constituted a geopolitical pivot connecting what was by this time the British-occupied (if still theoretically Ottoman-held) Suez Canal region, and thereby "the Suez route to the farther East which lies between Aden and Singapore," with "the Levant," "Euphrates valley" (i.e., present-day Iraq), and "India . . . to the East beyond."[10] Mahan's classic, pre-WWI articulation implies a remarkably broad geographic scope. As such, "Middle East" could come to connote a sphere of influence extending from the Mediterranean basin, through the Arabian Peninsula, Persian Gulf region, and Afghanistan. While promising access to Asian realms beyond, this strategic vision stretched, as is sometimes quipped, from the Straits of Gibraltar to the Straits of Malacca.[11] Further noteworthy is that, from Mahan's vantage point some 120 years ago, naval power reigns supreme, proliferating railways notwithstanding:

---

8. Yilmaz, "Eastern Question and the Ottoman Empire," 24.

9. Yilmaz, "Eastern Question and the Ottoman Empire," 23.

10. Alfred Thayer Mahan, *Retrospect and Prospect: Studies in International Relations, Naval and Political* (Boston: Little, Brown, 1902), 235–39.

11. See Zachary Lockman, *Contending Visions of the Middle East: The History and Politics of Orientalism* (Cambridge: Cambridge University Press, 2010), 97.

The Middle East, if I may adopt a term which I have not seen, will someday need its Malta, as well as its Gibraltar; it does not follow that either will be in the Gulf.... The British Navy should have the facility to concentrate in force, if occasion arise, about Aden, India, and the Gulf.

In summary ... there exists now the sea route by Suez, which is, and probably must remain, supreme to all others. Alternative to it, in part of the way, the future will doubtless bring railways. These, however, on account of the greater cheapness of water carriage, will pretty surely do their principal business in expediting special transit between the two seas—the Mediterranean and the Indian Ocean.... Between them and the Suez route there will be the perennial conflict between land and water transport, between natural and artificial conditions, in which the victory is likely to rest, as heretofore, with nature's own highway, the sea. But, however that prove, the beginning and the end, the termini, of both routes, land and sea ... will be substantially the same: the Levant Sea [i.e., the eastern Mediterranean], the Straits of Bab-el-Mandeb [i.e., the outlet from the Red Sea lying between the southwestern Arabian Peninsula and the eastern "horn" of Africa] and the Persian Gulf.[12]

Writing against the immediate historical backdrop of the US's conquest of Cuba, Puerto Rico, Guam, and the Philippines in the 1898 Spanish-American War, as well as the (projected) Panama Canal, the American Mahan serves to augur a future historical environment in which rising, interventionist US global power would help shape conceptions of the Middle East.

Still pre-WWI, Mahan's paradigm "was soon taken up by various individuals, most of whom were related to the Anglo-Indian world": on Daniel Foliard's evocative assessment, among them were "constructive imperialists, Greater Britain sycophants, and Curzonian expansionists."[13] Yet regional circumstances shifted during the lead-up to the war. Through early twentieth-century events that we will soon discuss, like the 1907

---

12. Mahan, *Retrospect and Prospect*, 237–39.

13. Daniel Foliard, *Dislocating the Orient: British Maps and the Making of the Middle East, 1854–1921* (Chicago: University of Chicago Press, 2017), 212–13.

Anglo-Russian agreement dividing Persia into British and Russian spheres of influence, and revolutions within both the Ottoman Empire and Persia, "long-standing categories . . . [like] the 'Eastern Question' [were 'condemned'] to obsolescence":

> New problems required new conceptualizations, new phrases, new categories. The emergence of the "Middle East" was therefore much more than a footnote in specialized articles. It was evidence of the reinvention of the region as a key component in the global European imperial structures by powers who would play a crucial role in shaping it after the First World War.[14]

This brings us to the heart of the matter explored throughout this book: How did a vast, 600-plus-year-old, Anatolia-based Eurasian Islamic empire—one that by 1914 had contracted to essentially comprise Anatolia plus the Levant—transform, together with Persia/Iran and Afghanistan, depending on one's perspective, into what we today regard as the modern Middle East? This is a story hinging on European colonial ambitions for carving the Ottoman Empire and Persia, as well as Asian and African lands beyond, into spheres of influence. No less significant, though, are the competing nationalist (e.g., Arab, Zionist, Turkish, Iranian, Afghan, and Kurdish) and further forms (e.g., Islamic activist) of ambition for people to shape their own destinies.

---

14. Foliard, *Dislocating the Orient*, 232.

CHAPTER ONE
1798–1914

A Brief Survey of the Long Nineteenth Century

Historically framed on one end by Napoleon Bonaparte's attempted conquest of Ottoman-held Egypt and on the other by the eruption of World War I, this chapter begins with an extended overview of the "long nineteenth century" (1798–1914) from which the post-WWI Middle East emerged.[1] The chapter then proceeds to provide greater detail about the main themes and subjects, which are echoed throughout later sections.

Though European encroachment on Ottoman lands had been going on for some time, Napoleon's 1798 invasion of Egypt is "conventionally" viewed, on at least a symbolic level, as initiating the modern history of Western intervention in the Middle East.[2] Beyond aiming to outflank British access to India, Napoleon sought to style himself as a reembodied Alexander the Great. He thereby laid claim to ancient "Eastern" legacies for the benefit of modern "Western" virtues of "progress" and "civilization," supposedly exemplified by postrevolutionary France.[3] Edward Said's (1935–2003) deeply influential late-1970s inquiry into the phenomenon of "Orientalism" critically examined how Western colonial consciousness imagined itself as rightfully dominant over the Eastern "Other." The episode of Napoleon in Egypt reveals how the French conceived of themselves as rational, enlightened colonizers who had come to

---

1. A still-broader chronological framing is offered by Ian Rutledge, *Sea of Troubles: The European Conquest of the Islamic Mediterranean and the Origins of the First World War, 1750–1918* (London: Saqi, 2023).

2. Rashid Khalidi, *Resurrecting Empire: Western Footprints and America's Perilous Path in the Middle East* (Boston: Beacon Press, 2005), 10.

3. Juan Cole, *Napoleon's Egypt: Invading the Middle East* (New York: Palgrave Macmillan, 2008).

bestow deliverance on a supposedly irrational, exotic East.[4] It has become commonplace—especially in the wake of the troubled US-led invasions of Afghanistan and Iraq in 2001 and 2003—to draw on Said's insights in observing that Napoleon helped establish an ill-fated pattern of Western attempts to "rescue the East."

The East/West binary clouds a much more nuanced reality. As will be demonstrated throughout this book, Europe's regard for itself as the embodiment of rationality and enlightenment exemplifies the enduring resonance of Orientalist conceptions of self and other. Yet the fact that, in the wake of the Cold War, US "hyperpower" arguably saw Americans as chief wearer of the Orientalist mantle underscores how fraught is any attempt to equate Europe with the West. For that matter, the Ottomans' status as a Eurasian empire constituting an ongoing re-blending of Eastern with Western elements offers perhaps the ultimate demonstration, for our purposes, that the East/West binary is a fictive projection.[5]

In surveying the intricate relationship between the events of the long nineteenth century and the making of the modern Middle East, one is struck by the ceaseless machinations of European colonial powers. From the vantage point of imperial capitals like London, Paris, St. Petersburg, and Vienna, the East was being framed as a supposed "question" inviting resolution for the strategic benefit of those empires. While Orientalist caricatures depict an irrational, pre-enlightened East subjected to the rightful mastery of a modern, enlightened West, historiographical trends have increasingly emphasized how actors within the Middle East perceived, and sought to mold, their own objectives and identities. The Ottoman Empire and Persia did not merely stand as passive targets of colonial machinations. Both Istanbul and Tehran, from the French Revolutionary Wars (1792–1802) onward, strove to channel fortune, as best they could, in their own directions. This is illustrated by the Ottomans' temporary cooperation with British forces to drive French invaders out of Egypt in 1801, the 1906-initiated Persian constitution blending post–French revolutionary discourse with Shi'i Islamic motifs, and the Ottomans' forging of a WWI-sealed alliance with Germany. In each

---

4. Edward Said, *Orientalism* (New York: Vintage, 1979).

5. For an illuminating discussion extending the geopolitical dimensions of Eurasian empires to contemporary Russia, Iran, and China as well as Turkey, see Jeffrey Mankoff, *Empires of Eurasia: How Imperial Legacies Shape International Security* (New Haven, CT: Yale University Press, 2022).

instance, European encroachment occurring between 1798 and 1914 was met with strategizing and innovation.

By the latter 1800s, the European-led onset of industrialization—together with the worldwide extension of trade, transportation, and communications networks—created an initial era of modern globalization. Within this rapidly transforming world, the Middle East took on pivotal economic and strategic significance, positioned at the geographic nexus of imperial rivalries between France, Britain, Russia, Austria-Hungary, and Germany. As the Ottoman Empire and, to a lesser but still notable degree, the Qajar dynasty in Persia were drawn into these global networks, they faced domestic pressure to undertake military, political, social, and economic reforms. Known as the *Tanzimat* era, this signal 1839–1876 period of Ottoman reforms aimed at strengthening the empire by centralizing government authority. Leading reformers placed much emphasis on modernizing systems of administration, education, and law based on the principle of equality and security for all citizens. One of the *Tanzimat*'s most profound legacies was the emergence of an extraordinarily cosmopolitan (if not conflict-free) milieu. It built an ethos of social cohesion known as Ottomanism, which drew on interchanges among the diverse religious, ethnic, and cultural communities living within Ottoman territories. At times, a series of military and economic upheavals stalled the direction of Ottoman reforms. But by the early 1900s, reformist demands generated revolutionary outgrowths across the emerging Middle East. These included the Young Turk Revolution of 1908–1909 that eventually overthrew Sultan and Caliph Abdülhamid II (1842–1918, r. 1876–1909), and the Persian Constitutional Revolution of 1905–1911 (notably influenced by the 1905 Russian Revolution). Each was instrumental in the subsequent establishment of modern Turkish and Iranian state structures.

Napoleon's attempted takeover of Egypt was repulsed in 1801 by a temporary Anglo-Ottoman alliance. Competition between France and Britain for dominance over Ottoman territories remained a central motif throughout the 1800s. The Anglo-Ottoman convention of 1838, or the Treaty of Balta Limanı, widely opened Ottoman lands to British commerce. Further, during the 1820s and 1830s, Britain secured coaling stations around the coastline of the Arabian Peninsula. These enhanced access to the Indian subcontinent, where the East India Company expanded trading monopolies and British influence. For London, a paramount concern became the security of imperial communications routed through the Middle East to Britain's valuable economic interests lying beyond. Simultaneously, France conquered Algeria in the face of fierce local resistance in 1830. Intersecting with British and French ambitions was the so-called Great Game. Coined amid the 1839–1842 Anglo-Afghan War, in which Britain suffered a notoriously devastating defeat, the Great Game commonly refers to the British-Russian contest, persisting for nearly a century, to hold sway over a wide swath of Asia. While the Great Game culminated in the 1907 division of Persia into two spheres of influence, the British-Russian rivalry continued manifesting even following the late 1917 Bolshevik Revolution, as with British support for the Mensheviks during the 1918–1921 Russian Civil War.

Of particular importance to Russia were the strategic series of waterways (including the Bosporus and Dardanelles) connecting its vital Black Sea ports to the Mediterranean. During the 1820s, European powers competed with each other in support of the Greek War of Independence against the Ottomans; and during the 1853–1856 Crimean War, French, British, and Ottoman interests aligned against those of Russia. Further exemplified by the Crimean War was the emergence of the so-called Eastern Question. This phrase indicated the concern within European capitals over how to preserve the territorial integrity of the Ottoman Empire against a possible collapse that might benefit rivals, and thereby upset the balance of power in Europe. Especially emblematic of this concern was London's trepidation that Russia, and thereafter Germany, might be first to fill any breach. As Britain's Foreign Office clarified in 1833, "H.M.'s Government attach great importance to the maintenance of the integrity of the Ottoman Empire, considering that state to be a material element in the general balance of power in Europe."[6]

Nonetheless, beginning with the 1830s loss of Balkan territories to a newly independent Greece, the Ottomans' European lands were continually diminished at the hands of European-backed nationalist movements. These territorial losses grew in the wake of the 1877–1878 Russo-Ottoman War and then during the two Balkan Wars of 1912–1913. Meanwhile, in North Africa, French-British rivalry formed the backdrop for France's domination of the Suez Canal project, whose 1869 completion cut through Egypt in order to connect the Mediterranean and Red Seas. The canal created a time-saving maritime route facilitating trade and communication between the European continent and Asia—above

---

6. Quoted in Malcolm Yapp, *The Making of the Modern Near East, 1792–1923* (London: Longman, 1987), 71.

all, India. Accordingly, Britain came to regard the canal as the "jugular vein" of its global empire, coursing through the Middle East lying between London and British holdings east of the Suez. Soon thereafter, Britain seized on deepening Egyptian indebtedness to European financiers. First, Britain purchased Egypt's own stocks in the Suez Canal Company. Then, in the aftermath of the Egyptian government's bankruptcy, Britain invaded the country in 1882, launching an occupation that would keep British soldiers on Egyptian soil until the 1956 Suez Crisis. Simultaneously, France added Tunisia to its North African holdings in 1881.

When Sultan Abdülhamid II rose to power in 1876, he responded to the ongoing European encroachment by retreating from some of the *Tanzimat* reforms. Subsequently, he also engaged in violence against what he came to regard as subversive Christian communities within the Ottoman Empire, such as ethnic Armenians and Bulgarians. "More harshly judged by history than any other sultan," Abdülhamid II's violent actions earned a characteristically malign assessment from those who have regarded him as the epitome of Ottoman decline and despotism.[7] However, such interpretations need not lend themselves to a pejorative reading of Ottoman history. The postulating of a "sick man of Europe" thesis, whereby the Ottomans are viewed as a moribund empire in decline, has been all too pervasive in Western historiography. In fact, it is remarkable that the Ottomans were able to achieve all that they did under the multidimensional pressures that they faced throughout the long nineteenth century.

Napoleon's Entry into Egypt

Upon landing in July 1798 at the Egyptian port of Alexandria (appropriately enough, given Napoleon's emulation of the ancient conqueror), French forces quickly pushed inland to rout local forces in the so-called Battle of the Pyramids. The French victory proved short-lived. For one thing, British admiral Horatio Nelson (1758–1805) had pursued Napoleon's ships to Egypt and devastated them off the coast: French troops were now effectively stranded in a scorching, summertime desert environment. Further, Napoleon's audacious claims to have come as a friend

---

7. Caroline Finkel, *Osman's Dream: The History of the Ottoman Empire* (New York: Basic Books, 2007), 488.

of Islam who wished only to "liberate [Egypt's] inhabitants from Mamluk tyranny"[8] fell on deaf ears: by October 1798, a rebellion in Cairo arose, provoking a brutal, further alienating response from aspiring French colonizers. By 1799, Napoleon personally abandoned the enterprise in favor of political ambitions within France. Remaining troops were driven out two years later by a joint Anglo-Ottoman force. The Middle East's modern strategic condition as a region repeatedly struggled over, and occupied, by rival outside actors had been initiated.

As chronicled by the Egyptian scholar and cleric Abd al-Rahman al-Jabartī (1754–1825), the French invaders, far from representing enlightened paragons of liberty, equality, and fraternity, in fact sowed evil, heresy, and vengeful brutality (see Document 1). Al-Jabartī allowed that the French expedition had some administrative skills, as well as technical and scholarly knowledge, worth admiring (notably, Napoleon introduced the printing press into Egypt). However, Napoleon's force was, in the Egyptian narrator's view, contemptible on the whole for its deceitful determination to turn Egyptians against one another. Napoleon's decision to preferentially grant key powers of administration and taxation to Egypt's minority Coptic Christian and Jewish communities foreshadowed the ways in which modern European colonizers throughout the Middle East (as elsewhere) employed tactics of divide and rule to devastating effect. From North Africa to Palestine, Lebanon, Syria, and Iraq, this strategy would enable colonial powers to forge alliances with religious and ethnic communities who became beholden to colonizers' administrative paradigms and patronage. Simultaneously, colonial officials managed to set differing communities in competition against one another, seeking to forestall the coalescence of nationalist opposition to colonial rule.

Reverberations in Egypt and Greece

The power vacuum created by the withdrawal of French forces from Egypt was soon filled by Muhammad Ali (1769–1849, r. 1805–1848), an Ottoman military officer of Albanian-Macedonian descent. Egypt

---

8. Quoted in Robert Tignor, "Introduction" to Abd al-Rahman al-Jabartī, *Napoleon in Egypt: Al-Jabartī's Chronicle of the French Occupation, 1798*, expanded edition in honor of al-Jabartī's 250th birthday, trans. Shmuel Moreh (Princeton, NJ: Markus Wiener, 2010), 8.

would technically remain part of the Ottoman Empire until becoming a British protectorate in 1914. However, the emergence of a modern (semi-)sovereign Egyptian state is typically associated with Muhammad Ali, who sought to modernize his army along European lines and centralize political, commercial, agricultural, and industrial control. At the same time, he sought to draw on European culture and knowledge. A key instance came when Muhammad Ali developed an educational program teaching technical rather than religious knowledge. In the 1820s, he sponsored a mission to France, notable among whose members was Rifa'a Rafi' al-Tahtawi (1801–1873), who then returned to build a Parisian-modeled School of Languages in Cairo.

Muhammad Ali's establishment of an empire-within-an-empire exposed his own expansionist aims. His imperial desires were abetted, ironically, by the Ottomans' need to enlist his forces in fighting two internal threats. The first was a politico-religious force that had initially emerged in the Hejaz region of Arabia during the mid-1700s. The Wahhabi movement, a strictly conservative form of Sunni Islamic revivalism, had joined with the warriors of a local chieftain from the Nejd, Muhammad al-Saud (d. 1765). By 1807, this force had captured Karbala (the pilgrimage site of Shi'i Islam), as well as Islam's focal holy cities of Mecca and Medina. This ideological and strategic alliance would not only continue in the twentieth century to create the Kingdom of Saudi Arabia, but it would also promote the late-twentieth and early twenty-first-century global spread of Wahhabi-influenced Islamic activism.

The second threat that forced the Ottomans to seek an alliance with Muhammad Ali was the Greek independence movement that erupted during the 1820s. The Greek nationalist revolt against the Ottomans almost immediately became an arena for international rivalry. Russia asserted itself as the protector of Orthodox Christian communities, and various European governments and citizenries (including even some philhellenic volunteers from the US) drew on Orientalist tropes of "Eastern despotism" to champion the rescue of the ostensible birthplace of Western civilization from Turkish domination.[9]

In the end, the European alliance defeated the Ottoman and Egyptian forces in Greece. Then, a joint British and French intervention compelled all Egyptian forces to retreat home. Europeans feared

---

9. Mark Mazower, *The Greek Revolution: 1821 and the Making of Modern Europe* (London: Allen Lane, 2021).

what Muhammad Ali's prospective regional primacy over the Ottomans in the 1830s might mean for their own commercial and strategic interests. It was within this context that Britain secured the 1838 Anglo-Ottoman commercial agreement, also known as the Treaty of Balta Limanı. The treaty provided for free trade within Ottoman territory and limited tariffs on foreign goods to the low rate of 3 percent. Together with the favorable terms of previous commercial treaties known as the Capitulations, which since the 1500s had granted Europeans and their merchant allies special trading privileges within Ottoman territories, the powerful instruments of economic control granted by the terms of the 1838 treaty intensified Europe's military and economic dominance. Though European opposition had forced Muhammad Ali to end his imperial ambitions, he did secure from the Ottoman sultan a grant of hereditary rule over Egypt. Thus was launched an Egyptian dynasty that would preside, in various Turco-European–dominated formulations, until the 1952 Free Officers' coup overthrew the monarchy in the name of revolutionary Arab nationalism.

European Strategizing

Europe's strategic and economic encirclement of the Ottoman Empire was becoming ever more palpable. Britain further asserted itself in the Persian Gulf, signing in 1820 the first in a series of treaties with the so-termed Trucial States (forerunners of today's United Arab Emirates) who aided Britain in securing the trade corridor to India. Britain's effort to dominate the waters around the Arabian Peninsula culminated in its securing a protectorate over Aden in 1839, later followed by an 1861 treaty with Bahrain. Russia, meanwhile, under the expansionist reign of Tsar Nicholas I (1796–1855, r. 1825–1855), fought successful wars against both the Ottomans and Persia as the Romanovs pushed into the Caucasus during the late 1820s.

By expanding into Transoxiana (corresponding to present-day Uzbekistan), Russian holdings encompassed key locales from the ancient Silk Road and classical Islamic history. Britain perceived a potential Russian threat to its growing dominance in India and sought to consolidate its own power along the northwest flank of India. In what Adeeb Khalid construes as a truer "Great Game," China's Qing dynasty countered Russian power in Central Asia from the east. China came to dominate Eastern Turkestan (encompassing an area like Xinjiang, whose Uyghur Muslim population today remains oppressed by Beijing).[10] Against this geostrategic backdrop, Afghanistan remained an independent confederacy of Muslim tribal dynasties.[11] The 1839–1842 Anglo-Afghan War culminated in the notorious near-annihilation of the invading British contingent. A second Anglo-Afghan War (1878–1880) enabled London to "demarcate Afghanistan's boundaries" vis-à-vis further Russian expansion into Central Asia and turn Afghanistan into "a client state."[12] This demarcation marked the boundary between Afghanistan and the northwestern area of the British imperial Raj in India, but it divisively cut through the tribal lands of the Pashtun people (who continue to straddle what is now the Afghanistan-Pakistan border). In a third Anglo-Afghan War of 1919, Afghanistan proved able to assert its independence from the British Indian orbit behind the leadership of Amanullah Khan (1892–1960, r. 1919–1929). Amanullah's military successes foreshadowed Afghanistan's modern reputation for repelling incursions by global powers, eventually the Soviet Union and US alike.

The *Tanzimat*

From Istanbul's standpoint, the need to respond to the encroachment of European political, economic, and military power, as well as intellectual and cultural influences, was pressing.

The *Tanzimat* Reordering of Ottoman Life

The main era of reforms known as the *Tanzimat* is associated with the reign of Sultan Abdülmecid (1823–1861, r. 1839–1861). Abdülmecid was primarily motivated by military concerns over how to counter European expansionism. But his wide-ranging reform program would profoundly

---

10. Adeeb Khalid, *Central Asia: A New History from the Imperial Conquests to the Present* (Princeton, NJ: Princeton University Press, 2021).

11. Tariq Ali, *The Forty-Year War in Afghanistan: A Chronicle Foretold* (London: Verso, 2021), xix.

12. Khalid, *Central Asia*, 84.

influence numerous aspects of Ottoman social and economic life, with the creation of administrative and bureaucratic structures surrounding matters like law, commerce, property and taxation. The 1839 Gülhane Edict, with which the process was inaugurated, provided for the security of all citizens' (Muslim as well as non-Muslim) "life, honor, and fortune," a regularized system of taxation, and new procedures for the conscription and mobilization of troops (see Document 2).[13]

Ultimately, the *Tanzimat* reforms came to rearticulate what it meant to be an Ottoman citizen. As the empire sought to reorient itself as a participant within the modern, European-dominated arena of nation-states, it also needed to bind together its religiously, ethnically, and linguistically diverse population under a unified political identity and centralized system of governance. The resulting form of identity was Ottomanism, "a new [nationalist] ideology that advocated the loyalty of all subject peoples, no matter their religion or ethnicity, to [the sultan's] person and to the empire."[14] In reaching across the empire's differing religious communities, the *Tanzimat* promised to update the long-standing system through which the Ottomans had administered their Christian, Jewish, and Muslim subjects. Under the *dhimmi* principle, Muslim rulers had extended legally protected status to "people of the book," that is, Christians and Jews (with protection generally also applied to Zoroastrians), in exchange for payment by those communities of a poll tax called the *jizya*. As the empire's diverse populations interacted ever more closely, this hierarchical millet system (as it was termed in the Ottoman instance) became increasingly incompatible with moves toward constitutional liberalism.

Thus, the *Tanzimat* hinged on the integration of the Ottoman Empire's underlying Islamic legal postulates with nineteenth-century conceptions of equality before the law. Such a profound juridical transformation was necessarily ambiguous. Together with the seeming unalloyed good of equal rights, regardless of one's religious affiliation, came a displacement of deep-seated norms and institutions. In terms of the lived experiences of members from diverse religious communities, matters were complex and contradictory. Within an empire that remained Islamic at its foundation,

---

13. "The Rescript of Gülhane—Gülhane Hatt-ı Hümayunu (3 November 1839)," https://www.anayasa.gen.tr/gulhane.htm.

14. Marc Baer, *The Ottomans: Khans, Caesars, and Caliphs* (New York: Basic Books, 2021), 347.

while being subjected to increasing intervention by European rivals, the ingredients for intercommunal divergences and rivalries were ironically multiplied. Moreover, when the accumulating pressures of European interventionism precipitated an end to the *Tanzimat* era after 1876, there followed the Ottomans' reemphasis of a distinctly Islamic identity.

Imperial Rivalries and Revolt in Qajar Persia

Analogous political, social, and religious transformations simultaneously affected Persia. The Qajar dynasty (1789–1920s) faced great pressure from the Great Game contest between the Russian Empire in the north and the British Empire in the south. Territorial and war indemnity losses to Russia during the 1820s brought the Qajars to the brink of bankruptcy, and the Persian socioeconomic balance was altered to the detriment of lower classes. The situation was worsened by Europeans' search for new global import markets fueled by the Industrial Revolution, in conjunction with modern banking and communications technology like telegraph lines, and Persia's growing economic reliance on the export of cash crops like tobacco and opium.[15] Further unsettling were pandemics and agricultural pests whose introduction was exacerbated by increased trade. Notwithstanding the initiatives of figures like crown prince Abbas Mirza (1789–1833), who sought to modernize the military with European aid, and Mirza Saleh (c. 1790–1845), a Persian answer to al-Tahtawi whose European travels brought in innovations like the printing press, the *Tanzimat* reforms were not matched by equivalent measures on the part of the Qajars.[16]

The Qajar dynasty thus found itself ripe for the 1844–1852 Babi revolt. During the nineteenth century, Shi'i Islamic communities—forming the majority populations of Persia and neighboring Ottoman Iraq—were shaken by both the Wahhabi assault on Karbala and an 1842 Ottoman suppression of Shi'a that contrasted greatly with the intent of the *Tanzimat* era. Within this setting, a Persian arising from within Shi'ism's messianic tradition, Sayyed 'Ali Mohammed (1819–1850),

---

15. Abbas Amanat, *Iran: A Modern History* (New Haven, CT: Yale University Press, 2017), 177.

16. Christopher de Bellaigue, *The Islamic Enlightenment: The Struggle Between Faith and Reason, 1798 to Modern Times* (New York: Liveright, 2018), 107–53.

proclaimed himself the "gate" (*bāb*) to the truth, opening the way for the Mahdi—the savior from injustice and corruption who would return at the end of time. The Babi movement exemplified an emerging modern global trend in which socioeconomic and intellectual upheavals, from industrialization to Darwinian evolutionary theory, prompted a diversity of visions that promised salvation amid a perceived, impending apocalypse.[17] Executed by a European military-styled firing squad, the Bab would assume a prophetic role in the world religion stemming from the revolt, the Baha'i faith.

The Baha'i faith's modernist emphasis on purported theological, social, and scientific progressivism was augured by the Bab's follower Fatemeh Baraghani (c. 1817–1852), who came to be known as Qurrat al-'Ayn (connoting "solace"), as well as Tahirih ("The Pure One"). As evoked in a poem of hers, Qurrat's radical 1848 gesture of removing her face veil before addressing a gathering of male Babi theologians has come to symbolize her place as a "revolutionary proto-feminist":[18]

> Should I unveil my scented hair
> I'll captivate every gazelle
> Should I line my narcissus eyes
> I'll destroy the whole world with desire
> To see my face, every dawn
> Heaven lifts its golden mirror
> Should I chance to pass the church one day
> I'll convert all Christian girls.[19]

As for the revolutionary dimension, Qurrat reputedly said to Qajar ruler Nāsir ad-Dīn Shah (1831–1896, r. 1848–1896):

> No!
> Kingdom, wealth and power to thee
> Beggary, exile and loss for me

---

17. Juan Cole, *Modernity and the Millennium: The Genesis of the Baha'i Faith in the Nineteenth-Century Middle East* (New York: Columbia University Press, 1998).

18. Amanat, *Iran*, 241.

19. From Susan Gammage, "A Gathering of the Poems of Tahirih," trans. Farzaneh Milani, *Nine Star Solutions*, https://www.ninestarsolutions.com/a-gathering-of-the-poems-of-tahirih/.

If the former be good, it's thine
If the latter is hard, its [sic] mine.[20]

Great Power Competition across Ottoman and Asian Lands

By the 1850s, the growing salience of the Eastern Question hinged on contending European claims to represent the presumed interests of distinct Christian denominations residing within Ottoman lands. France at this time was emerging into the fullness of its imperial "civilizing mission" ambitions and regarded itself as the protector of Catholic Christians.[21] This support extended both to the leadership of the Maronite Christians of Lebanon, who had been bound to France since the 1700s due to the influence of Jesuit missionaries, and to Catholics' claims in Palestine to Christian holy sites in Bethlehem and Jerusalem. In opposition, Russia asserted itself as the protector of Orthodox Christians and supported local Orthodox Christian leaders' competing claims for controlling access to holy sites. For its part, Britain saw itself as the guardian of Protestant interests in the region.

This all came to a head in the Crimean War, the immediate causation of which was a "monk's dispute."[22] When Tsar Nicholas I's forces moved against the Ottomans in July 1853 in a bid to champion Orthodox claims to holy sites, a joint British-French military venture backed the Ottoman defense. Fighting during 1854–1855 centered on British and French attempts to damage Russian naval power in the Black Sea, with the Crimean port of Sevastopol besieged by the Allies amid the carnage chronicled by Tolstoy.

While Russia managed to push into the Caucasus as far as northeast Anatolia, the 1856 Treaty of Paris concluded the war on the Allies' terms. The Ottomans regained key Balkan territories seized by Russia. Above all, though, the Ottoman Empire attained official recognition as one of

---

20. From Negar Mottahedeh, "The Mutilated Body of the Modern Nation: Qurrat al-'Ayn Tahirah's Unveiling and the Iranian Massacre of the Babis," *Comparative Studies of South Asia, Africa, and the Middle East* 18, no. 2 (Fall 1998): 45.

21. Krishan Kumar, *Visions of Empire: How Five Imperial Regimes Shaped the World* (Princeton, NJ: Princeton University Press, 2017), 397, 405.

22. Heather Sharkey, *A History of Muslims, Christians, and Jews in the Middle East* (Cambridge: Cambridge University Press, 2017), 137–38.

the powers belonging to the Concert of Europe. Crucially, the Treaty of Paris was preceded by the Ottomans' February 1856 Reform Edict, a landmark of the *Tanzimat* enterprise (see Document 3). In the edict, Istanbul guaranteed freedom of religion as well as equal opportunity to all of the empire's non-Muslim communities. The timing raises a host of complicated questions. As asked by Heather Sharkey:

> Were the edicts merely attempts at window-dressing, to make the empire look modern on the world stage and to curry favor with the powers of Europe, while actually sticking to old ways beneath the surface? Did they represent a sincere belief on the part of Sultan Abdulmajid and his statesmen in egalitarian ideals, or simply a pragmatic effort to make inclusion in the empire more appealing at a time when ethnic nationalist movements were gaining momentum among some of the empire's Christians?[23]

Thus, the complexities and ambiguities flowing from the events of 1856 are many. On the one hand, the Ottoman Empire's strategic pivot toward Ottomanism supplanting the empire's diverse religious and ethnic identities sought to stem the tide of European interventionism and concomitant internal, nationalist fracturing of the empire. On the other hand, the appearance of equality acted, if unintentionally, to accelerate this tide. There came a heightened growth of Christian missionary activity, especially foreign schools that gave rise to the mingling of Christian and Muslim students.[24] Within this setting, Americans became increasingly influential in Ottoman realms: the Syrian Protestant College was established in 1866 (later renamed the American University of Beirut), and Robert College opened in Istanbul in 1878. These schools helped develop the urban intellectual environments within which new nationalist identities would germinate.

In other key public arenas like the military, the privileged position once accorded to Islamic religion and culture gave way to "a crisis of identity."[25] For example, significant numbers of non-Muslims enjoyed the opportunity to prosper economically in emerging global networks. While

---

23. Sharkey, *A History of Muslims, Christians, and Jews*, 116.
24. Sharkey, *A History of Muslims, Christians, and Jews*, 256.
25. Finkel, *Osman's Dream*, 447–87.

theoretically equal citizens of the empire, non-Muslims were able to buy their way out of conscription through the payment of an exemption tax to a revenue-hungry government bending under the competitive pressure of European financial might.

Further, while the *Tanzimat* precepts enunciated in the 1856 Reform Edict were instrumental to fostering a multireligious and multiethnic cosmopolitan culture, an especially notorious backlash manifested in Lebanon and Syria. In 1860, intercommunal violence erupted between Muslims and Christians, hinging on the perception that some prosperous Christians who had already benefited from European interventions on their behalf now stood to gain added advantages. As Ussama Makdisi argues, it was due to the distorting effects of European interference that *Tanzimat*-era policies of nondiscrimination actually bear much responsibility for the cleaving of hostile divides between differing religious communities.[26] "[W]hen coexistence among Muslims and Christians was . . . identified as a problem that had to be managed, contained, and manipulated for contending Ottoman and European imperial ends," the result was a "culture of sectarianism" that beset locations like modern Lebanon and Syria.[27] As we will see, the "culture of sectarianism" would be greatly exacerbated by colonial France and its post-WWI divide-and-rule policies.

The Coda to the *Tanzimat* Era

The year 1876 proved a tumultuous passage to the end of the *Tanzimat* era. The empire's severe financial difficulties, along with damage inflicted by natural disasters in rural areas, led first to bankruptcy and then to raising taxes to pay European creditors. Unpopular taxation increases in turn brought unrest, especially in the Balkans. One such Balkan uprising, resulting in the massacre of Bulgarians by Ottoman Circassian irregulars, prompted British politician William Gladstone's (1809–1898) publication of the well-known *Bulgarian Horrors* pamphlet

---

26. See Ussama Makdisi, *Age of Coexistence: The Ecumenical Frame and the Making of the Modern Arab World* (Oakland: University of California Press, 2019); and Ussama Makdisi, *The Culture of Sectarianism: Community, History, and Violence in Nineteenth-Century Ottoman Lebanon* (Berkeley: University of California Press, 2000).

27. Makdisi, *Age of Coexistence*, 56.

decrying the "barbarian Turks."[28] Meanwhile, as Britain and other rapacious European rivals of the Ottomans circled and intervened, internal Muslim disquiet percolated. For instance, the adaptation of purportedly secular, European-styled law had undermined long-embedded forms of knowledge and social organization embodied in influential Muslim communities and institutions like the *ulama* (i.e., Muslim religious scholars) and Sufi mystical orders.[29] Among dissatisfied Muslim ruling elites, poet and journalist Namık Kemal (1840–1888) was influential. "A fervent Muslim" and at the same time a European Romantic-influenced proponent of patriotism toward the Ottoman homeland (*vatan*), Kemal expressed his concerns with how the *Tanzimat* reforms "were [suspect for being] products of foreign pressure."[30]

Kemal was integrally involved with one of the chief proponents of organized political opposition—the Young Ottomans, which emerged from the mid-1860s forward.[31] The Young Ottomans' advocacy for a greater degree of nationalist identity and political reform culminated, by spring 1876, in a call for representative constitutional governance. They had support from influential reformist statesman Midhat Pasha (1822–1883), who had formerly served as grand vizier to Sultan Abdülaziz (1830–1876, r. 1861–1876). Midhat was central not only to Ottoman

---

28. Cited in Baer, *Ottomans*, 365.

29. Wael B. Hallaq, *Reforming Modernity: Ethics and the New Human in the Philosophy of Abdurrahman Taha* (New York: Columbia University Press, 2019), 7; Baer, *Ottomans*, 401. While largely beyond the scope of this text, it is important to note that even though common perceptions of modernity tend to equate modern European ideas and institutions (especially in the wake of the eighteenth-century Enlightenment, but often also following from the seventeenth-century Scientific Revolution) with secularity, i.e., the presupposed absence of religion, the truth is much more complex. The categories "religion" and "secularity" are artificially constructed ideas, whose creation overlaps with power dynamics attendant to such developments as the rise of the modern state after the sixteenth-century Reformation. See William Cavanaugh, *The Myth of Religious Violence* (Oxford: Oxford University Press, 2009). Moreover, ostensibly secular structures like modern European law—including legal reformulations that were then colonially engrafted around the world—carry deep religious residues from Christianity, in particular, which is the tradition from within which the idea of secularity distinctly emerged. Consider, for example, the ongoing courtroom practice of giving an oath on a Bible before delivering testimony.

30. de Bellaigue, *Islamic Enlightenment*, 89–94.

31. Serif Mardin, *The Genesis of Young Ottoman Thought: A Study in the Modernization of Turkish Political Ideas* (Syracuse, NY: Syracuse University Press, 2000), 12.

constitutionalism, but also to one of the most significant modernization projects in latter Ottoman history: the "making [of] citizens" through the development of distinct state educational systems that produced professional soldiers as well as civil servants.[32] Students emerging from the Ottoman state schools, systematized with the education law of 1869, "came to form a self-conscious elite" who would lead the Ottoman military effort during WWI and continued to play a central role in former Ottoman lands well after the war ended.[33] Emblematic is Mustafa Kemal, a product of the late-Ottoman military education system (distinct from the civil education system), who was foremost among the "saviors of the [Ottoman] nation." Yet he would then guide the creation of a Turkish Republic from out of the Ottoman ashes he himself would be eager to bury during the 1920s.[34]

Thus began the eventful, contentious reign of Abdülhamid II, who inherited an exceptionally difficult set of circumstances over which loomed impending war with Russia. In December 1876, European powers met in Istanbul (termed by Europeans the Constantinople Conference) to debate new territorial arrangements necessitated by the Balkan conflagration. Meanwhile, Abdülhamid II oversaw the promulgation of a constitution and the creation of an Ottoman parliament, the seeming *Tanzimat* capstones (see Document 4). Drawing as models on the 1831 Belgian constitution and 1850 Prussian constitution, the Ottoman version emulated the Prussian emphasis on a "kaiser [who] granted some of his subjects the right to share in governance yet retained full authority."[35] Although the constitution conferred personal liberty and equality on each Ottoman citizen regardless of their religion, ultimate sovereignty remained vested in the sultan, named the "supreme caliph." Thus, Islam remained the official creed of the Ottoman Empire, even as the free practice of all other recognized religions within the empire was guaranteed, subject to the dictates of public order.

It would not be long before absolutism won out. By the rights that the sultan-caliph reserved for himself, Abdülhamid II used constitutional

---

32. Michael Provence, *The Last Ottoman Generation and the Making of the Modern Middle East* (Cambridge: Cambridge University Press, 2017), 9–55.

33. Provence, *Last Ottoman Generation*, 10, 18.

34. Provence, *Last Ottoman Generation*, 32–45.

35. Baer, *Ottomans*, 361.

measures to prorogue the first Ottoman parliament in early 1878 and abrogated the constitution that same year.[36] In this manner, Abdülhamid II drew some important aspects of the *Tanzimat* reforms to a close, on the basis that liberal constitutionalism was not what the empire needed to save itself from abounding threats. Douglas Howard illustrates the distinctly modern fashion through which the sultan reclaimed an averred, age-old prerogative:

> Thanks to modern bureaucratic and communications technology, especially the telegraph and railroads, Abdülhamid became an autocrat such as none of his ancestors ever were. Abdülhamid closed the debate over *Tanzimat* aims decisively, in favor of the centrally directed development of Ottoman Islamic society.[37]

Yet, in important senses, there could be no turning back from the hope of a more open political environment. Resistance to Abdülhamid II's reign would manifest in dissent, separatism, and eventually the 1908–1909 Young Turk Revolution, all abetted by yet further European interventionism.[38]

Geographic Pivot of an Emerging Middle East: Egypt and North Africa

As with the episode of Napoleon's short-circuited venture decades before, during, and in the wake of the *Tanzimat* era, Egypt proved central in the dynamic whereby European encroachment helped gradually carve out the geographical space now regarded as the modern Middle East. An idea first explored by Napoleon-commissioned engineers, the Suez Canal project was ultimately initiated by Muhammad Ali's son Said (1822–1863, r. 1854–1863), as its feasibility materialized through the plans of French engineer Ferdinand de Lesseps (1805–1894). Said accepted

---

36. Douglas Howard, *A History of the Ottoman Empire* (Cambridge: Cambridge University Press, 2017), 280; Finkel, *Osman's Dream*, 490.

37. Howard, *History of the Ottoman Empire*, 279.

38. Howard, *History of the Ottoman Empire*, 278.

Egyptian workers digging the Suez Canal.

de Lesseps's proposal, to the initial consternation of Britain. Britain's fear for the weakening of its dominance over trade routes led London to go so far as to try to undermine the project by backing a canal worker protest.[39]

Beginning in 1859, the building of the canal was overseen with ongoing French support by a grandson of Muhammad Ali's, the noted Francophile Ismail (1830–1895, r. 1863–1879). When the canal opened a decade later, it would radically alter the geographic configuration of imperial power—helping give rise to an area imaginable as the "Middle East."

As Ismail set about remaking Egypt in a European mold, Egypt became indebted to Europe in more than one respect. Paralleling *Tanzimat* developments emanating from Istanbul, Ismail pursued reforms ranging from European-inspired urban construction, including streetlights and roundabouts, to telegraphs, railways, ports, waterworks, courts, and schools (including for girls). For example, his wish to transform Cairo into "a New Paris on the Nile" followed a visit to the 1867 world exhibition in France.[40] The price of it all, however, proved unsustainably high. Egypt's

---

39. Terje Tvedt, *The Nile: History's Greatest River* (London: I. B. Tauris, 2021), 42–43.

40. M. E. McMillan, *From the First World War to the Arab Spring: What's Really Going On in the Middle East?* (New York: Palgrave Macmillan, 2016), 15–16.

cotton-rich agricultural sector drew it into a triangular relationship of dependency with Britain and the British Raj in India (to which British textiles were ultimately shipped for purchase). Egypt relied on increasingly unfavorable loans from European banks to finance the costs of the canal and other infrastructure. Meanwhile, Ismail's own personal ambitions further encumbered Egypt's treasury: in return for a new title, *khedive* (Persian for sovereign), Ismail agreed in 1866 to double the yearly tribute to the Ottoman sultan.

With Egypt's foreign debt under Ismail growing to the size of its entire economy, "the entire house of cards collapsed" by 1876.[41] The prospect of Egyptian insolvency prompted Britain to make a move at the expense of its French imperial rival (itself still reeling from defeat in the 1870–1871 Franco-Prussian War), to say less of the Ottomans. In 1875, Ismail was forced to sell Egypt's 44 percent stake in the Suez Canal Company to the British government. In 1876, Egypt essentially declared bankruptcy. By 1879, Britain together with France pressed Abdülhamid II to depose Ismail and replace him with Ismail's son Tawfiq (1852–1892, r. 1879–1892), clearing the way both for European domination of Egyptian finances and, soon thereafter, London's outright occupation of Egypt. An 1881–1882 uprising led by Ahmad 'Urabi (1841–1911), the first Egyptian to attain high rank in the Turco-Mamluk–dominated Egyptian military, posed a significant challenge to the rule of European-favored Khedive Tawfiq. In response, British troops defeated Egyptian forces at the 1882 Battle of Tell al-Kabir. Egypt had become, in effect, a British colony, and London was able to control the Suez Canal, by now the proverbial jugular vein of Britain's global empire.

European Interventions in North Africa

At this point, the Eastern Question converged with the unfolding Scramble for Africa, a term generally associated with the 1884–1885 Berlin Conference that addressed the proliferation of competing European colonial claims to the African continent. As Britain was tightening its colonial hold in northeast Africa, France was similarly securing the Maghreb, or northwest Africa. France had already moved to seize Algeria in 1830 and

---

41. McMillan, *From the First World War to the Arab Spring*, 17.

established a protectorate over Tunisia in 1881. From its new redoubt in Cairo, Britain launched a campaign in 1884 to secure rule over Sudan. Seeking to compete with Britain, as well as with a rapidly ascending German imperial rival, France's furious effort to expand its global empire led to North African confrontation, in the first instance with London. In the 1898 Fashoda Incident, a French expedition confronted British forces in an area of Sudan to which Britain had laid claim on behalf of the Ottomans' continued nominal sovereignty over Egypt. France stopped short of war, accepting a British domination of the Nile valley. Britain was thereby enabled to press on with its own plans for a continuous empire stretching across the African continent, from the southern Cape to Cairo.[42]

Throughout much of the pre-WWI period (1882–1907), British interests in Egypt were overseen by consul general Evelyn Baring (1841–1917). Best known as Lord Cromer, he worked to readminister Egyptian finances to European benefit. Advantages long conferred by the Capitulations, together with associated legal immunities, would be most infamously exposed in a 1906 incident at Dinshaway, a village in the Nile delta. When British officers on a hunting party accidentally shot an Egyptian woman, a local uprising ensued. The disparate punishment then inflicted by British officials on Egyptians underscored the stark injustices of colonial rule and helped stimulate anticolonial nationalist consciousness, especially in the burgeoning local press.

Colonial Encroachment and Revolution in Persia/Iran

During the period of Persian history corresponding to Abdülhamid II's 1876–1909 reign, Russia and Britain continued to vie for influence in Tehran. For his part, Nāsir ad-Dīn Shah made diplomatic overtures to the European powers as well as the Ottomans, in attempting to recover from a famine that had beset Persia into the early 1870s. In 1879, Russia sought to further its own influence through a small military unit within Persia, later known as the Cossack Brigade. Recruited mainly from among Muslim émigrés from the Caucasus, this unit would later provide one of its brigadier generals, Reza Khan Pahlavi (1878–1944, r. 1925–1941), with the force to overthrow the Qajar dynasty. The shah's

---

42. Kumar, *Visions of Empire*, 411.

financial difficulties led him in the late 1880s to grant a British military official a monopoly on tobacco. In response, the monopoly-disadvantaged members of the Persian merchant class, some high-ranking Shi'i clerics, and political dissidents made common cause against the Qajar shah. Another important commodity—oil—attained a preeminence in modern Iranian history that has not abated. In 1901, Nāsir ad-Dīn Shah's successor, Mozaffar ad-Dīn Shah (1853–1907, r. 1896–1907), granted British financier William Knox D'Arcy (1849–1917) a concession that has become infamous in terms of the exploitative role of oil extraction in the history of modern Western imperialism across the Middle East (see Document 5). In return for granting D'Arcy a monopoly on the discovery and export of the country's southern oil reserves, the Qajar government received a small advance, some stocks, and only 16 percent of the annual profits. In 1909, the Anglo-Persian Oil Company, a forerunner to British Petroleum, was established to exploit Persian oil, and in 1914 the British government became a major shareholder in the company. This would prove strategically invaluable when First Lord of the Admiralty Winston Churchill (1874–1965) began converting the Royal Navy fleet from coal to oil.

With a loosening of opportunities for public dissent under Mozaffar ad-Dīn Shah came the Persian Constitutional Revolution of 1905–1911. In numerous ways, the Constitutional Revolution was a signal episode in the history of modern Iran, and the Middle East as a whole. It presaged subsequent currents of transformative, sociopolitical revolution that would play out nationally and regionally over decades to come. This was a broad-based uprising, drawing on elements of society—ranging from workers to merchants, reformist intellectuals, and Shi'i Muslim clerics—against the Qajar monarchy's perceived corruption and subservience to European interests. As an emerging articulation of a "new national community conscious of itself," the Constitutional Revolution helped to create a modern Iranian nation-state.[43] Moreover, it resulted in a constitution that "with the true hallmarks of twentieth-century Islamic constitutionalism . . . prefigured not only the debates after the 1979 Islamic revolution in Iran but also much twentieth-century constitutional thought throughout the Muslim world."[44]

---

43. Amanat, *Iran*, 314.

44. Andrew March, *The Caliphate of Man: Popular Sovereignty in Modern Islamic Thought* (Cambridge, MA: Belknap Press, 2019), 5; Kevan Harris, *A Social Revolution: Politics and the Welfare State in Iran* (Berkeley: University of California Press, 2017).

The Persian revolutionary order crystallized by 1906–1907 with the creation of a parliament and fundamental law (see Document 6). This established a constitutional monarchy with a separation of powers between the legislative *majles* and the shah as chief executive, as well as a guarantee of basic liberties. Over the three decades that had elapsed since the promulgation of the Ottoman constitution, notions of popular franchise were constantly evolving. Whereas members of the Ottoman parliament were, on paper, indirectly selected through layered electoral colleges, the *majles* membership elected in 1906 featured direct voting, at least by people in Tehran.[45]

As with many revolutions, constitutionalists soon had to contend with a violent counterrevolutionary regime. Mohammad 'Ali Shah (1872–1925, r. 1907–1909) dissolved the first *majles* and undertook an artillery bombardment of the Tehran parliamentary building. However, the counterrevolution occurred against the backdrop of a new Anglo-Russian agreement consummated in August 1907 that effectively concluded the Great Game. It also helped seal the British-French-Russian Triple Entente among the soon-to-be WWI Allies. Under the agreement, Persia was divided into two zones of influence. Russia was allotted the north, abutting areas like the Transcaucasus and Caspian Sea. Britain held sway in the south, adjacent to British India as well as the Strait of Hormuz strategically leading into the Persian Gulf. In central Persia, Qajar sovereignty was recognized; at the same time, it is telling that neither the *majles* nor the constitutional arrangements were acknowledged. Still, the legacies of the Constitutional Revolution were long-lived: the Qajar dynasty was fatally weakened, modern Iranian nationalism was born, and anti-imperialist political consciousness was galvanized, in ways that continue to resonate today.

Abdülhamid II's Reign: European Encroachments and Local Challenges

Recent scholarship tends to suggest that if Abdülhamid II has been typically maligned as paranoid, he certainly faced plenty of dangers about which to worry. These ranged from political opponents' plots to remove

---

45. de Bellaigue, *Islamic Enlightenment*, 291.

him from rule by both coup and assassination, to uprisings by religious and ethnic minorities, to European powers' plans to utilize such uprisings and further strategic rationales in order to whittle away at the Ottomans' shrinking but still expansive territories. As supreme caliph, Abdülhamid II sought ways to counter these dangers. Most prominent was his reinvigoration of both the Ottomans' Islamic identity and the idea of imperial succession to the Prophet Muhammad (c. 570–632) that the term "caliphate" connotes.

During spring 1877, Russia again attacked the Ottomans through the Balkans and Caucasus. By early 1878, they were advancing on Istanbul, which for Russia represented Constantinople, the ancient seat of Orthodox Christianity. Echoing the strategic alignments that marked the Crimean War (and in particular London's ongoing wish to stave off Ottoman collapse, lest the security of essential trade routes be compromised), Britain threatened to intervene to forestall the Russian advance. The resulting Treaty of San Stefano, signed between Russia and the Ottomans in March 1878, imposed vast territorial losses upon the latter. In the Balkans, autonomy was granted both to Bulgaria and to Bosnia and Herzegovina, while independence was accorded to Romania, Serbia, and Montenegro. Beyond this, the Ottoman territories of Kars, Batum, and Ardahan, which became known as the three lost provinces, were ceded to Russia.[46]

At the ensuing 1878 Congress of Berlin, a concert of European powers, concerned over Russia's territorial gains, adjusted the disposition that had occurred at San Stefano. Crucially, autonomous Bulgaria was divided three ways: Macedonia was restored to the Ottoman Empire; an autonomous province to be administered by a Christian Ottoman governor, called Eastern Rumelia, was formed in the south; and the rest became the vassal principality of Bulgaria. Russia did manage to add southern Bessarabia, situated to the west of the Black Sea, and the Habsburgs received their coveted Bosnia and Herzegovina. Further, Britain received a vital eastern Mediterranean foothold on the island of Cyprus. Not least, foisted upon the Ottomans was the establishment of European rights to intervene inside Ottoman territory on behalf of the Armenian ethnic minority. By this juncture, the Armenian population had reached between 1.5 and 2 million (although the numbers were contested, with Ottoman authorities typically undercounting and local

---

46. Kumar, *Visions of Empire*, 126.

Chapter One: 1798–1914 35

A graphic representation from a 1908 journal depicting Habsburg emperor Franz Joseph and Russian tsar Nicholas II struggling over the Eastern Question, while Ottoman sultan-caliph Abdülhamid II looks on sullenly.

Christian officials overcounting).[47] Nonetheless, "the empire had survived, and had been spared the worst": Russia was stopped short of key aims, and bore enormous financial losses that further destabilized the Romanovs' domestic politics.[48] Perhaps above all from the Ottomans' strategic vantage point, movement began toward greater cooperation with Germany that would bear significant fruit over the following decades.

Amid British and French gains at the Ottomans' expense, and especially once the kaiser had compelled the politically cautious Chancellor Otto von Bismarck (1815–1898) to retire in 1890, Germany took the opportunity from the 1880s onward to contribute diverse forms of support to the Ottoman Empire. These ranged from military training and materiel to engineering aid for the construction of Ottoman railways reaching throughout Asia Minor and beyond to Baghdad and the Hejaz. During the 1890s, German enhancement of Ottoman fighting power, as well as German diplomatic support, helped buttress the Ottomans' violent suppression of a series of uprisings by various Christian ethnic communities. These suppressive campaigns earned Abdülhamid II some of his most malign reputation.

Growing Armenian opposition to the Ottomans from within eastern Turkey was met with the use of Hamidiye regiments comprising

---

47. Benny Morris and Dror Ze'evi, *The Thirty-Year Genocide: Turkey's Destruction of Its Christian Minorities, 1894–1924* (Cambridge, MA: Harvard University Press, 2019), 23–24.

48. Sean McMeekin, *The Ottoman Endgame: War, Revolution, and the Making of the Modern Middle East, 1908–1923* (New York: Penguin, 2016), 23.

Kurdish tribal fighters. This empowerment of Kurdish communities, who had an antagonistic relationship with Armenian revolutionaries, to police remoter areas of eastern Anatolia offers an important foreshadowing of later Kurdish separatist efforts.[49] By the mid-1890s, thousands of Armenians were killed in effective civil war and mob violence across Turkey. Some historians have regarded this as the commencement of a three-decade-long process of concerted Ottoman-Turkish killing of Armenian and other Christian communities, lasting through the mid-1920s establishment of the Republic of Turkey.[50] In 1897, an uprising by Greek Christians in Crete was also met with a fierce Ottoman military response. Russian opposition, in particular, compelled a political arrangement, further backed by Britain, France, and Italy, in which Crete was granted autonomy.

German-Ottoman Affinities

Displaying Germany's pro-Istanbul influence, the kaiser undertook a lavish state visit to Ottoman territories in 1898. It featured triumphal entrances into Jerusalem as well as Damascus.[51] This visit was soon followed by Germany's increase in financial aid and technical assistance for building Ottoman transportation and communication infrastructure. Kaiser Wilhelm's geopolitical posture was illustrative of his "fin-de-siècle *weltpolitik* [i.e., turn-of-the-twentieth-century 'world politics,' as opposed to the deposed Bismarck's pragmatic, balance-of-power-oriented *realpolitik*], which aimed to rival British imperial aspirations on the global stage."[52] The *weltpolitik* mindset would drive Germany's pre-WWI naval arms race with Britain, as well as growing popular nationalism supporting the global spread of German military power and cultural influence.

Within the context of German-Ottoman relations, a key dimension of Kaiser Wilhelm's cultural vision was his idealized, Romantic affinity

---

49. Finkel, *Osman's Dream*, 502.

50. Morris and Ze'evi, *Thirty-Year Genocide*.

51. McMeekin, *Ottoman Endgame*, 27.

52. Tony Ballantyne and Antoinette Burton, "Empires and the Reach of the Global," in Emily Rosenberg, ed., *A World Connecting: 1870–1945* (Cambridge, MA: Harvard University Press, 2012), 399.

Comparison of imperial entries into Jerusalem: Kaiser
Wilhelm II in 1898 and Lord Edmund Allenby in 1917.

for Islam.[53] Such an affinity had roots in the Germanic tradition reaching back to the seminal Romantic poet Johann Wolfgang von Goethe (1749–1832), who gravitated especially toward Persian Islam. (Notwithstanding Ottoman-Persian rivalry, Persian language, culture, and literature had also long been influential on Ottoman high culture and royal court life.) Kaiser Wilhelm thus styled himself as a worldwide defender of Muslims, a sentiment manifested most prominently in the financial support extended to the building of the Hejaz railway to Mecca.[54] Wilhelm's mocking moniker Hajji underscores the contentious assertion that, as will be explored in Chapter 2, the Ottomans' joining the Central powers in WWI and declaring a *jihād* against the Allies came chiefly at the behest of Germany.[55]

---

53. Romantic, as in the sense of the spiritually infused, nineteenth-century Euro-American Romantic movement arising in reaction against the eighteenth-century Enlightenment's perceived excessive rationalism.

54. de Bellaigue, *Islamic Enlightenment*, 260.

55. Wael Hallaq, *Sharī'a: Theory, Practice, Transformations* (Cambridge: Cambridge University Press, 2010), 324; Mustafa Aksakal, "'Holy War Made in Germany'?: Ottoman Origins of the 1914 Jihad," *War in History* 18, no. 2 (2011): 184–99.

Turns toward Competing Islamic Identities

Abdülhamid II's own propounding of a pan-Islamic identity aimed to galvanize the unifying sentiments of not only the empire's Muslim subjects but also people across the Muslim world.[56] From India to the Caucasus region to West and North Africa, diverse Muslim communities found themselves dominated by three European imperial powers: Britain, Russia, and France. Naturally, Berlin was all the more enthusiastic about supporting a sultan-caliph whose appeals to Muslim solidarity worried Germany's rival colonial overlords. As Pankaj Mishra usefully elaborates, Abdülhamid II "needed an ideological justification for his despotism, and some kind of leverage over European powers who ruled millions of restless Muslims in colonized countries; pan-Islamism served him well on both counts."[57]

Along the way, Abdülhamid's supporters made strategic use of burgeoning strands of anti-colonial, pan-Islamic thought. They called for "Muslim societies to return to the basic rules set out in the Koran and to the 'meanings that could be extracted' from Prophet Mohammed's life," as a means for "improv[ing] the lives of . . . [Muslim] believers and the conditions of . . . [Muslim societies]" in the face of stagnation and colonial encroachment.[58] It is important to note that these late nineteenth-century Islamic renewal movements were not necessarily opposed to the West; rather, they saw engagement with Western modernity as an opportunity to revitalize Islam.[59]

The Egyptian Muhammad 'Abduh (who served as Egypt's grand mufti between 1899 and 1905) and the Lebanese-born Rashid Rida, who moved to Egypt and became a student of 'Abduh's, each represents distinct variants of Islamic reformism impelled by the anti-colonial impulse. 'Abduh called for an Islamic renaissance that took inspiration from the

---

56. Nikki Keddie, *Sayyid Jamāl ad-Dīn "al-Afghānī": A Political Biography* (Berkeley: University of California Press, 1972), 130.

57. Pankaj Mishra, *From the Ruins of Empire: The Intellectuals Who Remade Asia* (New York: Farrar, Straus and Giroux, 2012), 90.

58. Tarek Osman, *Islamism: A History of Political Islam from the Fall of the Ottoman Empire to the Rise of ISIS* (New Haven, CT: Yale University Press, 2017), 47–51. See also Michael Cook, *A History of the Muslim World from Its Origins to the Dawn of Modernity* (Princeton, NJ: Princeton University Press, 2024), 779–846.

59. Osman, *Islamism*, 48.

example set by the Golden Age (roughly the first four centuries of Islam).[60] Rida's approach diverged from his teacher's in seeking to "live according to the original Shari'a of the Salaf, which was based on the teachings of Muhammad and the Qur'an."[61] Here, we can recognize two key (and often misunderstood or misappropriated) Arabic terms manifesting in present-day affairs within the Middle East and many other places around the world. One is Sharī'a, which as previously observed is often translated as "Islamic law," but which carries much broader connotations, more in the spirit of a person's overall approach to life and the entirety of God's creation (as distinguished from the modern English-language sense of law as being the specific realm of state governance, legislation, and courtrooms). The other is *salaf*, referring to the pure or pious ancestry of the Prophet Muhammad and his followers, from which is derived the notion of Salafism as a variable form of modern Islamic thought and practice advocating, in general, a turn toward the example of the Salafs.

Another reformist advocate of pan-Islamism who was emblematic of the conditions in the late stages of the Ottoman Empire was Jamāl ad-Dīn al-Afghānī (c. 1839–1897). During his life, al-Afghānī traveled widely, from India throughout Central Asia, Ottoman lands, Russia, and western Europe. Al-Afghānī preached that the "independence and self-strengthening" of the Muslim world, together with the protection of "traditional Islamic ways and beliefs against the encroachments of modernization," were essential to the struggle against imperialism (see Document 7).[62] Intriguingly, al-Afghānī worked persistently to make inroads into Abdülhamid II's court. However, he ran afoul of the sultan's suspicious nature and wish to control the charismatic preacher, not least after al-Afghānī was accused of complicity in the 1896 assassination of Nāsir ad-Dīn Shah in Persia.

Consistent with the falling-out between al-Afghānī and Abdülhamid II, some Ottoman *ulama* who had been opposed to the *Tanzimat* were similarly unenthusiastic about the notion of modernizing Islamic reforms. The sultan-caliph sought to cultivate these conservative perspectives in support of his instrumentalization of Islam against unwanted

---

60. Suleiman Mourad, *The Mosaic of Islam* (London: Verso, 2016), 69.

61. Mourad, *Mosaic of Islam*, 70.

62. Keddie, *Sayyid Jamāl ad-Dīn "al-Afghānī,"* 422.

European interference.⁶³ This period thereby proved pivotal to the subsequent—and very much ongoing—global development of diverse forms of politicized Islamic activism. Some such movements are conservative to highly variable degrees; some are reformist to the extent they seek to integrate liberalism; and some are radically populist in their opposition to colonial and neocolonial elites (as with the enduringly influential Muslim Brotherhood originating in late-1920s Egypt).⁶⁴

Nationalist Identities

The latter stages of Ottoman history supplied the setting for the growth of several species of nationalist identity that would come to challenge the predominance of Ottomanism. The concept of nationalism is highly complex and contested. Theoretical and specific historical accounts range from those regarding nationalism as primordially rooted in the deep past of a people who are bound together by traits (like a shared religion, culture, ethnicity, language, or territory) to Benedict Anderson's influential view that nationhood involves a peculiarly modern social and material construction of an "imagined community."⁶⁵ For present purposes, it is sufficient to observe the following generality: the nineteenth century brought into Ottoman lands a post–French Revolution European trend toward the idea that people (some people at any rate, for racialized assumptions certainly factored in) are primarily defined by their belonging to distinct nations. This trend drew on a spectrum of intellectual influences, from Enlightenment rationalism, to Romanticism's imparting of a spiritual dimension, to the connection between a community of people and a piece of land that ostensibly belongs to that people. Within the context of late nineteenth-century Ottoman history and territory, it is especially important to consider the emergence of three competing nationalist identities: Arabism, Turkism, and Zionism.

For much of the past century or so, an ongoing historical debate with powerful political ramifications has surrounded the question of whether

---

63. Mishra, *Ruins of Empire*, 71; Sami Zubaida, *Beyond Islam: A New Understanding of the Middle East* (London: I. B. Tauris, 2011), 91.

64. Zubaida, *Beyond Islam*, 91.

65. Benedict Anderson, *Imagined Communities: Reflections on the Origins and Spread of Nationalism* (London: Verso, 2006).

Chapter One: 1798–1914   41

Arab nationalism can be said to have concretely taken hold prior to WWI. One side of the interpretive spectrum is exemplified by George Antonius's (1891–1942) 1939 book *The Arab Awakening*. Antonius was an Orthodox Christian of Lebanese descent, who addressed contending Zionist and Palestinian claims to Palestine amid the 1936–1939 Arab revolt against Britain. On Antonius's perspective, Arab nationalism germinated together with the literary societies characterizing the *Nahda*, or Arab cultural "'arising' or 'awakening'" that began flowering in cosmopolitan urban locales during the *Tanzimat* era.[66] On the other hand are those who argue that more widespread popular Arab nationalism would not occur until the end of WWI replaced Ottoman imperial rule with British and French imperialism. Historian of Arab nationalism Adeed Dawisha illustrates that, by the time of the late nineteenth- and early twentieth-century Ottoman milieu, a key distinction had arisen between *Tanzimat*-empowered Christian Arab thinkers and activists, who promoted a separate Arab identity, and Muslim reformers like 'Abduh, Rida, and al-Afghānī, whose pan-Islamic ideas promoted Turkic-Arab cooperation.[67] Dawisha asserts (while critiquing Antonius's interpretation) that even if Arab nationalists had sown nationalist seeds amid the *Nahda*, this would have held limited public appeal prior to WWI.[68] By and large, Arabs "remained loyal to the Empire and committed to it as a political framework at least until 1914, notwithstanding their differences with a given Sultan, or regime, or government."[69]

At this time, Arab elites were centered on a group of landowning families often referred to as "notables."[70] These local leaders were integral

---

66. George Antonius, *The Arab Awakening: The Story of the Arab National Movement* (Safety Harbor, FL: Simon Publications, 2001 [1939]), 13. See Document 19.

67. Adeed Dawisha, *Arab Nationalism in the Twentieth Century: From Triumph to Despair* (Princeton, NJ: Princeton University Press, 2016), 25.

68. Dawisha, *Arab Nationalism in the Twentieth Century*, 28. Dawisha cites the "seminal" insights of "C. Ernest Dawn [who] asserts that prior to October 1914, only 126 men were known to have been 'public advocates of Arab nationalism, or members of Arab nationalist societies.'" Dawisha, *Arab Nationalism in the Twentieth Century*, 29, citing C. Ernest Dawn, *From Ottomanism to Arabism: Essays on the Origins of Arab Nationalism* (Urbana: University of Illinois Press, 1973), 152–53.

69. Rashid Khalidi, *Palestinian Identity: The Construction of Modern National Consciousness* (New York: Columbia University Press, 1997), 86.

70. See Albert Hourani, "Ottoman Reform and the Politics of the Notables," in William R. Polk and Richard L. Chambers, eds., *Beginnings of Modernization in the Middle East* (Chicago: University of Chicago Press, 1968).

to the Ottoman political system. As semi-independent intermediaries between state and society, they nonetheless competed with each other to acquire, or merely keep, power and influence. When some Arab families saw their positions threatened by Istanbul's efforts at greater centralization, they responded favorably to ideas of greater autonomy, expressed through Arab sentiments such as a love for language and literature. Still, their opposing government policies in this way reflected a desire for reforming and preserving the system; it did not erode the loyalty of most notables to Ottomanism. Those who argued that Arabs should break from the Ottoman Empire remained a small minority until the end of the war.

As we will discuss in Chapter 2, the British helped instigate a 1916 Arab revolt against the Ottomans that Antonius portrays as the culmination of Arab nationalism. In fact, it was more the other way around: Ottoman defeat in 1918 pushed Arab nationalist energies to the fore. The first such full-fledged nationalist entity was the Ottoman Empire's brief replacement (1918–1920) by an Arab kingdom based in Damascus. As we will see in Chapter 3, however, that project would have its independence "stolen" by the victorious WWI Allies.[71] European powers instead deployed their well-honed colonial policies of divide and rule in an effort to control Arab societies by co-opting the notable families and their intermediary networks.

Distinct from Ottoman identity, Turkish nationalism was somewhat more inchoate during the late nineteenth century. During the 1890s, a group of intellectually diverse, multiethnic, and multireligious activists who opposed Abdülhamid II's autocracy from within Parisian exile formed the Committee of Union and Progress (CUP). The CUP's European setting allowed for the influence of French revolutionary tradition and positivist philosophy. This yielded the quintessentially modernist notion that scientific thought could propel progress toward social and political utopias. The CUP's full force would manifest in the 1908–1909 Young Turk Revolution that it spearheaded, to which we will return shortly. Abdülhamid II's reemphasizing of the Ottoman Empire's identity as a Sunni Islamic caliphate offered a pillar of legitimacy that would be built upon even by the ostensibly modernizing and secularizing

---

71. Elizabeth Thompson, *How the West Stole Democracy from the Arabs: The Syrian Arab Congress of 1920 and the Destruction of Its Historic Liberal-Islamic Alliance* (New York: Atlantic Monthly Press, 2020).

resistance organization opposing his rule. In the aftermath of the Young Turk Revolution and lead-up to WWI, CUP member Mehmed Ziya Gökalp (1876–1924) undertook an influential articulation of the idea of Turkishness. Longtime CUP member Mustafa Kemal (Atatürk) fully brought to bear the concept of Turkish nationalism as a political reality, providing the state context within which Gökalp's idea could be applied.

Jewish nationalism, or Zionism, entails the notion that Jewish identity cannot be defined solely in religious terms. Instead, Zionism embodies a nationalism in which shared traits of religion, culture, ethnicity, and language bind together a political community whose historical genealogy is rooted in a specific piece of territory: the biblical Land of Israel. Numerous influences combined to produce this idea within the overall context of post-1789 European culture. Following the French Revolution, and the promised emancipation of Jews as citizens of European nation-states, the Jewish *Haskala* (Enlightenment) movement prompted Jews to seek their own identity and self-determination.[72] The development of Zionism crystallized within the early 1880s setting of the western Russian Empire, when the destabilizing 1881 assassination of Alexander II led to pogroms, or massacres of Jews.

Among foundational proponents of the Zionist political project, the most prominent was Theodor Herzl (1860–1904). A Vienna-based journalist whose own lived circumstances were as "a typical product of . . . [Jewish] Emancipation" within the Habsburg realm, Herzl's experiences were markedly different than those of persecuted Jews from Russia.[73] However, during the 1890s, Herzl became convinced, especially while observing the unjust trial for treason of French military officer Alfred Dreyfus (1859–1935), that even ostensibly emancipated, secularized Jews like Dreyfus would never attain full and fair acceptance within Christian societies. As such, Herzl argued in 1896 that the pursuit of a Jewish state was necessary for a resolution to centuries of Jewish suffering. Herzl and other Zionists allowed for the possibility, as late as 1903, that such a state could be located in a location other than Palestine, if necessary (Argentina and Uganda were named as possibilities). Should "His Majesty the Sultan" grant it, though, "our ever-memorable historic

---

72. Shlomo Avineri, *The Making of Modern Zionism* (New York: Basic Books, 2017 [1981]), 11.

73. Avineri, *Making of Modern Zionism*, 97. See also Derek Penslar, *Theodor Herzl: The Charismatic Leader* (New Haven, CT: Yale University Press, 2020).

home" of Palestine was far preferable. Then again, critics who assert that Zionism constitutes yet another form of European settler-colonialism and ethnocentrism highlight Herzl's assertion that "we should form [in Palestine] a portion of a rampart of Europe against Asia, an outpost of civilization as opposed to barbarism" (see Document 8).[74]

Between 1882 and 1903, while two million Jews escaping persecutory violence in Russia and Romania emigrated to locales like the US, many fewer Jews moved to Ottoman-ruled Palestine. These several tens of thousands of Jewish immigrants comprised the first *aliyah* (Hebrew for "ascent"), which came to denote immigration to the Land of Zion). Settling in locations ranging from Jaffa (just south of where Tel Aviv would be established in the early 1900s) to Jerusalem and the valleys of the Galilee, some of the immigrants were aided in farming ventures by the French banker and Zionist Baron Edmond de Rothschild (1845–1934). The second and third *aliyot* (plural of *aliyah*) followed in 1904–1914 and 1918–1923, respectively, bringing another sixty-five thousand Jews, mostly from eastern Europe, who pursued a largely secular vision of life predicated on the ideals of land and labor. The fact that these Jewish immigrants were Ashkenazim, or Jews of central and eastern European descent, as opposed to the relatively small number of Mizrahim, or Jews of Middle Eastern descent already living in Palestine, is highly significant.[75] By the end of the 1800s, the majority of Jews in Palestine were Ashkenazi. This prefigured both the Palestinian claim that Zionism amounts to a European settler-colonial incursion and the discriminatory dominance that Ashkenazim would come to have over Mizrahim within Palestine, before and after the 1948 establishment of the State of Israel.[76] Inspired by "both socialism and romantic, back-to-the-land ideas," and enabled to purchase land by legal and market practices ushered in by *Tanzimat*, Ashkenazi Jewish immigrants focused on the development of farming

---

74. Theodor Herzl, "The Jewish State" (1896), https://www.jewishvirtuallibrary.org/quot-the-jewish-state-quot-theodor-herzl.

75. Tom Segev, *A State at Any Cost: The Life of David Ben-Gurion* (New York: Farrar, Straus and Giroux, 2020), 57. The term "Sephardim" literally indicates Jews of Spanish descent but has often been used to refer to Jews from throughout the Islamic world. Distinct from this more encompassing usage of Sephardim, the term "Mizrahim" is increasingly employed in reference to Jews hailing from the broader Middle East and Central Asia.

76. Segev, *A State at Any Cost*, 57.

settlements. They also initiated the "resurrect[ion] [of] the biblical language of Hebrew for use as the national tongue."[77] Withal, the prospect for conflict with the Muslim and Christian Palestinians who constituted the overwhelming majority of residents already living in the area lay in the immigrants' notion that the land was open and available for settlement.

The Abdülhamid II Legacy

At the turn of the 1900s, an Ottoman Empire entering into its remarkable seventh century of existence embodied a host of contradictions. Paranoid about criticism, and facing mounting territorial losses, Abdülhamid II was derided by Western observers as a violent despot. At the same time, the Ottomans' territorial losses meant that the empire contained a far lesser percentage of Christians than it had for centuries. Notable in this regard, the empire's Muslim population was forcibly increased. This came as a result of, for instance, Muslim Bulgarians being driven out of the Balkans and ethnic Tatars and Circassians being expelled from Russian-dominated lands in Crimea and the Caucasus.[78] By 1906, the empire's overall Muslim population comprised approximately three-quarters of an overall population of 21 million.[79] Within the immediate historical setting, then, an embattled Abdülhamid II's call on pan-Islamic identity was quite understandable, even if it earned him ever more European mistrust—other than from Berlin, that is.

It is instructive to think further in this light about the *Tanzimat* era. An apparent influx of liberalization helped yield impressively efficacious reforms. But the era was also characterized by a range of perils, such as the unsated interventionism of European powers. Then, the Ottomans' placating Reform Edict of 1856 was followed by an upsurge

---

77. James Gelvin, *The Modern Middle East: A History*, 5th ed. (Oxford: Oxford University Press, 2020), 235.

78. Sharkey, *A History of Muslims, Christians, and Jews*, 185.

79. McMeekin, *Ottoman Endgame*, 30. Abülhamid II's census-taking was an important indicator of his burgeoning efforts at modern, systematized administration. The census "serv[ed] state aims, both as a defense against additional diplomatic aggression and to facilitate taxation and conscription"; moreover, "[w]omen were counted for the first time" and "[i]dentity documents were issued." Howard, *History of the Ottoman Empire*, 281.

of "sectarianism." Ultimately, *Tanzimat* ran up against what Abdülhamid II understandably perceived as weakness in the face of European rivals. Yet he held to the Ottoman Empire's continuing modernization—albeit a variant of modernization that was more in keeping with the burgeoning movement of pan-Islamic anti-colonialism than European secularism. Further to a more-nuanced reading of Abdülhamid II's legacy, not only did the Ottomans' putative terminal decline seem to have been held in check during his reign, the empire's cosmopolitan character also continued to develop. As was intimated in the Preface, a case in point was Salonica, the "Jerusalem of the Balkans," with its long-standing Jewish population descended from post-1492 exiles fleeing the Spanish Inquisition.[80] The empire's sizable Jewish community sought to demonstrate its fealty to Abdülhamid II when it commemorated the year 1892 as the four hundredth anniversary of the welcome proffered by Ottoman sultans to Jews expelled from Spain. Furthermore, in these early days of Zionist immigration to Palestine being tolerated by Istanbul, Herzl sought to sway European public opinion in favor of the Ottomans when the 1890s Armenian massacres brought opprobrium to the sultan-caliph.[81] Poignantly augured by Jews' wish to show loyalty to the sultan-caliph, the coming demise of Ottoman suzerainty would only spell disaster—annihilation, in fact. As a result of the Balkan Wars, the city became Thessaloniki, Greece. During the Nationalist Socialist (Nazi) invasion and occupation of Greece, Nazi-perpetrated genocide devastated the remaining Jewish community in Thessaloniki, which lost 98 percent of its members by the end of World War II.[82] Within the pre-WWI environment, though, the fundamental understanding of what it meant to be a citizen of the unified Ottoman Empire was once again undergoing transformation. Abdülhamid II's eventual fall in the Young Turk Revolution was received hopefully by the diverse religious, ethnic, cultural, and linguistic communities living in Ottoman provinces—provinces that had their own local cultures and interests, and even interprovincial relations. Informed by efflorescing conceptions of nationalism, and revolutionary ideals of "liberty, equality, fraternity, and justice" newly emanating from Persia as well as from within the French tradition, residents of a provincial region

---

80. Sarah Abrevaya Stein, *Family Papers: A Sephardic Journey Through the Twentieth Century* (New York: Farrar, Straus and Giroux, 2019), 14.

81. Baer, *Ottomans*, 379.

82. Stein, *Family Papers*, 5.

Ottoman public celebrating the constitutional regime, which was reinvigorated by the 1908 Young Turk Revolution.

like Palestine sought what has been described as an evolving form of "civic Ottomanism."[83] This objective entailed "a grassroots imperial citizenship project that promoted a unified sociopolitical identity of an Ottoman people struggling over the new rights and obligations of revolutionary political membership."[84]

The Young Turk Revolution and the Coming of World War I

At the same time, discontent with the darker side of Abdülhamid II's rule mounted. The activism of exiles in Paris, where the CUP held its first congress in 1902, revolts in the Anatolian heartland over grain shortages, burdensome taxes, and feared conscription all indicated growing discontent. This unrest was compounded by an overall economic downturn

---

83. Michelle U. Campos, *Ottoman Brothers: Muslims, Christians, and Jews in Early Twentieth-Century Palestine* (Stanford, CA: Stanford University Press, 2011), 3–4.

84. Campos, *Ottoman Brothers*, 3.

within the empire due to both agricultural failures and the pressures of European competition. Of especial concern to the Ottoman government, dissatisfaction reached across religious and ethnic communities. The 1906–1907 revolt in the eastern Anatolian city of Erzurum included Armenians as well as Muslims. By the time a second opposition congress took place in Paris in 1907, various opposition movements were "unanimous in resolving to overthrow the Ottoman government in order to save the empire."[85]

The revolution and counterrevolution unfolded over the course of a tumultuous year between 1908 and 1909. In summer 1908, there was a revolt among Ottoman troops in Macedonia, together with the assassination of several Ottoman generals. Now based in Salonica, the CUP seized the opportunity to call for reinstatement of the 1876 constitution. In an attempt to stave off imminent overthrow, the sultan-caliph hurriedly restored the constitutional order and promised far-reaching reform concessions. As we can see in the excerpt from feminist writer Halide Edib's (1884–1964) *Memoirs*, where she recounts her 1908 experiences in Istanbul, there was a flush of excitement in a city that thought it had found a "panacea" to "[cure]" "all the old evils."[86] Celebrations then spread to provincial centers across the empire (see Document 9).[87]

In this manner, Abdülhamid II's reign survived the remainder of 1908, seemingly against the odds. However, early 1909 was beset by factionalism. The rising power of the CUP was countered both by liberal parliamentary opponents accusing the now-dominant organization of its own authoritarianism (with which Edib too would grow disenchanted) and by the newly formed Society of Islamic Unity, which opposed the CUP's secularism. A short-lived counterrevolution coalesced by April 1909, with Abdülhamid II as the temporary beneficiary of an uprising against the CUP that was led by Muslim activists and loyalist troops. However, within a couple of weeks, CUP-allied troops struck back forcibly, executing Hamidian loyalists, reconvening the parliament, and deposing the sultan-caliph. Abdülhamid was exiled (ironically, to Salonica) and spent his last days practicing carpentry in an Istanbul palace on the Bosporus.

---

85. Campos, *Ottoman Brothers*, 26.

86. Halide Edib Adīvar, *Memoirs of Halidé Edib* (New York: Century, [n.d.] [1926]), 266, 271; de Bellaigue, *Islamic Enlightenment*, 262, 276; Campos, *Ottoman Brothers*, 26–27.

87. Campos, *Ottoman Brothers*, 32.

In the midst of intercommunal recriminations and a breakdown in governance, there was a massacre of thousands of Armenians, as well as over a thousand Assyrian Christians, in the southern Turkish city of Adana. Abdülhamid II's brother Reşad was installed as Sultan Mehmed V, as the CUP quickly proceeded to impose authoritarian measures in order to assert its control over the Ottoman Empire. Under the slogan "Unity of the Elements," which espoused "common purposes across the diverse Ottoman communities," the CUP program advanced several noteworthy policies. Limitations were placed on the sultan-caliph's governing power, notwithstanding the secularizing CUP's improbably renewed strategic emphasis on pan-Islamic identity. Military reforms emulating a Western model proceeded, including universal conscription across religious communities, Muslim and non-Muslim alike. Meanwhile, an attempted centralizing of authority in Istanbul ended up prompting provincial uprisings in favor of decentralization, from Albania to the Arabian Peninsula.[88]

North Africa

Given the CUP's commitment to preserving the territorial integrity of the empire, the maneuverings of European powers in North Africa during this period would prove especially damaging to Istanbul's position. Italy—a party to the 1882 Triple Alliance with Germany and Austria-Hungary now countering the Triple Entente of Britain, France, and Russia—was eager to demonstrate its own relevance to the growing European competition for African colonies. Italy ignited a 1911–1912 war with the Ottoman Empire when it occupied the Ottoman provinces of Tripolitania and Cyrenaica (two of three provinces, the other being Fezzan, that would subsequently be merged to create modern Libya). At this time, the Ottomans' provincial forces were off fighting in Yemen. But CUP military officers in Libya—including a young Mustafa Kemal—enlisted local fighters from the Sanusi Sufi order in a tenacious guerrilla struggle against the Italians.

In a war whose markedly modern character featured the first use of airpower, the Italians' vastly superior naval capabilities proved determinative.[89] The Italian navy defeated the Ottomans in several engagements,

---

88. Howard, *History of the Ottoman Empire*, 298.
89. McMeekin, *Ottoman Endgame*, 64–65.

spanning from the Red Sea to the Mediterranean and Aegean. In April 1912, it even began shelling the Dardanelles that guarded access to the Ottoman capital. Any Italian advance toward Istanbul carried the potential for a wider conflict involving Russia, which immediately felt threatened by the Ottomans' resulting closure of the Bosporus waterway leading into the Black Sea. However, Ottoman defeat was soon sealed by an October 1912 treaty in which Tripolitania, the empire's last remaining colony in North Africa, was ceded to Italy. Made painfully aware of its naval deficiency, Istanbul placed an order for two new British dreadnought battleships, paid for by raising public contributions from across the empire.

The Balkan Wars

The Italo-Turkish War led directly into the two Balkan Wars of 1912–1913 which, by stoking a cauldron of Balkan conflict, can be plausibly construed as the initiation of WWI. While the Ottomans were busy battling Italy in North Africa, an unlikely coalition—given the countries' contending nationalist and territorial claims—among the Balkan League of Bulgaria, Serbia, Greece, and Montenegro emerged to take advantage of Istanbul's diverted energies. Between October and December of 1912, the coalition members launched a war against the Ottomans. They made shocking headway into the remaining Balkan territories of an empire whose population dwarfed that of the Balkan League. Negotiations began in London during December and extended into January 1913, at which point Istanbul's delegates agreed to peace terms including the surrender to Bulgaria of Edirne (known in English as Adrianople), a venerable Ottoman historical city in Thrace. Outraged at their government's capitulation, a group of Ottoman military officers spearheaded by Ismail Enver (1881–1922) undertook a coup d'état in Istanbul, overthrowing the cabinet led by grand vizier Kâmil Pasha (1833–1913). When the new, post-coup cabinet refused the European powers' demand to surrender Edirne to Bulgaria and the Aegean islands to Greece, war resumed in February. After suffering further losses, the Ottomans were finally compelled to cease fighting, and the resulting May 1913 Treaty of London ended the First Balkan War. The Ottomans were forced, at least temporarily, to relinquish all of their remaining European territory.

Chapter One: 1798–1914

Festering grievances among the short-lived Balkan League alliance brought about the Second Balkan War. In June 1913, Serbia and Greece, joined now by Romania, allied with one another against Bulgaria, which quickly found itself on the defensive against its new Balkan enemies. By July, the Ottomans seized the opportunity to strike back against reeling Bulgaria. By entering the Second Balkan War, the Ottomans were able to retake territory in Thrace, including Edirne, behind a cavalry march led by Enver (who thereupon attained heroic status). Under the September 1913 Treaty of Constantinople, the Ottomans regained European territory, if merely the small corner of the southeastern Balkans that continues to represent present-day Turkey's western boundary.

Notwithstanding the symbolically as well as strategically significant reconquest of Edirne, the North African and Balkan Wars left the Ottoman Empire shaken. Not least was the inflaming of intercommunal tensions in the wake of the Balkan Wars. Hundreds of thousands of Muslim refugees were driven out of the Balkans, destined for Istanbul. Similarly, hundreds of thousands of Orthodox Christians were driven westward out of Ottoman territory, including Thrace, Smyrna (known in Turkish as Izmir), and the Aegean region. Thus foreshadowed were the further, violent population transfers that would occur approximately a decade later in the wake of another Greco-Turkish war.

The Ottomans' concern for their own security and legitimacy now turned toward the empire's Arab provinces, representing the single largest non-Turkish ethnic group in the empire. This shift was underscored by the Arab-Syrian Congress held in Paris during June 1913. Calling for such measures as the recognition of Arabic "as an official language in Syrian and Arab countries," the congress's main resolutions challenged the perceived official efforts to promote the integration of imperial citizens under a banner of Turkish identity (see Document 10).[90] Though the congress is often seen as a sign of burgeoning Arab nationalism, most Arabs at this juncture retained allegiance to Ottomanism: many supported moves toward greater decentralization but not separatism.[91]

---

90. "Resolution of the Arab-Syrian Congress at Paris, June 21, 1913," in J. C. Hurewitz, ed., *The Middle East and North Africa in World Politics: A Documentary Record*, 2nd ed., *Volume I: European Expansion, 1535–1914* (New Haven, CT: Yale University Press, 1975), 566–67.

91. Dawisha, *Arab Nationalism in the Twentieth Century*, 33; Makdisi, *Age of Coexistence*, 108.

The CUP met the Congress's demands by allowing for the official use of Arabic. The CUP also determined that an overarching emphasis on the empire's Islamic identity continued to offer the most effective strategy for binding together Ottoman citizens—particularly Muslim Arabs.

Challenges to the CUP Leading Up to WWI

Adding to the challenges faced by the Ottomans within Arab territories was another upsurge of Wahhabi power in Arabia. 'Abd al-'Aziz ibn al Sa'ud's (1880–1953) early nineteenth-century ancestors had been defeated in Muhammad Ali's Arabian campaign, but in 1902 he successfully reestablished a base of political control in Riyadh. By 1913, Ibn Saud forged a formidable alliance with the *ikhwan* (brothers), a group of Wahhabi fighters from various tribes, to help vanquish the Saudis' opponents within the region, including Ottoman garrisons. In consolidating his position, Ibn Saud even began to explore the possibility of support and recognition from Britain, which had become the dominant power in the Persian Gulf. Agreements signed with Kuwait, the Trucial States, and Oman effectively converted them into British protectorates by the turn of the twentieth century.

Consistent with the growing confidence shown by the empire's Arab citizens, a new Ottoman parliament elected in 1914 saw more Arab representatives than ever before.[92] For "members of the elite of the Arab provinces of the Empire who had spent their careers in the service of the state, their Ottomanism was natural and ingrained."[93] However, at the same time, the Istanbul government that was about to be confronted with the unprecedented challenges of 1914 was unapologetically authoritarian. Buttressed by the overall institutional dominance of the CUP, power came to be dominated by the dictatorial rule of the so-called Three Pashas. The triumvirate consisted of the personal primacy of Enver, the "hero of Edirne" who became minister of war in January, alongside Ahmed Cemal Pasha (1872–1922), minister for the navy, and Mehmed Talat Bey (best known as Talat Pasha, 1874–1921), minister of the interior (and also later serving concurrently as minister of finance). The challenges facing the new government were many.

---

92. Finkel, *Osman's Dream*, 525.
93. Khalidi, *Palestinian Identity*, 86.

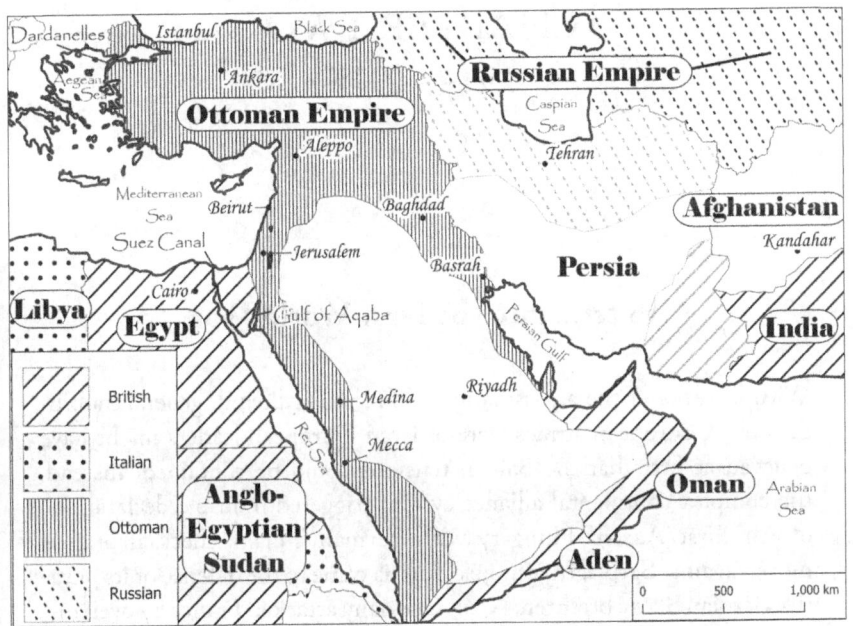

Middle East 1914

Then, on June 28, 1914, in Sarajevo, a young Bosnian Serb nationalist (Gavrilo Princip, 1894–1918) assassinated the Austro-Hungarian crown prince Archduke Franz Ferdinand (1863–1914) and his wife, Sophie (1868–1914). An unchecked flow of strategic and nationalist rivalries and ambitions converged just when the triumvirate already faced the perilous job of negotiating Istanbul's place amid Europe's alliance system.

CHAPTER TWO
1914–1918

Entries into the First World War

Within weeks of the assassination of Franz Ferdinand, general mobilizations of European armies were ordered. European leaders might have believed at first that the Balkan tensions could be contained. Instead, the complex continental alliance system triggered multiple declarations of war. First, Austria-Hungary, with Germany's blank check assurance, moved against Serbia. In response, Russia came to the defense of its putative Serbian Slavic brethren. Next, Germany attacked France by overrunning neutral Belgium, followed by the British Empire's entering on the Allied side. (Notwithstanding the 1882 Triple Alliance, Italy remained neutral until 1915, when it actually entered on the Allied side.)

There is an immense historiography on the European origins of World War I. Less studied are the factors which, over the course of fall 1914, drew the Ottomans into the Great War on the side of the Central powers—Germany and Austria-Hungary. While it is generally accepted that WWI was a decisive turning point in the history of the modern Middle East, it can equally be said that the Ottoman front played a pivotal role in the history of the conflict. As Eugene Rogan observes, the fighting on this front represented "a veritable tower of Babel."[1] With soldiers from North America, North Africa, West Africa, and the Indian subcontinent joining European soldiers sent to the region, the Ottoman front quickly turned the European conflict into a global one. Moreover, as Malcolm Yapp conjectures, the war might well have ended much sooner, and with a very different impact on the shaping of the modern world, had the Ottomans

---

1. Eugene Rogan, *The Fall of the Ottomans: The Great War in the Middle East* (New York: Basic Books, 2015), 13.

stayed neutral or sided with the Allies.² With their control over such strategic waterways as the Suez Canal and Bosporus, the Ottomans diverted millions of Allied soldiers, both European and colonial, and vast amounts of materiel, away from the Western and Eastern Fronts in Europe.

Hitherto detached from the interlocking system of European alliances, the Ottoman government set about considering its options. In the end, however, the final decision was mainly orchestrated by the Young Turk triumvirate of pashas—Enver, Cemal, and Talat. While there was little that was preordained about the Ottomans' ultimate decision to ally with Germany, the previous chapter explored how connections between Berlin and Istanbul developed from the 1880s onward. The relationship had become quite robust on many levels—infrastructural, diplomatic, military, economic, and even ideological if one takes into account Kaiser Wilhelm's Islamophilia.

Although the Ottoman government waited until October 1914 to actually join the war, the Ottoman military mobilized immediately at the beginning of hostilities in Europe. The Ottoman leadership was determined that the empire not be caught as underprepared for another war as it had been during the previous Balkan Wars. Under a policy referred to as "armed neutrality," general mobilization was announced at the start of August. The general mobilization, referred to as *seferberlik*, adopted increasingly interventionist measures. From the initial announcement proclaimed by newspapers and posters, through the massive movement of men from rural villages, to the subsequent appropriations and controls in trade and agriculture, the empire militarized all facets of life.³ It is testament to the devastating impact of the mobilization that across the empire, the suffering of the Great War would continue to be broadly referred to by the word *seferberlik*.⁴

---

2. Malcolm Yapp, *The Making of the Modern Near East, 1792–1923* (London: Longman, 1987), 266.

3. Yiğit Akin, *When the War Came Home: The Ottomans' Great War and the Devastation of an Empire* (Stanford, CA: Stanford University Press, 2018).

4. Najwa al-Qattan, "When Mothers Ate Their Children: Wartime Memory and the Language of Food in Syria and Lebanon," *International Journal of Middle East Studies* 46, no. 4 (2014): 719–36.

Ottoman Entry into the War

While the military mobilized under the shadow of both the escalating crisis in Europe and the secret scheming of the triumvirate, the Ottoman government remained divided about whether and how to choose sides. On the one hand were those officials who advised in favor of Ottoman neutrality. They understandably advocated for a necessary reprieve from the endless wars of the previous decade, given the destruction and suffering during recent entanglements in the Balkans and Libya. They asserted either that the empire did not have a stake in "a third Balkan war"[5] or that this most recent conflict could be successfully contained within Europe. On the other hand were those officials who counseled against the notion that the Ottoman Empire could afford to sit out the war. They argued that the geostrategic significance of the empire's relation to key global trade arteries would inevitably force a pan-European struggle upon Istanbul. In the minds of these officials, the century-long European imperial competition for advantage in the Ottoman Empire loomed large. For them, the situation demanded that Istanbul seek an alliance with at least one European power to protect its own interests.

Those who advised that the empire ought to enter on the side of the Triple Entente stressed the need to safeguard the empire against a direct Entente attack. They highlighted, too, the economic and military interconnections that had developed with France and Britain. France, for example, had long been looked upon as a model for Ottoman administrative reforms. France was also a major investor in the empire's economic infrastructure. Moreover, Cemal Pasha in particular admired France: he had lived in Paris and spoke French. Britain, too, was a major trading partner. More important, Britain was widely recognized as the world's greatest naval power. For a long time, British officers had been closely engaged in training the Ottoman navy and, most recently, it was from British shipyards that the Ottoman government had ordered its two new dreadnoughts.

For their own part, neither Britain nor France tried very hard to court the Ottoman Empire as an ally. Compared to the more immediate and intensely experienced battle lines in western Europe, operations in the

---

5. As WWI has sometimes been dubbed by historians, e.g., Robert Bideleux and Ian Jeffries, *A History of Eastern Europe: Crisis and Change*, 2nd ed. (New York: Routledge, 2007).

Chapter Two: 1914–1918

East were widely dismissed in these early stages as a minor sideshow. Both countries vastly underestimated the contributions the Ottoman military could make. More to the point, neither was willing to provide Istanbul with a guarantee against Russian war aims, which, as everyone knew, included control over the Dardanelles. Russia had been the Ottoman Empire's chief adversary over the previous century, and it would have been very difficult for the Entente allies to assuage Ottoman fears of further Russian encroachment along their borders.

As for the possibility of the Ottoman Empire's pursuing an alliance with the Central powers, Enver Pasha played a key role, holding to his certitude that Germany would win the war. He had been posted previously to Germany as a military attaché, and he had his own close links with German military advisors who had long been involved in reorganizing the Ottoman Army. Moreover, German money and arms were on offer, as well as German promises both to end the intolerable Capitulations system and to help regain from Russian control former Ottoman territories in eastern Anatolia—Kars, Batum, and Ardahan, the so-called three lost provinces. In his capacity as minister of war, Enver was in an especially influential position to steer things his way. On August 2, 1914, he secretly secured an Ottoman-German treaty and negotiated German shipments of money and arms. Ottoman forces were mobilized but they remained uncommitted, and Enver did what he could to delay initiating operations on Germany's behalf. Perhaps he expected, as did many throughout Europe at the time, that the war would be over quickly. Still, Enver had to personally manipulate events in such a way as to overcome ongoing divisions among the Ottoman decision-makers over how to proceed.

Key to the Ottoman Empire's ultimately finding itself at war against the Entente powers was the subterfuge surrounding the transferred ownership of German warships to the Ottoman Empire. Two earlier events in naval procurement and deployment helped bring about these machinations. First, as was indicated in Chapter 1, when the loss of Libya to Italy in 1912 exposed the empire's naval weakness, Istanbul negotiated the purchase of two new British battleships, named *Osman* and *Reşadiye*, paid for by public contributions raised from all over the empire. When war broke out in summer 1914, First Lord of the Admiralty Churchill decided to commandeer the ships, irreparably damaging the British-Ottoman relationship. Second, in early August, the German ships *Goeben* and *Breslau*, which had been deployed off the coast of Algeria in an effort to disrupt vital French army transports, were forced to make their way eastward across the Mediterranean to avoid capture by the British navy. When they arrived at the Dardanelles, the Ottoman government eventually agreed to allow the two German ships safe passage. Arrangements were then made for their formal transfer into the Ottoman navy, as replacements for the two withheld Ottoman-purchased ships that had been commissioned into the British navy. While British warships were forced to wait outside the Dardanelles, the Ottomans' new German-supplied ships moved into the Black Sea. Their use in the bombardment of the port of Odessa on October 29, 1914, officially launched the outwardly neutral Ottoman Empire into war against Russia, surprising some Ottoman cabinet ministers and infuriating others who resigned. Sultan Mehmed V (1844–1918, r. 1909–1918) declared war against the Allies on November 11, calling for a *jihād*, or holy war (see Document 11). Though we need to remain mindful of the term's complexities, the British took very seriously the sultan's "summon[ing] [of 300 million Muslims] by sacred Fetva to a supreme struggle."[6]

The Call for *Jihād*

The CUP-dominated government had already chosen to continue the Hamidian strategy of pursuing pan-Islamic identity to bind the Ottoman Empire. So it is perhaps best to first locate the sultan's call for *jihād* within the domestic context of seeking a mobilizing narrative to justify expected sacrifices from the population. Nonetheless, this call for *jihād* also factored significantly into German considerations, and visions, of an alliance with the sultan-caliph and the serious threat it posed to British and Russian imperial communications (at the Suez Canal and the Dardanelles, respectively). Moreover, the prospect of Ottoman forces tying down Russian forces in the Caucasus, and thus preventing their deployment on the more vital fronts in eastern Europe, carried much weight. An especially important role was played by Kaiser Wilhelm, who was greatly roused by the potential of the Ottoman sultan to call for a *jihād* against the Allied powers, in whose global empires resided large Muslim populations. "Our consuls in Turkey and India," the kaiser

---

6. From Charles F. Horne and Walter F. Austin, eds., *Source Records of the Great War*, Volume II (USA: National Alumni, 1923), 400.

Chapter Two: 1914–1918

insisted, "must inflame the whole Mohammedan world to wild revolt . . . ; for if we are bled to death [by their encirclement policy], at least England shall lose India."[7] Britain remained as fearful of the Central powers' plan to inflame the world's Muslims against the Allies as Germany was excited by the prospect. These fears would be captured especially well by the novelist John Buchan, who served in the war propaganda bureau (see Document 12).[8] In the end, however, the sultan's call for *jihād* would in fact have little measured impact in terms of desertions on the battlefronts or uprisings in the far-flung colonies.

The term *jihād* continues to be frequently employed in a warped sense today—by violent activists within the Middle East and elsewhere, as well as by Western political actors and media commentators. These distortions require us to understand that there exist various meanings of the concept. Originating from within early Islamic history, *jihād* can be literally translated as "struggle." Though *jihād* is commonly connected to making war, this form of external striving in service of the faith has always stood alongside the inner, "greater" *jihād* associated with one's personal struggle to follow in the path of God (inclusive of spiritual, moral, and intellectual efforts).[9] Any reading and application of the concept of *jihād* necessarily depends on individual interpretations within specific historical contexts. Also worth noting here is, of course, the extent to which all European powers pursued their own modes of religion-inflected politics. In the Caucasus, Orthodox Russia sought to foment Christian solidarities on both sides of the Ottoman-Russian border (again, with limited success but, as we shall see, especially tragic implications when it comes to the 1915 Armenian genocide). Further, Britain was eager to mobilize domestic Protestant as well as Jewish religious sentiments in support of their own "liberation" of Jerusalem and the Holy Land. (Britain had emerged by 1917 both as a bastion of the ever more significant

---

7. Quoted in Rob Johnson, *The Great War and the Middle East* (Oxford: Oxford University Press, 2016), 75.

8. John Buchan, *Greenmantle* (London: Hodder & Stoughton, 1916).

9. John Kelsay, "Jihad," in Gerhard Bowering, ed., *Islamic Political Thought: An Introduction* (Princeton, NJ: Princeton University Press, 2015), 86. It is illustrative to observe that within the vital context of Islamic jurisprudence, the "general term for legal reasoning was *ijtihad* (to strive or struggle intellectually)," which "comes from the same root as *jihad* (to strive or struggle in God's path)." John Esposito, *Islam: The Straight Path* (Oxford: Oxford University Press, 1988), 83.

phenomenon of evangelical Protestant advocacy for Zionism and as a key redoubt in Jewish Zionist leaders' search for support.)

Ultimately, the military effects of the sultan's call were relatively few. Underscoring the degree to which the Ottoman leadership had little global pull on Muslims around the world, the interests of most communities were more localized. Questions of loyalty and allegiance are tied in complex ways to evolving interests in which politics, ethnicity, and language can all play as significant a role as religious solidarity. Even religious authorities in territories such as Egypt and India did not back the Ottoman call for *jihād*, and many Muslim soldiers fought bravely for the British Empire against the Ottoman Empire. One of the more consequential reactions among Ottoman religious figures to the sultan's call for *jihād* was the rather muted and ambiguous response by Sharif Husayn (1853–1931), custodian of the Muslim holy cities of Mecca and Medina. Husayn's hesitancy to engage with the Ottoman sultan's call can be explained by two main factors. First, Husayn had in recent years become increasingly unsettled by the Ottomans' continued push for centralizing reforms. Istanbul's intrusive infrastructure projects, such as railways and telegraphs, progressively threatened to curtail his own autonomy in the Hejaz. Second, the dominant presence of the British navy in the Red Sea led Husayn to either fear British reprisal or seek Britain's help for his own Hashemite family's dynastic ambitions. The emirate of Kuwait, for example, had earlier benefited from establishing cordial British diplomatic relations through the 1899 Anglo-Kuwaiti Agreement. With Sharif Husayn increasingly open to entertaining negotiations with London, British officials appeared eager for an alliance with a prominent Muslim leader that might mitigate the much-feared pan-Islamic influence wielded by the Ottoman sultan. Husayn's position as guardian of the holy places, and his status as a member of the Hashemite clan descended from the Prophet Muhammad's Quraysh tribe, could be construed as a religious authority rivaling the Ottoman sultan. The context was thus set for Britain's alliance with Sharif Husayn's family, the first of many competing undertakings that helped ensure the Middle Eastern theater became much more than a sideshow.

The main campaigns directly involved the Entente powers on four fronts: in Egypt and Palestine, the Caucasus, the Dardanelles (that is, Gallipoli), and Iraq (often referred to as the Mesopotamian campaign). Although there are benefits to examining these campaigns in turn, one must be wary of studying them in isolation from one another. Though

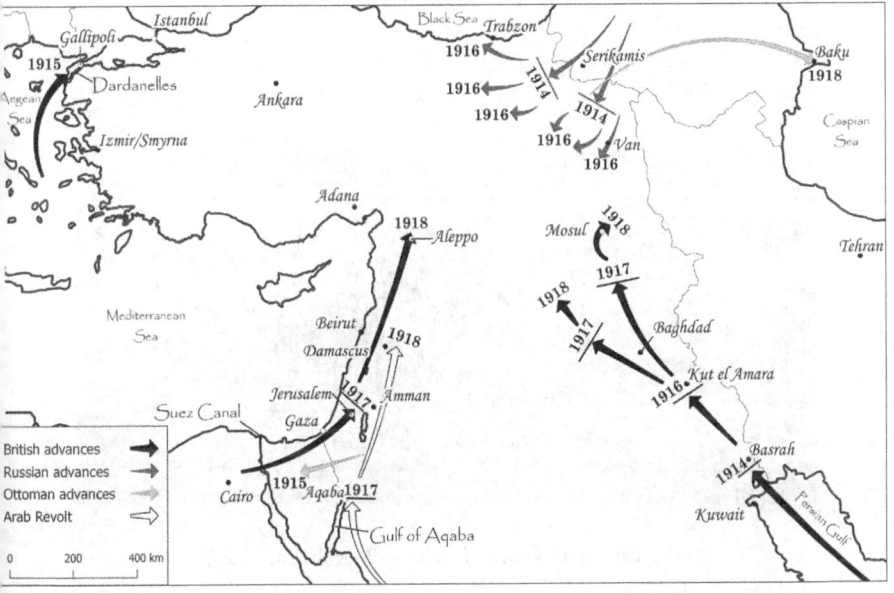

World War I battlefronts in the Middle East

geographically far apart, they were fundamentally interconnected, in terms of competing demands on resources and infrastructure, and with respect to concurrent strategies of international diplomacy.[10]

Egypt and Palestine

On November 21, 1914, Cemal Pasha set off from Istanbul to attack British positions on the Suez Canal. Germany was pushing hard for an Ottoman strike at the British Empire's key line of communications. At the very least, such an operation would force a diversion of Allied troops away from the Western Front. For his part, Cemal sought to reimpose Ottoman rule over Egypt. (Recall that, officially, Egypt had remained part of the Ottoman Empire even as it suffered under the rule of an occupying British administration since 1882.) Cemal's military operation was constructed on the inflated premise that a surprise attack on the Suez

---

10. See Kristian Coates Ulrichsen, *The First World War in the Middle East* (London: Hurst, 2014).

The Ottoman Camel Corps at Beersheba, 1915.

Canal must surely inspire a sweeping pan-Muslim uprising against the British. Expectations of rousing such religious sentiment had further led Cemal to expect a constant stream of volunteers to join his troops as they advanced through Syria to the Sinai Peninsula.

Ottoman forces' numbers, however, remained relatively small (especially compared to the British forces they sought to defeat). Nonetheless, given the limits to the Ottoman transportation infrastructure, it was a considerable achievement for Cemal just to move whatever forces he had across the forbidding Sinai desert and pull off a surprise attack on the Suez Canal on February 2, 1915. In the end, British defensive positions on the waterway had been well prepared. Cemal's overextended forces were beaten back by the determined resistance of two British Indian divisions (Egypt's own army being deployed on security duties in the Anglo-Egyptian condominium of Sudan). Cemal's anticipated uprising of Muslim compatriots against their colonial overlords never happened. But the German goal of tying down the British was successful enough.

Britain maintained a large military presence in Egypt throughout WWI and beyond. Joining the British soldiers and Indian divisions were the ANZAC forces (the Australian and New Zealand Army Corps) who disembarked in Egypt, ostensibly on their way to Europe. Fearing the pan-Islamic sentiments the Ottomans had hoped to rally, Britain declared a protectorate over Egypt during late 1914 (see Document 13). Finally bringing an official end to the lingering claims of Ottoman sovereignty, Sir Henry McMahon (1862–1949) was appointed as high commissioner. Britain also proclaimed military rule and, as a theatrical show of dominance, marched units of the British Army through the streets of Cairo. With the launch of its offensive campaigns at Gallipoli in 1915 and Palestine in 1916, Britain gradually turned the port of Alexandria into "half camp and half hospital."[11] Though Egyptians did not rise against British colonial rule during the course of the war, wartime tribulations transformed relations on the ground. British demands greatly aggravated the growing resentment against colonial occupation. The peasantry was hit especially hard by economic scarcities related to rising food prices, food shortages, and the requisition of farm animals, as well as by being dragged into serving for the Egyptian Labour Corps and deployed in fields of operation far from home.[12]

The British Capture of Jerusalem

Throughout 1916, British forces made major efforts to push back against the Ottomans and advance across the Sinai Peninsula. Their main achievement—invaluable support for which came from the hard labor of Egyptian "volunteers" of the Egyptian Labor Corps and Egyptian Camel Transport Corps—was the construction of both a railway line and water pipeline to provide necessary logistical support across challenging terrain. By early 1917, British forces were at the borders of southern Palestine. There, they met stiff resistance from Ottoman defenses set up at Gaza. But the Ottoman Empire's overall infrastructural limitations, and the impossible burdens imposed on society, caused fatal delays in Ottoman attempts to reinforce the Palestine front. By contrast, over the course of 1917, the commander of the British forces, Lord Edmund Allenby (1861–1936), successfully amassed ever more firepower. This support was thanks to the determination of Prime Minister David Lloyd George (1863–1945, prime minister 1916–1922) to capture Jerusalem "as a Christmas present" for the British public, yet another reminder of how

---

11. Sir Ronald Storrs, *Memoirs* (New York: G. P. Putnam's Sons, 1937), 214.

12. See Kyle Anderson, *The Egyptian Labour Corps: Race, Space, and Place in the First World War* (Austin: University of Texas Press, 2021).

Punch magazine cartoon depiction of the Allied capture of Jerusalem as a new crusade.

deploying religious symbolism for political aims factored in for all sides.

The capture of Jerusalem was achieved on December 11, 1917. Much to Allenby's relief, the holy city itself was surrendered without a fight. Allenby theatrically entered the walls on foot—a deliberate contrast to Kaiser Wilhelm's extravagant visit in 1898, seated on a horse and with banners flying.[13] Allenby's declaration of martial law and establishment of a military administration for Palestine's conquered southern districts were notably accompanied by highly publicized declarations of respect for the religious status quo of the city. Further northward advances by the British imperial Egyptian Expeditionary Force slowed over the first part of 1918. But they progressed more rapidly in the fall. By the time the Ottoman Empire signed the Armistice of Mudros on October 30, the retreating Ottoman Army held a defensive line just north of Aleppo, Syria.

The Balfour Declaration

Developments on the ground in Palestine during late 1917 coincided with London's next major round of diplomacy regarding the future distribution of Ottoman territory. Having already negotiated the future status of Palestine with Sharif Husayn (in the Husayn-McMahon correspondence, to be discussed shortly, see Document 16) and with the French (in the Sykes-Picot Agreement, also to soon be discussed), Palestine became the thrice-promised land. As described in Chapter 1, Zionist leaders had, since the late 1800s, pursued a nationalist response to the alienating and oppressive rule suffered by Jews as minorities in European states. In seeking to build a state of their own, Zionist leaders turned to great powers for support. But little progress was made on

---

13. Please recall the contrasting images in Chapter 1.

Chapter Two: 1914–1918

```
                          Foreign Office,
                          November 2nd, 1917.

Dear Lord Rothschild,
         I have much pleasure in conveying to you, on
behalf of His Majesty's Government, the following
declaration of sympathy with Jewish Zionist aspirations
which has been submitted to, and approved by, the Cabinet
         "His Majesty's Government view with favour the
establishment in Palestine of a national home for the
Jewish people, and will use their best endeavours to
facilitate the achievement of this object, it being
clearly understood that nothing shall be done which
may prejudice the civil and religious rights of
existing non-Jewish communities in Palestine, or the
rights and political status enjoyed by Jews in any
other country"
         I should be grateful if you would bring this
declaration to the knowledge of the Zionist Federation.
```

Balfour Declaration, 1917.

the diplomatic front, until the maelstrom of WWI. Wartime circumstances radically changed things. Reminiscent of the Ottoman Jewish community's 1890s display of fealty to Abdülhamid II, the war's initial stages saw the fledgling Zionist leadership in Palestine, not least the future founding prime minister of Israel, David Ben-Gurion (1886–1973, prime minister 1948–1953, 1955–1963), advocate "loyalty to the Ottoman regime" as the best way to "promote Zionist interests."[14] However, by 1917, negotiations in London between high-placed government officials and leading members of Britain's Jewish community who represented the Zionist movement (especially the biochemist Chaim Weizmann [1874–1952]) helped secure the November 1917 Balfour Declaration.

---

14. Tom Segev, *A State at Any Cost: The Life of David Ben-Gurion* (New York: Farrar, Straus and Giroux, 2020), 118.

As with all wartime correspondence, the Balfour Declaration presents the need to parse deliberately vague formulations of British foreign policymaking. While Britain asserted some degree of support for a national homeland for the Jewish people, it refrained from specifying the creation of a state as such, and there was never consensus on what a home looked like constitutionally. Nor was it clear how exactly a national home was to be facilitated: in this regard, note how British support was further qualified by the stipulation that civil and religious rights of "non-Jewish communities" in Palestine should not be compromised, a phrase that raises several questions of its own. On the one hand, the phrase "nothing shall be done which may prejudice" the rights of Palestinian Arabs clearly sets significant limits on what could actually be achieved on behalf of Zionists' plans for Palestine. On the other hand, the term "non-Jewish communities" reveals a cold neglect for the rights and aspirations of the indigenous Arabs who constituted 90 percent of Palestine's population. During a period when Zionists sought to depict world Jewry as a nationalist entity, and Britain presented itself as their champion, the lack of such recognition of Palestine's Arabs was telling. As Balfour later explained:

> In Palestine we do not propose even to go through the form of consulting the wishes of the present inhabitants of the country. . . . Zionism, be it right or wrong, good or bad, is rooted in age-long traditions, in present needs, in future hopes, of far profounder import than the desires and prejudices of the 700,000 Arabs who now inhabit that ancient land.[15]

The final phrase regarding "the rights and political status enjoyed by Jews in any other country" reflects London's response to the concerns expressed within world Jewry that overt Zionism could open recently emancipated communities in Europe, North America, and elsewhere to charges of dual national loyalties.

Much historiographical debate persists over the motivations that drove Britain's declaration. Several factors have been emphasized. One argument focuses on the biblical romanticism of evangelical Protestant-inflected support for Zionism (notwithstanding ample British antisemitism), and the importance some British leaders attached to the restoration

---

15. Doreen Ingrams, *Palestine Papers, 1917–1922: Seeds of Conflict* (London: John Murray, 1972), 73.

of a Jewish nation in the Holy Land. Another stresses the larger political and diplomatic context, within which the role that grateful Jewish communities in Russia and America could play in pushing their governments for more support in the war effort was advocated. A third argument references British diplomat Sir Mark Sykes's (1879–1919) 1916 diplomatic commitment to an international administration shared with France, underscoring Britain's new determination a year later to push out those French interests. By using European Jewish immigrants to circumvent Sykes's deal with his French counterpart François Georges-Picot (1870–1951), Britain sought to implant its colonial footprint in the eastern Mediterranean, neighboring the Suez Canal.

Although there is no straightforward explanation of the Balfour Declaration's origins, historians have reached one dominant conclusion. Rather than operating either with grand geostrategic foresight or ideological idealism, London was essentially grasping at straws for whatever heightened strategic advantage it could gain at the end of 1917, a year of terrible losses and paltry gains.[16] The grinding intractability of the Israel/Palestine conflict over the ensuing century and beyond would continuously assert the significance of November 1917 as a basic stepping stone in the historical trajectory of Zionism. Yet the genealogy of documents such as the Balfour Declaration in fact indicates the importance of chance, contingency, and haphazard decision-making under conditions of stress.

The Caucasus

For the Ottoman leadership, the major irredentist war aim was recapturing the three lost provinces of eastern Anatolia—Kars, Batum, and Ardahan—previously annexed by Russia following the 1877–1878 Russo-Ottoman War.[17] Enver Pasha, the ambitious "hero of Edirne," assumed that overextended Russian forces would quickly collapse in the

---

16. Jonathan Schneer, *The Balfour Declaration: The Origins of the Arab-Israeli Conflict* (London: Bloomsbury, 2010); Ian Lustick, *Paradigm Lost: From Two-State Solution to One-State Reality* (Philadelphia: University of Pennsylvania Press, 2022).

17. "Irredentism" is a term derived from the formative period of nineteenth-century Italian nationalism, in reference to the reclaiming of territories; the idea has become associated with WWI and its aftermath, particularly the postwar emergence of Italian fascism.

face of a swift offensive strike. When confronted by the Ottoman Army's overwhelming lack of resources necessary for a winter campaign, ranging from ammunition to footwear, he confidently and simply responded by forecasting that "the supply base is in front of us."[18] Enver's first major offensive was launched on December 22, 1914, against the strategically located Russian railhead at Sarikamis. The weather changed dramatically and Ottoman forces suffered major casualties, as much from the cold weather conditions as from the resistance they encountered. Successful Russian counteroffensives over 1915 and 1916 then resulted in a series of Ottoman defeats. In the end, the Ottoman campaigns in the Caucasus would be responsible for colossal losses: of the 120,000 forces that marched on Sarikamis in December 1914, almost 90 percent were killed, wounded, captured, or died of disease and exposure. It has been estimated that Ottoman losses in the Caucasus amounted to three-quarters of all casualties suffered by the Ottoman Army between November 1915 and March 1917.[19] Ultimately, it would be the 1917 Bolshevik Revolution in Russia, and the subsequent extraction of the Russian Army from the war, that saved what remained of Enver's forces.

The massive Ottoman defeats in the Caucasus were both self-inflicted and highly demoralizing. Though they undoubtedly served the German war aim of diverting Russian forces from the European Front, they also diverted Ottoman forces from engaging in campaigns against the British Empire to the south. Most catastrophic was the consequent destruction of the Armenian communities, caught in the middle of overlapping tensions and territorial claims in an epic clash of Eurasian empires.

The Armenian Genocide

At the outset of the war, prominent leaders of the Ottoman Armenian community (approximately two million in size) pledged loyalty to the sultan, and tens of thousands mobilized to join the ranks of the Ottoman Army. This did not, however, stop the Ottoman leadership from seeing the Armenian community as an impending fifth column tied to their Christian coreligionists in Russia, and thus as a collective danger in the eastern territories (see Document 14). In the previous chapter, we examined earlier perceptions of

---

18. Quoted in Johnson, *Great War and the Middle East*, 159.
19. Yapp, *Making of the Modern Near East*, 274.

Armenians as potentially disloyal Ottoman subjects, as evidenced by previous massacres and periods of persecution (1894–1896 and 1909 in particular). Such suspicions were greatly exacerbated and radicalized by the war in the Caucasus. The stakes grew even higher with the panic that set in after the series of Ottoman military defeats during the winter of 1914–1915, followed by the Allies' landing at Gallipoli in April 1915.

In April 1915, Russia supported an Armenian uprising in the city of Van, seeking to exploit the notion of Christian solidarities. After fierce fighting with Ottoman forces, the city was occupied by Russia. On April 24, the Ottoman government rounded up and killed large numbers of Armenian leaders, artists, and intellectuals in Istanbul, an event which is now annually commemorated as Armenian Genocide Memorial Day. Though an increasing number of countries officially recognizes the date as such (recently notable, the US in 2021), Turkey continues to deny a genocide, instead regarding the events as a tragic by-product of wartime. But, once Ottoman leaders framed Armenians as an existential danger, the cruel policies that resulted from this view made the perceived threat a self-fulfilling policy. Each side now feared the worst from the other. It is true that Armenian communities engaged in local sabotage, perhaps out of fear of Ottoman authorities who for generations had failed to protect them, or out of vengeance for decades of violence and persecution, or out of treason and betrayal on behalf of Russia. But whatever the reasons for Armenian violence, the widespread fears held by the Ottoman government that some rebellious Armenians might assist Russia influenced decisions to unleash crimes against humanity.[20]

Ostensibly as a way to prevent both what they feared was the imminent collapse of Ottoman authority and the usurpation of control by Russian forces in the eastern provinces, the Ottoman government administered brutal policies of deportation. Some authors have viewed these deportation policies as being in line with prewar efforts at radical demographic engineering, premised on the "unmixing" of populations. As we have seen, the Ottoman government had engaged during the Balkan Wars in the resettlement of Muslim refugees while simultaneously displacing Christian populations, who were driven into Greece or shot. But the 1915 plans for Armenians were also categorically different from previous relocation programs: no provisions whatsoever were made for displaced Armenians. The program pursued by Ottoman authorities followed a

---

20. Ronald Grigor Suny, *"They Can Live in the Desert but Nowhere Else": A History of the Armenian Genocide* (Princeton, NJ: Princeton University Press, 2015).

Armenians who escaped from the Turkish
starvation zone approach British lines.

two-track approach. First, verbal but secret orders for mass murder were forwarded. Second, an open deportation policy was declared. This forced Armenians to abandon their homes in strategic areas—where locals were feared to be providing refuge for insurgents—for what proved to be death marches into the harsh terrain of the Syrian and Iraqi deserts. There, irregular militias and local Kurdish tribesmen contributed to the killing of hundreds of thousands.

Recognizing the trauma of the Armenian genocide has been one of the main challenges faced by scholars of the First World War. Again, the Turkish government has refused to recognize it as a genocide. In fact, calling it such has been penalized as a criminal offense in Turkey, as Turkish law instead asserts the contingency of the context. Yet increasing numbers of Turkish scholars—drawing upon new research into records left by the series of courts-marshal established by the Ottoman government from 1919 to 1920—have exposed what Taner Akçam calls the "Young Turks' crimes against humanity."[21]

---

21. Taner Akçam, *The Young Turks' Crime against Humanity: The Armenian Genocide and Ethnic Cleansing in the Ottoman Empire* (Princeton, NJ: Princeton University Press, 2012). See also Uğur Üngör and Mehmet Polatel, *Confiscation and Destruction: The Young Turk Seizure of Armenian Property* (London: Continuum, 2011).

The Dardanelles

Of all the terribly destructive campaigns of the war, the Gallipoli invasion holds a paramount place in the Western popular imagination. The Dardanelles strait, a narrow strip of water dividing Europe from Asia, had for centuries lain at the center of both European Romantic consciousness and imperial strategizing. When Britain and France settled on launching an operation at the Dardanelles in early 1915, championed in large part by First Lord of the Admiralty Winston Churchill, the prospect of victory promised several gains (see Document 15). Foremost was the urgent need to reopen trade routes to the Black Sea and help supply the Russian Front with much needed materiel. Combined with the German blockade of Russian ports in the Baltic, the Ottomans' closure of the Dardanelles (as part of the move which had spelled the Empire's entry into the war on the side of Germany) had left Russia solely dependent on its Pacific ports. When not completely ice-bound during winter months, these ports were accessible only by a single-track railway.[22] Furthermore, it was widely expected that a successful breakthrough in the Dardanelles, followed by the ensuing Allied occupation of Istanbul, would effectively drive the Ottomans out of the war. Not least, it was hoped that shaking up the grinding stalemate on the Eastern Front would lead the way for neutral powers such as Italy, Greece, Romania, and possibly Bulgaria to join the Allied side.

Certainly for the Ottomans, an operation at Gallipoli, so close to Istanbul, was the most feared Allied attack. Thus, much effort was expended by both the Germans and Ottomans to exploit as best they could the natural defensive advantages of the region. Trenches were dug and barbed wire laid down along the jagged untraversable valleys of the European Gallipoli Peninsula, while mines were laid in the narrow waterways of the Dardanelles strait, and land batteries were bolstered along the coastal fortifications of the strait. This ensured that large ships could not enter without significant damage.

Thus, when the frontal Anglo-French assault was launched in the Dardanelles on March 18, 1915, it was met with huge losses in ships and

---

22. Notably, Russia's loss of its Pacific reach in the Russo-Japanese War of 1904–1905 came at the hands of Japan, a rising Asian power that was now among the WWI Allies. Following the war, Japan gained further influence with the acquisition of German imperial territories in the Pacific.

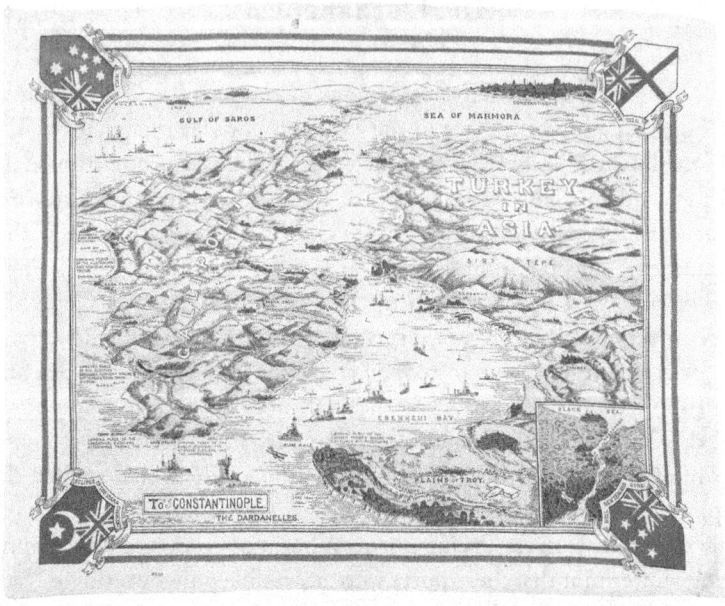

A pictorial cotton map of the Gallipoli campaign.

fatalities. The Allies were now gripped by the fear that an admission of failure here would be too damaging in the hands of the enemy, who could be allowed no boost to their morale. Accordingly, the Allies expanded operations and undertook an amphibious landing on the Gallipoli Peninsula. A successful invasion of the peninsula could allow for a land assault on the coastal fortifications of the Dardanelles, and thus remove the batteries that were preventing sweepers from clearing the lethal mines. The landings at Gallipoli are most often recognized for the engagement of the British-led ANZAC forces. But it is also important to recognize the military contributions of the French, whose commitment to the campaign was fueled in part by mistrust of their British allies regarding the potential spoils of war in the event of a victory. On April 25, 1915, British and French troops attacked Cape Helles, while ANZAC forces landed further north. Under a constant hail of Ottoman gunfire from the ridges above, the invading forces dug into narrow stretches of beachhead dissected by the deep gullies running crosswise. ANZAC forces pushed to gain the high ground against Ottoman forces who held it, but there was a clear advantage to the defensive positions. The Ottoman soldier tasked

Chapter Two: 1914–1918   73

with holding the line was Mustafa Kemal: when facing an approaching ANZAC column, Kemal famously rallied the troops by telling them that "I don't order you to attack, I order you to die."[23] Immortalized for this inspired defense of the Ottoman Empire, Kemal would within a few years become the founder of the secular Turkish nation—and earn the moniker Atatürk.

The failure of the Allies to break out of the beachheads that spring led to a bloody stalemate throughout the long, hot summer. It would take until October 1915, and an actual visit to the battlefields, for Britain's military leaders to finally admit to the overwhelming challenges. The Allied evacuation, concluded by January 1916, has since been remembered as the only real success of the whole Gallipoli campaign. The death toll is estimated at 230,000 Allied losses and 300,000 Ottoman losses, with the harsh environmental conditions of the region—that is, climate (both summer heat and winter hypothermia), flies, and dysentery—being held more responsible than combat for overall casualties. The political ramifications were significant as well. In London, for example, the ruling government and Churchill's political career appeared to be over, as he was relieved from command of the Royal Navy. And Bulgaria, whose allegiances had until then swung in the balance, decided in the wake of the Allied defeat to enter the war on behalf of the Central powers.

Diplomacy after the Dardanelles Campaign

The Dardanelles campaign led to a historic agreement among the Allies (see Document 15). It was Russia who first called for the Dardanelles campaign, as a necessary show of force to divert Ottoman resources from the Caucasus. But given their own clear interests in Istanbul, Russian leaders were wary of an Allied victory leading to an Anglo-French occupation of this vital region. Russia thus sought firm assurances from her allies. We saw in the last chapter how, until the outbreak of war, the Allies had for decades settled, more or less, on a policy of maintaining the integrity of the Ottoman Empire, if only out of fear that its partition would force a European conflict. But in the midst of war, Britain and France were now prepared to give Russia what she had so coveted.

---

23. Quoted in Rogan, *Fall of the Ottomans*, 128.

In the planning of the Dardanelles operation, France too expressed reservations about Britain's dominant military position in the Ottoman theater. Accordingly, France desperately sought to find troops to spare for the Dardanelles operation, refused to consider an alternative operation along the Syrian coast (which might actually have been more propitious for the whole operation), and then laid French claims for a vaguely defined Syria which also included Jerusalem and the Holy Land. These claims built especially on France's well-established cultural and religious links between the French Catholic Church and the Maronite Christian population of Lebanon (which was at this time part of so-called Greater Syria). French claims also reflected the growing extent of economic relations that had developed, from the running of railways to investments in silk production. In Paris, highly influential military and colonialist organizations campaigned for as large a sphere of influence as would befit a Mediterranean power.

For its part, London responded to the assertion of Russian and French territorial demands by demarcating its own interests. If Russia was to be recognized as the dominant power in eastern Anatolia and the Dardanelles, then Britain demanded control over southern Mesopotamia, which was viewed as a logical extension of its interests in the Persian Gulf. From the point of view of London, France's position on the Syrian coast, stretching as far east as possible, could serve as a useful buffer between the Russian and British Empires. Britain also sought the deepwater harbor at Haifa, from where railway connections could build a land bridge to Basra, at the headwaters of the Persian Gulf. The port at Haifa aside, the three Christian powers could not agree on Palestine, in which all held interests. So Palestine was provisionally declared an international administration. A year after the Constantinople Agreement, British and French representatives Sykes and Picot secretly sketched provisional lines on a map to mark out the agreed-upon spheres of influence. A British head of military intelligence quipped that "it seems to me (...) that we are rather in the position of the hunters who divided up the skin of the bear before they had killed it."[24]

---

24. Quoted in James Barr, *A Line in the Sand: Britain, France, and the Struggle That Shaped the Middle East* (London: Simon & Schuster, 2011), 32.

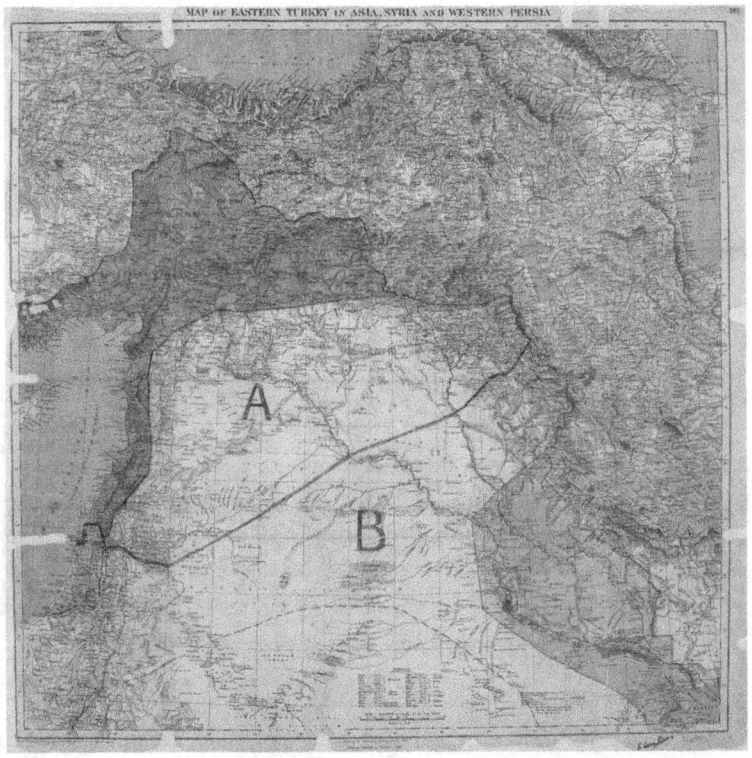

Map of the Sykes-Picot Agreement borders, 1916.

The Arab Revolt

At the same time as British officials were negotiating with their European allies, officials in Cairo were conducting negotiations with Sharif Husayn. As a descendant of the Prophet Muhammad and custodian of the holy cities of Mecca and Medina, Husayn offered Britain the prospect of mitigating the much-feared Ottoman call for *jihād*. In response, the British high commissioner in Cairo, McMahon, struck a deal with Sharif Husayn, outlined in an exchange of letters from July 1915 to January 1916 (see Document 16). Husayn not only provided Britain with his own effective endorsement of another holy war, to potentially offset the Ottoman sultan-caliph's, he also promised an Arab revolt that would divert resources from the Ottoman forces threatening Egypt. By this point, Britain had been led to believe, from some intercepted documents, that Arab leaders

Hanging of Arab nationalists in Damascus, 1916.

were making preparations to mobilize in a widespread uprising against the Ottomans. No such action was in fact being contemplated. But the repressive wartime policies of the Ottoman government certainly took their toll on local allegiances (see Document 17). Following the June 1916 arrest and hanging of Arab notables for treason, Cemal Pasha was henceforth identified as al-Saffah, "the blood shedder," or "the butcher"—while Sharif Husayn warned Istanbul that "blood will cry for blood."[25]

Shortly after these hangings, Sharif Husayn's son Faysal (1885–1933) launched the Arab revolt, together with (and made famous by) British military officer T. E. Lawrence (1888–1935). In acting as the main liaison between the British and Faysal, Lawrence clearly exploited the position to develop his own legendary reputation and style but did become a trusted adviser of Faysal's.[26] After first aiming to secure the Hejaz region,

---

25. Quoted in Rogan, *Fall of the Ottomans*, 240.

26. Ali A. Allawi, *Faisal I of Iraq* (New Haven, CT: Yale University Press, 2014); Scott Anderson, *Lawrence in Arabia: War, Deceit, Imperial Folly and the Making of the Modern Middle East* (New York: Doubleday, 2013).

the revolt followed a strategy of guerrilla warfare against Ottoman forces. This mostly involved acts of sabotage on the Hejaz railway in an attempt to further undermine the Ottomans' stretched infrastructure capacity. Over the course of 1917–1918, Faysal and the leaders of the Arab revolt would play a key role in securing Allenby's right flank before ultimately entering Damascus and setting up an Arab administration. This administration, made up of Arabs from the Hejaz, Iraq, and Syria, can be seen as the first real bid to create and showcase an independent Arab entity. But the modest number of adherents to the Arab revolt (often estimated at six thousand fighters) pales in comparison to the hundreds of thousands of Arabs who remained loyal to the Ottoman Army (though as conscripts, not necessarily volunteers). This was despite the best efforts of British pilots who dropped leaflets aiming to convince Arabs "to take advantage of the opportunities to escape and come to us" (see Document 18).[27]

What did Sir Henry McMahon offer Sharif Husayn in return for launching the Arab revolt? In highly equivocal terms, and at the risk of running his own policy in this distant region, McMahon promised Sharif Husayn an "independent" Arab kingdom, subject to the rendering of British "advice." As for the borders of this kingdom, they remained ill-defined. The key passage of the Husayn-McMahon correspondence in this regard can be found in a letter dated October 24, 1915. McMahon agreed to support the independence of the Arabs "within the limits demanded by the Sherif of Mecca," with the exception of "portions of Syria lying to the west of the districts of Damascus, Homs, Hama and Aleppo."[28] These qualifications reflected the official concessions simultaneously being made to French claims in Syria and Lebanon, but were subject to much debate over the following years, largely in regard to whether Palestine was excepted from the promised independence. The ambiguities and omissions of McMahon's phrasing would be subject to intense parsing, as Britain sought in later years to build a case for Palestine's being excluded.[29] But

---

27. Great Britain, *Palestine Commission on the Disturbances of August, 1929, Volume 1. Evidence Heard During the 1st to 29th Sittings* (London: His Majesty's Stationery Office, 1930), 908.

28. "The Husayn-McMahon Correspondence, 14 July 1915–10 March 1916," in J. C. Hurewitz, ed., *The Middle East and North Africa in World Politics: A Documentary Record*, 2nd ed., Volume 2: *British-French Supremacy, 1914–1945* (New Haven, CT: Yale University Press, 1979), 50. (See Document 16.)

29. See, for example, the 1922 Churchill White Paper (Document 30).

Sharif Husayn, guardian of the holy places.

the basic nature of British policy is captured at the time in a remark by McMahon himself: "What we have to arrive at now is to tempt the Arab people into the right path, detach them from the enemy and bring them on to our side. This on our part is at present largely a matter of words, and to succeed we must use persuasive terms and abstain from academic haggling over conditions."[30] The point of the promise was to mobilize an ally. Mere details could be worked out later.

Ultimately, the whole mess was a sign of just how fractured Britain's own policymaking process was during wartime. It also shows how desperate Britain was in 1915 and 1916 to negotiate whatever support they could for a grinding, stalemated war effort (especially in the immediate context of the potential loss of prestige emanating from the Gallipoli defeat). All would soon enough be superseded by other developments in the region. Yet, importantly, the contradictory documents do live on in perfidy as the ultimate accusation of British betrayal and, as George Antonius described it, "the bitterness and revulsion of feeling which the post-War provisions engendered" (see Document 19).[31]

The Mesopotamia Campaign

From the late nineteenth century on, British hegemony in the Persian Gulf was secured by a series of alliances formed with local sheikhdoms whose allegiance brought them protection under the British imperial

---

30. Quoted in Schneer, *Balfour Declaration*, 85.

31. George Antonius, *The Arab Awakening: The Story of the Arab National Movement* (Safety Harbor, FL: Simon Publications, 2001 [1939]), 277.

umbrella. These include, for example, the al-Sabah family in Kuwait and the al-Thani family of Qatar. Shoring up relations with these families was a primary concern of Britain's from the outset of the war. So too (given the 1912 conversion of British naval ships from coal to oil) was the protection of oil installations at Abadan in southern Iran. Regard for these interests led the British to immediately assemble a military force at the head of the Persian Gulf on November 6, 1914, the day after declaring war on the Ottoman Empire.

Meanwhile, the Ottoman leadership had given relatively little attention to defending southern Mesopotamia. The remoteness of the port of Basra meant that Istanbul simply could not consider it as worthy of diverting resources from other fronts. The Berlin to Baghdad railway begun during the early 1900s remained far from completion, and access to the region was still mostly lacking necessary modern infrastructure. Local transportation remained highly dependent on the Tigris-Euphrates river system. But this waterway posed several navigation challenges: for example, each season brought its own variations in the depth of the water, and spring flooding caused particular problems for land transport. Regarding overall defenses, Istanbul did make some effort to mobilize regional leaders, not unlike the manner in which local Libyan militias had been employed against Italy's 1911 invasion. But most local sheikhs weighed their options. For example, Ibn Saud in neighboring Nejd might have been expected, given his *ikhwan* alliance, to respond positively enough to the Ottoman Empire's call for support in its *jihād*. But he showed no intention of fighting the British Empire. Not only were the British the much more powerful force in the region, but they were also willing to pay more compensation for an alliance. Ibn Saud's own main objective was to procure much-needed resources in his local conflicts with rivals, such as the al-Rashidi family (who stayed within the Ottoman sphere), and Sharif Husayn's family too. As J. C. Hurewitz observes, competing British ministries were in effect "subsidizing antagonistic Arabian chieftains" (see Document 20).[32]

Given the sharp disparities in British and Ottoman mobilization in the area, the easy capture of the port of Basra on November 21, 1914, by the Indian Expeditionary Force was not surprising. Basic war aims were quickly achieved. However, such early success encouraged Britain's military leaders to press their advantage. They advanced further up the

---

32. Hurewitz, *The Middle East and North Africa in World Politics, Volume 2*, 57.

"British Maurice Farman Attacked by a German Fokker While Dropping Sacks of Corn on Kut," painting by Sydney W. Carline, 1916.

river and, by April 1915, successfully reinforced their position by defeating Ottoman forces in southern Mesopotamia. As news of mounting setbacks at Gallipoli and the worsening of the stalemate on the Western Front piled up, the pressure to continue their advance was hard to resist. Capturing such a famed historical city as Baghdad could provide a desperately needed boost to British prestige. But further military advances up the river were highly dependent on proper communication and supply networks. Overreach would be dangerous, given the extreme challenges posed by climate and terrain, and the prospect of eventually meeting with a more effective Ottoman fighting force.

By the end of August 1915, General Charles Townshend (1861–1924) was halfway to Baghdad when, at Salman Pak, he met with stiff resistance. So he decided to fall back to the town of Kut al-Amara for the 1915–1916 winter and await reinforcements. This proved to be a huge mistake. Townshend soon found himself besieged, and he had miscalculated supplies. With river levels dropping, the British did not have the capacity to supply the necessary relief. The siege of Kut brought terrible starvation and forced an unconditional surrender in April 1916. Prisoners (who largely comprised colonial soldiers fighting on behalf of Britain) were marched into captivity across the Syrian Desert to internment camps, though Townshend was looked after near Istanbul until the armistice. It is worth stressing that far from the campaign's providing an overall boost to British standing, the overall blow to British prestige in fact had a significant impact on concurrent regional diplomatic efforts. Kut contributed to growing fear of *jihād* and, in turn, buttressed the rationale for building an alliance with Sharif Husayn.

In the wake of its defeat at Kut, Britain remained on the defensive in Mesopotamia for the rest of 1916. During this time, they successfully completed an overhaul of supply lines, lessening their overall dependence on river craft. One year later, in March 1917, in what would

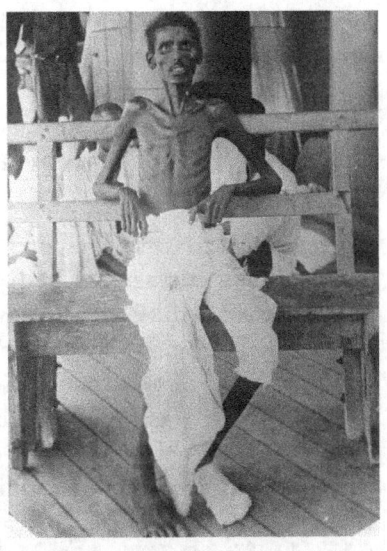

Liberated prisoners, Kut al-Amara.

prove to be one of the war's first major turning points in the Middle East, British forces under General Stanley Maude (1864–1917) entered Baghdad. Maude immediately delivered a proclamation promising that "our armies do not come into your cities and lands as conquerors or enemies, but as liberators."[33]

Having so "liberated" the Ottoman provinces of Basra and Baghdad, British forces continued to advance north over the course of 1918. Interestingly, the final push for the Ottoman vilayet of Mosul in fact came *after* the October 30, 1918, signing of the armistice. In this sense, the last-minute rush to bring Mosul (which on paper had been apportioned to France according to the line drawn by Sykes-Picot) within the British orbit can be viewed less as the final campaign against the Ottomans, and more the opening gambit in postwar diplomacy with the French. With a civil war–wracked, postrevolutionary Russia no longer the worrisome factor for the British Empire that it had been throughout the nineteenth-century Great Game, Britain held little interest in a French buffer zone. With the added prospect of securing Mosul's rich oil fields, Britain hastily sought

---

33. Quoted in Rashid Khalidi, *Resurrecting Empire: Western Footprints and America's Perilous Path in the Middle East* (Boston: Beacon Press, 2005), 37.

facts on the ground, so to speak, that might help it renegotiate previous promises to France.

End of the Fighting

Overextended and under-resourced, exhausted and sick, Ottoman forces faced several setbacks in 1917, especially on the Palestinian and Mesopotamian fronts. In the Caucasus, however, the situation evolved somewhat differently. The Bolshevik Revolution of fall 1917 and the March 1918 Treaty of Brest-Litovsk combined to remove Russia from the war. This allowed the Ottomans to successfully push forward and even take temporary control of the key oil center of Baku, Azerbaijan. But in Syria, two parallel Allied fronts moved steadily toward Damascus over the course of 1918—one led by Allied forces under Allenby and the other pushed forward by the Arab revolt under Faysal. They both reached Damascus at about the same time, but then (as we shall see in the next chapter) each pursued their own aims.

Following the Battle of Megiddo in September, Mustafa Kemal held the last defensive Ottoman positions at Aleppo. He might not have known it then, but these lines north of Aleppo effectively drew the borders demarcating the new Turkey from the old Ottoman Empire. The war ended in their final defeat in late October 1918, just before the German surrender, with the armistice signed aboard a British ship anchored off Mudros in the north Aegean Sea. Allied forces, led by Britain and France as well as Italy, occupied Istanbul, where contending European ambitions to reclaim the erstwhile Constantinople portended bitter intercommunal violence. Meanwhile, the Ottoman government resigned and key CUP leaders fled Istanbul for Europe. As for the Ottoman military hero, Mustafa Kemal, he repaired into Anatolia, making secret military plans to fight another day.

Allied forces (especially those under British command) now controlled most of the Arab lands of the defeated Ottoman Empire. In the Greater Syria region, Allenby laid down the parameters under which the large land mass, then mostly occupied by the Egyptian Expeditionary Force, would be organized. He divided areas under his military rule into zones known as Occupied Enemy Territory Administrations [OETAs]: OETA South incorporated almost all of Palestine under the control of

Jerusalem; OETA North (later renamed OETA West) was established for Mt. Lebanon and coastal Syria and was placed under a French administration based in Beirut; and OETA East, consisting of the interior of Greater Syria, was placed for a time under the Arab administration of Emir Faysal. In this way, Allenby's dismemberment of the Arab lands of the former Ottoman Empire served to inaugurate the notorious process by which Europe imposed upon the Middle East the borders of the present modern state system.

On the ground, however, the major force acting upon Allenby's (supposedly temporary) military administration of these territories was the pressure to adhere to the doctrine of the status quo. The stated commitment to maintain a status quo owed much to recently established norms and guidelines of military occupation, as drawn up at the Hague Conferences of 1899 and 1907, which prohibited occupying forces from completely ignoring the rights of the inhabitants. In this regard, it is also vital to consider the role played by US president Woodrow Wilson's (1856–1924, president 1913–1921) widely publicized wartime promises, propounding American support for principles of national self-determination. While these ideas had already been proclaimed by Bolshevik leaders in Russia, they became a cornerstone of Wilson's foreign policy (though of course in a manner ideologically and strategically counterpoised to the Bolsheviks' outlook). "No peace can last, or ought to last," exhorted Wilson in January 1917,

> which does not recognize and accept the principle that governments derive all their just powers from the consent of the governed, and that no right anywhere exists to hand peoples about from sovereignty to sovereignty as if they were property.[34]

Often referred to as "the spirit of the age," nationalist ambitions for independence on the part of varying communities throughout the broader Middle East would clearly place them at odds with expansionary European powers. Yet, at the time, the new emphasis on powerful notions of self-determination and freedom forced rhetorical adjustments even

---

34. Quoted in Erez Manela, *The Wilsonian Moment: Self-Determination and the International Origins of Anticolonial Nationalism* (Oxford: Oxford University Press, 2007), 24.

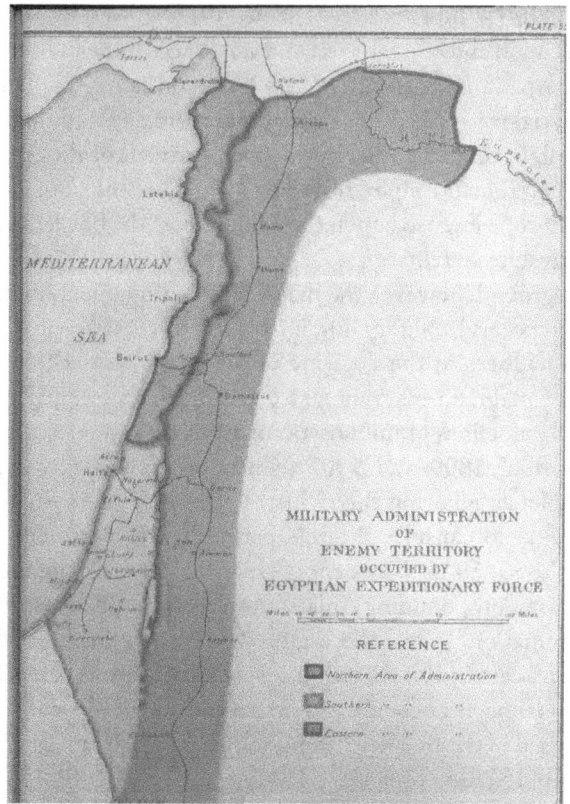

Zones of Allied administration in
occupied territory after WWI.

from Britain and France. On November 7, 1918 (at about the same time that Britain was violating the armistice in its rush to occupy Mosul), Britain and France declared that the authority of new governing institutions would be derived from the will and interests of the indigenous populations themselves (see Document 21).[35]

Public wartime pronouncements raised hopes and expectations, yet Ottoman citizens' destiny was now in the hands of European powers.

---

35. As it happens, the formerly secret Sykes-Picot Agreement had been made public in fall 1917, much to the Allies' consternation, by a new Russian Bolshevik regime anxious to condemn imperial machinations—not least, those of the Bolsheviks' loathed Romanov predecessor, who had been party to the negotiations.

British forces seemed to be in a dominant military position in late 1918, occupying most of the Arab lands of the defeated Ottoman Empire. But their conflicting wartime promises would necessarily leave a terrible legacy of bitterness and betrayal. This shifting ground was captured by Sykes when, in June 1917, he wondered:

> are the relations of European peoples towards subject Asiatic peoples going to be the same after the war as before the war? If there is anything in the tendency of the age, in the advance of democracy, in the expressed view of the powers with regard to small nationalities, I concluded that the answer is in the negative. . . . If we and the French intend to work towards annexation then I am certain that our plans will sink in chaos and failure.[36]

---

36. "Notes by Sir Mark Sykes on Sir Reginald Wingate's Telegram, No. 609," June 22, 1917, FO/371/3054.

CHAPTER THREE
1918 Onward

War's Aftermath

Four years of wartime hardship for the inhabitants of the Ottoman Empire had brought unimaginable sorrow: the calamity of Armenian deportations; the increasingly blurred lines between civilians and combatants; the toll inflicted by four years of conscription, with more Ottoman soldiers dying of disease and malnutrition than were killed in battle; relentless sequestration by the Ottoman Army; the parallel extra burdens of labor falling on women;[1] the devastating wartime famine wrought in large part by the Allied blockade; and multiple local infestations (e.g., locusts). Historians have placed the death rate for Greater Syria alone at 18 percent (compared to France and Germany losing approximately 5 percent of their prewar populations).[2]

How does one convey such terrible calamities? To provide a sense of how the people themselves found language to describe the profound ruptures, Najwa al-Qattan emphasizes the need to draw upon a variety of literary sources and singles out the poetry of Antun Yamin:

> Cry for a beloved country bereft of its people,
> Cry for the corpses stacked in roads, squares, plains, and valleys,
> Cry for the mothers whose children are dying,
> Cry for children who nurse on their mothers' tears,

---

1. One source concludes that a decade after the war, 30 percent of adult women were widows. Yiğit Akin, *When the War Came Home: The Ottomans' Great War and the Devastation of an Empire* (Stanford, CA: Stanford University Press, 2018).

2. See Elizabeth Thompson, *Colonial Citizens* (New York: Columbia University Press, 1999), 23.

Cry for the virgins who sell themselves for slices of black bread.³

Further wracked by the 1918–1920 influenza epidemic, the inhabitants of the Middle East continued in the immediate postwar period to experience profound upheaval. These years of human deprivation and displacement inspired Western colonial governments, international organizations like the newly created League of Nations, and such nongovernmental organizations (NGOs) as the Red Cross to extend measures like food aid, medical relief, and refugee resettlement. Keith Watenpaugh asserts that, in terms that are especially resonant, "the Eastern Mediterranean was where much of modern humanitarianism was born."⁴ Thus initiated, though, was the double-edged sword whereby humanitarianism—or more to the point, humanitarian intervention entering through military means—also came to constitute a neocolonial mechanism for paternalistic domination.⁵

"Spirit of the age" rhetoric aside, the postwar leaders of London and Paris fixed their attention on the spoils of war. European allies were determined to impose on the Middle East a new political and economic order corresponding solely to their own interests and concerns. Some European officials were clearly motivated by the need to vindicate their own nation's sacrifices. Others sought justification in delusions of "liberating" populations from what was alleged as "the murderous tyranny of the Turks" (while at the same time expelling from Europe the Ottoman presence they felt had "proved itself so radically alien to Western Civilisation").⁶ Michael Provence points out that the clear contrast

---

3. Quoted in Najwa al-Qattan, "When Mothers Ate Their Children: Wartime Memory and the Language of Food in Syria and Lebanon," *International Journal of Middle East Studies* 46, no. 4 (2014): 723.

4. Keith Watenpaugh, *Bread from Stones: The Middle East and the Making of Modern Humanitarianism* (Oakland: University of California Press, 2015), 2.

5. The controversial geopolitical doctrine of Responsibility to Protect (R2P), which achieved prominence during the 1990s collapse of post-WWI Yugoslavia into intercommunal Balkan warfare, has been notoriously problematic. It was again invoked, disastrously, as a rationale for twenty-first-century Western military interventions throughout the Middle East.

6. Huseyin Yilmaz, "The Eastern Question and the Ottoman Empire: The Genesis of the Near and Middle East in the Nineteenth Century," in Michael E. Bonine, Abbas Amanat, and Michael Ezekiel Gasper, eds., *Is There a Middle East?: The Evolution of a Geopolitical Concept* (Stanford, CA: Stanford University Press, 2012), 32.

with the Allies' plans for central and eastern Europe was not lost on Ottoman intellectuals at the time.[7] Whereas the 1918 demise of the Austro-Hungarian Empire brought into being independent European states, the colonial structures Britain and France had in mind for the Middle East clearly reflected prejudiced views of the region as less civilized and less worthy of self-rule. Stretched thin on the ground, however, European forces struggled to exert and maintain control over local populations. Local movements of anticolonial resistance almost immediately mobilized political aspirations and socioeconomic grievances in opposition to European designs. To better understand how foreign imperial ambitions conflicted with nascent local nationalist movements, this chapter blends a chronological approach with region-specific treatments of the postwar period.

But first, a brief overview is in order. In Anatolia, opposition movements rallied under the effective leadership of Mustafa Kemal, the hero of Gallipoli, who successfully resisted European efforts to control large parts of western Anatolia. In Iran, too, a Qajar military leader, Reza Khan (1878–1944, r. 1925–1941), garnered enough authority to negotiate new international relationships with Russia and Britain, as well as to coronate himself the head of his own new Pahlavi dynasty. In a dramatic realignment of forces on the Arabian Peninsula, Ibn Saud asserted his independence over much of the area, even supplanting the Hashemite clan of Sharif Husayn in the Hejaz. Elsewhere in the Arab lands of the former Ottoman Empire, British and French efforts to secure their own strategic interests provoked multiple resistance movements that met with more limited success. The rapidly changing postwar situation led to the unraveling of conflicting wartime promises (with bitter legacies of recrimination continuing to seethe across the region) and a reordering of the region under newly invented forms of European tutelage. In these Arab territories, a particular definition of imperial expansion, known as a "mandate," was initiated under the newly created League of Nations' oversight. This novel structure owed its origins in part to US president Woodrow Wilson's stated commitment at the Paris Peace Conferences to principles of consultation and self-determination. As envisioned by the European imperial powers, however, the mandate idea was carried out more as a way to contain than fulfill rising nationalist demands.

---

7. Michael Provence, *The Last Ottoman Generation and the Making of the Modern Middle East* (Cambridge: Cambridge University Press, 2017), 6.

1918–1920: Military Occupations and Struggles for Self-Determination

Signed on October 30, 1918, by Britain and the Ottomans, the punitive terms of the Mudros Armistice rendered the Ottomans easy prey for European expansionist aims. In addition to establishing full control over the Dardanelles and the Bosporus waterways, these exacting demands included the demobilization of Ottoman forces and the availability for use by the Allies of strategic infrastructure such as ports and railways. The stage was thus set for Europe's desired partition of Ottoman territories, known as the 1920 Treaty of Sèvres (one of the five major treaties signed in Paris's suburbs, pursuant to the postwar Paris Peace Conferences).

At the outset of its military occupation of the defeated Ottoman Empire's Arab lands, Britain certainly appeared, if only to itself, to be in a privileged position. Controlling vast swaths of Ottoman territory, London set out to leverage whatever postwar advantage it could. The long war emphatically reaffirmed for Britain the importance of securing global trade networks throughout this pivotal region. It had also highlighted the new geostrategic importance of the oil that lay underneath the Middle East. Areas such as Palestine and Mosul had thus taken on added significance. Meanwhile, in sharp contrast to Britain's heavy postwar military footprint in the region, its erstwhile ally France lacked forces on the ground (having been forced during the war to concentrate its resources on the Western Front). As for former rivals Russia and Germany, they were now altogether removed from the scene.

Soon enough, however, Britain's efforts to maximize its position would be forced to reckon with several competing pressures. First was the need to contend with the resistance posed by local inhabitants. The longer British military forces occupied territory in the Middle East, the greater the resistance exercised by emerging opposition movements, driven both by local grievances and broadly circulating ideas of self-determination. Violent confrontations challenged British positions everywhere. Though mostly regionalized, these confrontations were nonetheless powerful enough to force British officials into compromises, and certainly ardent enough to quickly disabuse Britain of her attempts to justify occupation as liberation.

When responding to the growing resistance, Britain faced a further set of limitations imposed by its own domestic population. The war had exhausted Britain's economy, and people were increasingly frustrated by the hesitant pace of demobilization and reconstruction. There was therefore much aversion to any new spending on military adventures. Yet, as the huge costs of prolonged military occupation continued to be paid by the British government, even such conservative voices as *The Times* newspaper bitterly queried the redirection of funds from domestic reconstruction to colonial expansion (see Document 22).[8] It had always been a cardinal rule that colonized territories pay their own way and not be a drain on the British taxpayer. Accordingly, the classic colonial strategy of ensuring minimum costs with the least disturbance quickly led to the search for intermediaries and the establishment of a system of governance often referred to as "indirect rule." In the post-Ottoman Arab world this usually meant gaining the support, or at least acquiescence, of influential wealthy landowning families, that is, "notables." We saw in Chapter 1 how notables had grown accustomed under Ottoman rule to playing an intermediary role. To a significant extent, these families shared with Britain a similar vested interest in maintaining a conservative social order.

A further challenge facing Britain emerged from the prolonged and contested postwar negotiations that risked turning the victorious European allies—Britain, France, and Italy—back into rivals (in fact, Italy stormed out of the peace conference proceedings). With regard to the Middle East, Britain and France did of course have starting points for negotiation, as set by Sykes and Picot in 1916. But postwar relations between British prime minister Lloyd George and French prime minister Georges Clemenceau (1841–1929, prime minister 1906–1909, 1917–1920) quickly fell out. For a moment, Lloyd George rushed to convince Clemenceau to shift the spheres of influence in Britain's interest. Lloyd George knew that Clemenceau's great personal concern for the future status and boundaries of Germany did not match any similar degree of interest in the Middle East (though other officials in the French government felt differently). Seeking leverage, Lloyd George linked Britain's support for France's demands in Europe with France's acceptance of expanded British influence in Palestine and Mosul. However, as these tensions increased, there was mounting interest in France for a Middle Eastern empire of its own. Such fervor was driven by pride and prestige and the perceived need to maintain France's international position relative to

---

8. "Mesopotamia," *The Times* (UK), July 18, 1921, issue 42775. See also Simon Bromley, *Rethinking Middle East Politics* (Austin: University of Texas Press, 1994).

Britain's. Accordingly, Clemenceau became apprehensive about whether Britain would stick to the remaining commitments Sykes had made to Picot regarding Syria or would instead support the conflicting promises made to Faysal (in the Husayn-McMahon correspondence, see Document 16), who at the time was busy establishing an Arab government in Damascus with the support of a British subsidy.

In addition to the fissures dividing Britain and France, major tensions also materialized between those two European powers and President Wilson. During the war, Wilson had projected a different postwar vision than could be countenanced by British and French imperial aims. While Britain and France haggled over imperial expansion, the liberal internationalist Wilson espoused principles of "consultation" and "self-determination" in the peace negotiations. To be sure, one must be careful not to overexaggerate Wilson as an anticolonial force. For Wilson, these principles did not necessarily mean immediate independence for nations around the world (nor, for that matter, did Wilson believe in equality for Black Americans at home). Still, whatever Wilson's true intentions, colonized peoples around the world took significant hope from Wilson's apparent decision to base US foreign policy on principles of national self-determination. Their expectations were soon dashed.[9]

The Mandate System

At a bare minimum, the prevailing principles of self-determination demanded that Britain and France at least try to repackage their desire for colonial spoils of war in a pseudo-democratic international instrument known as a "mandate." As rationalized in the highly patronizing language of Article 22 in the 1919 Covenant of the League of Nations, "Certain communities formerly belonging to the Turkish Empire have reached a stage of development where their existence as independent nations can be provisionally recognized subject to the rendering of administrative advice and assistance by a Mandatory until such time as they are able

---

9. Erez Manela, *Wilsonian Moment: Self-Determination and the International Origins of Anticolonial Nationalism* (Oxford: Oxford University Press, 2007); Pankaj Mishra, *From the Ruins of Empire: The Intellectuals Who Remade Asia* (New York: Farrar, Straus and Giroux, 2012).

to stand alone" (see Document 23).[10] The mandate system essentially allowed Britain and France to disguise the imposition of imperial control without entirely disavowing national self-determination. All of the territories of the former Ottoman Empire were referred to as Class A Mandates, obliging the European mandatory powers to move the local communities toward national independence in the near term.[11]

Article 22 also declared that "the wishes of these communities must be a principal consideration in the selection of the Mandatory."[12] Accordingly, President Wilson proposed that an inter-Allied commission travel the eastern Mediterranean to determine what people in the region sought. While neither Britain nor France was prepared to outright oppose Wilson's initiative, neither was willing to participate in it. Thus, the commission became a solely American one when Wilson ultimately dispatched theologian and Oberlin College president Henry King (1858–1934) and wealthy Democratic Party political ally Charles Crane (1858–1939) to chair it in June 1919. Members of the so-called King-Crane Commission traveled from Palestine through Greater Syria to Istanbul, hearing similar demands wherever they went for the unity of Syria within its "natural" boundaries (see Document 24).[13] Their Arab audiences plainly repudiated the idea of a foreign mandate, and they dismissed completely the notion that they were unable to govern themselves. Regarding Palestine, for example, the King-Crane Commission was persuaded that if Wilson had any intent of taking the idea of self-determination seriously, there was simply no way to ignore the fact that Jews constituted only 10 percent of the population. The vast majority of Palestine's Arab population understood full well the threat that Zionism represented to their own patrimony of the land. As the commission forewarned, enacting Zionism

---

10. "The Covenant of the League of Nations (including Amendments adopted to December, 1924), Article 22," Avalon Project, Yale Law School, https://avalon.law.yale.edu/20th_century/leagcov.asp.

11. Class B and Class C Mandates, which were imposed over various former German colonies in African and Asian territories, were envisioned by the principal Allied powers as being far from ready for independence, if they ever would be (with Namibia's not-until-1990 postapartheid national sovereignty as a chief example of the latter presumption).

12. "Covenant of the League of Nations."

13. "Report of American Section of Inter-Allied Commission on Mandates in Turkey: An Official United States Government Report," Editor & Publisher, December 2, 1922, https://babel.hathitrust.org/cgi/pt?id=uiug.30112075996634&view=1up&seq=7.

against the will of this overwhelming majority could only be brought about by violence.

An intriguing early experiment in polling the wishes of a population, the King-Crane Commission's findings ended up making little impact.[14] By the time of its official release, President Wilson was back in the US trying to persuade Americans—who were at best ambivalent toward his internationalist visions of a new global political order—to accept the Treaty of Versailles and League of Nations (which they never did do). The report was finally delivered to the White House during late September 1919, only a few days before Wilson suffered a massive stroke. The findings thus remained "locked in a drawer," unpublished until December 1922.[15]

For their part, Britain and France simply ignored the commission's findings. By early 1920, they had patched up their differences and, at a meeting held in April in San Remo, Italy, the four principal Allied powers (Britain, France, Italy, and Japan) divvied up the mandates among themselves. The meeting thus essentially swept aside international law, under which such moves required a final acceptance of the terms of surrender (which, as we shall see, did not occur until the 1923 Treaty of Lausanne). Nonetheless believing that they now had a free hand to inscribe the new arrangements they sought, Britain and France cooperated in deploying the newly invented mandate system to construct colonial holdings for themselves. They subdivided Greater Syria into the French mandates of Lebanon and Syria and the British mandates of Palestine and Transjordan, while Britain also merged the three Mesopotamian Ottoman provinces of Baghdad, Basra, and Mosul to create the new mandate of Iraq. With inhabitants suddenly finding themselves cobbled into these newly created political entities, the resulting Arab proto-states ended up suffering "sectarian" effects from imperial tactics of divide and rule. For example, the replacement of Ottoman rule by French and British rule in the separated states of Lebanon and Palestine aimed to reward the loyalty of specific religious minorities, which would in turn

---

14. Michael Reimer, "The King-Crane Commission at the Juncture of Politics and Historiography," *Critique: Critical Middle Eastern Studies* 18, no. 2 (2006): 129–50.

15. Elizabeth Thompson, *How the West Stole Democracy: The Syrian Arab Congress of 1920 and the Destruction of Its Historic Liberal-Islamic Alliance* (New York: Atlantic Monthly Press, 2020), 128.

Allied Supreme Council at San Remo, 1920.

serve to foment ongoing intercommunal strife.[16]

The Treaty of Sèvres, which was meant to confirm these arrangements, was signed on August 10, 1920. It also imposed especially harsh terms on Istanbul. These included continuing the international control of the straits between the Aegean and Black Seas and reducing the sultan's rule to a small rump of territory in north-central Anatolia. Surrounding that small territory were European zones of influence: France was allotted the historic Cilicia regions bordering Syria; Italy was promised southwest Anatolia and the Dodecanese islands of the Aegean and Mediterranean; and Greece, which had entered the war late but found an enthusiastic sponsor in the philhellene Lloyd George, was allowed to expand its territory into western Anatolia and Thrace (including Edirne). Sèvres further granted conditional independence to Kurds and Armenians, but neither fledgling national entity endured for long. Within three years, sweeping changes on the ground would force the crafting of a new treaty at Lausanne.

Turkey

The October 1918 Mudros Armistice technically marked the end of the fighting for the Ottoman Empire. But invasions, battles, and massacres all continued until 1923. In part, the ongoing wars were an extension of European attempts to secure their territorial interests in Anatolia, with

---

16. Even Britain's support for the early 1920s building of the Baha'i temple in Haifa shows how London sought to create allies among minority communities. This connects with broader colonial principles, employed from Africa through India and beyond, of using the modern conceptual construct of religion, and the emerging discipline of comparative religion, as intellectual aids toward political dominance. See Tomoko Masuzawa, *The Invention of World Religions: Or, How European Universalism Was Preserved in the Language of Pluralism* (Chicago: University of Chicago Press, 2005).

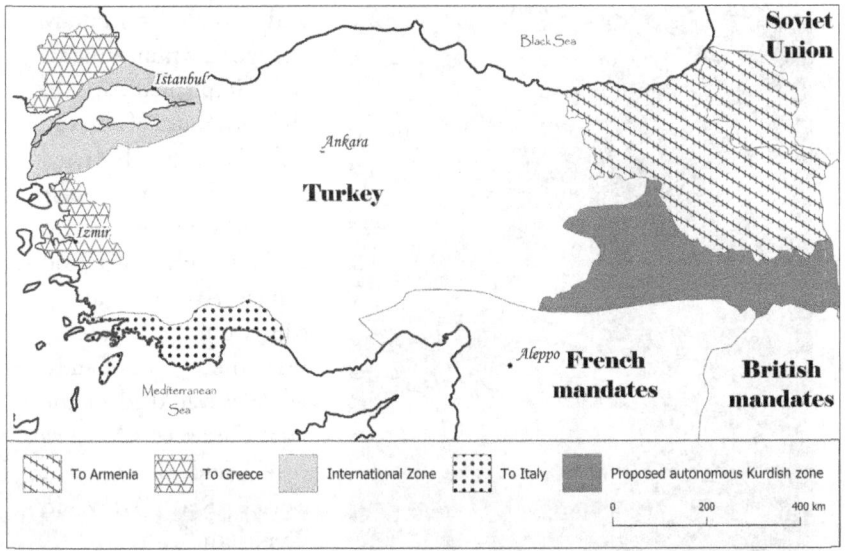

Treaty of Sèvres. Signed between the Allies and the Ottoman sultan in 1920, the treaty envisioned the future partition of the Middle East, with Turkey reduced to a central portion of Anatolia that was bounded by European-dominated territories, prospective states for Armenians and Kurds, and the soon-to-emerge Soviet Union.

Greece and Italy now joining Britain and France in securing territorial spoils. The violence can also be seen as a perpetuation of prewar communal and sectarian hostilities. A case in point is the effective Anatolian civil war between communal entities seeking vengeance both for the legacy of past deportations and massacres and for the uses to which such atrocities had been put by foreigners to justify their own interventions.

Upon the Allied occupation of Istanbul at the end of the war, the CUP leaders (Talat, Cemal, and Enver Pashas) all fled. A formal criminal inquiry into the crimes committed against the Armenians was launched in January 1919, constituting "the first war-crimes trials in history."[17] Hundreds of individuals were charged on the basis of written evidence

---

17. Caroline Finkel, *Osman's Dream: The History of the Ottoman Empire* (New York: Basic Books, 2007), 538. See also Taner Akçam, *The Young Turks' Crime against Humanity: The Armenian Genocide and Ethnic Cleansing in the Ottoman Empire* (Princeton, NJ: Princeton University Press, 2012).

Mustafa Kemal, 1919.

and oral testimony, though few punishments were implemented.[18] In the end, most of the top officials would be tried in absentia for their crimes. When it came to dealing with Talat and Cemal, Armenian assassins would take justice into their own hands, while Enver died in the fight between Muslim rebels and the nascent Soviet Red Army in Tajikistan.[19]

Chaos prevailed in the wake of the triumvirate's fall, in the midst of which control over the Ottoman Empire's government would be contested by two main groups. On the one hand was the recently crowned Sultan Mehmet VI Vahdeddin (1861–1926, r. 1918–1922). Though his position as sultan still garnered broad loyalty, his continued submission to the humiliating Allied occupation of Istanbul, in a vain attempt to hang on to some rump of Anatolian territory, only further encouraged European designs. On the other hand, a national movement coalesced under the leadership of Mustafa Kemal, who aimed to resist European dismemberment of Anatolia. Initially, Kemal had sought some kind of alliance with the sultan. But relations between the ancien régime and the new nationalist movement completely broke down following the sultan's signing of the Treaty

---

18. Still, the extensive documentation prepared by these tribunals has been a rich source for recent efforts to contest long-standing Turkish efforts to temper, or even deny, the complicity of CUP leadership in the Armenian genocide.

19. Sean McMeekin, *The Ottoman Endgame: War, Revolution, and the Making of the Modern Middle East, 1908–1923* (New York: Penguin, 2016), 427.

of Sèvres. When the nationalists emerged triumphant, Mustafa Kemal would come to renounce all that the sultan represented. Mustafa Kemal also forsook his own CUP background and dissolved the institution itself, though his personal ties and networks survived. So too did the party's centralized methods of coordination and unshakeable conviction to defend the state, if on the basis of a new nationalist identity. The resistance movements, generally referred to as "Societies for the Defence of National Rights," mobilized the widespread anger and humiliation. Following a series of congresses during the summer of 1919, representatives came together in September to sign the so-called National Pact. In line with prevailing modes of legitimation, the National Pact declared all territories within the national boundaries at the time of the armistice "which are inhabited by an Ottoman Muslim majority" to be an integral part of a new Turkish state.[20] On April 23, 1920, the new Grand National Assembly, meeting in Ankara (a central Anatolian redoubt that would become the capital of the new Turkish republic) as the representative of the self-styled Turkish nation, officially delegated executive authority to Kemal.

Asserting Turkish Borders and Boundaries

This opened the door for Kemal to extinguish the last Ottoman institutions, including both its sultanate in 1922 and the caliphate in 1924. Kemal's victorious military campaigns then determined the country's western and eastern borders. In the east, Kemal's forces effectively overwhelmed Armenian forces by November 1920 and, in March 1921, Turkey signed a treaty with Moscow that settled long-standing disputes. Whereas Armenia would be incorporated as a republic of the inchoate Union of Soviet Socialist Republics, the former Ottoman provinces of Kars and Ardahan were returned to Turkey. Relations between Turkey and Russia would continue to be tumultuous, but this would not be the last time the two historic rivals would cooperate in curtailing the influence of Western powers in the region. Turkish forces similarly erased the

---

20. "The Turkish National Pact, 28 January 1920," in J. C. Hurewitz, ed., *The Middle East and North Africa in World Politics: A Documentary Record*, 2nd ed., Volume 2: *British-French Supremacy, 1914–1945* (New Haven, CT: Yale University Press, 1979), 209–11.

Allied promise of an independent Kurdish space in eastern Anatolia, and they successfully pushed out the French from Cilicia. Turkey gained France's official recognition in late 1921, in return for Ankara's recognition of French rule in Syria.

In western Anatolia, European allies (especially Britain, who had lured Greece out of its initial wartime neutrality with the promise of territorial gains) encouraged Greek forces to block Italy's burgeoning irredentism. Much would hinge here on Prime Minister Lloyd George's personal relationship with the Greek prime minister Eleftherios Venizelos (1864–1936, several prime ministerial terms between 1910–1933). Venizelos was a major proponent of the Megali Idea, Greece's irredentist assertion of control over regions housing substantial Greek communities in western Anatolia.[21] Shortly following the 1918 armistice, Venizelos had launched a claim for those areas of the Ottoman Empire with large Orthodox Greek Christian populations. In 1919, he dispatched troops to take Smyrna (known by its Turkish name, Izmir, by 1930). At first, the Greek army made rapid gains far into the Anatolian interior. Perhaps more than any other event, it was the powerlessness of the sultan's government in responding to the Greek invasion of Anatolia that would stir the largest numbers of Ottomans to support Kemal. When Kemal mobilized the full Turkish counterattack, the overextended Greek forces suffered huge losses. The 1921 Turkish nationalist victory at Sakarya turned the war around, with fighting culminating in destruction, looting, and communal atrocities at Smyrna/Izmir in 1922 (see Document 25). As Greek forces were finally driven out of Anatolia, hundreds of thousands of Greeks were also pushed out of their homes. The brutal new nationalist reality generated by the Greco-Turkish War (which Turkey would come to regard as its own War of Independence) was finalized in an official agreement referring to the chaos as an "exchange" of populations. In fact, it constituted the forced transfer of about two million people whose religious identity alone was taken as the sole and primary indicator of nationality. Long-standing presence in one's ancestral home and local community was rendered incompatible with new nationalist claims to sovereignty. The terms and economic logistics of the population exchange were negotiated by the League of Nations' high commissioner for refugees Fridtjof Nansen (1861–1930), winner of the 1922 Nobel

---

21. See Arnold Toynbee, *The Western Question in Greece and Turkey: A Study in the Contact of Civilisations* (New York: H. Fertig, 1970 [1923]).

Peace Prize (though primarily for his work in Russia on behalf of the Red Cross). Facing the prospect by September 1922 of Kemal's victorious forces now marching from Smyrna to Allied-occupied Istanbul, Prime Minister Lloyd George sought to rally imperial forces to help hold the Dardanelles and the coastal city of Çanakkale. But only New Zealand and Newfoundland heeded the call. The evident assertion of independence by the dominions during the so-called Chanak Crisis would have great ramifications for the future of the British Empire. Moreover, Lloyd George's failure to rouse, at home or among Britain's allies, any support for another war against Turkey led to his own downfall in London.

In the end, the crisis was defused with the signing, in October 1922, of the Armistice of Mudanya. This recognition of the Grand National Assembly as the sole authority in Anatolia set the stage for Mustafa Kemal to assert sovereignty over the territory he now defined as the Turkish national homeland. For all practical purposes, the Ottoman government now ceased to exist. Sèvres had been rendered obsolete and a new peace settlement had to be negotiated in Lausanne, from November 1922 to July 1923. With Kemal's nationalist movement representing Turkish interests, the July 1923 Treaty of Lausanne ultimately buried earlier proposals for the dismemberment of the Ottoman Empire, including those for Armenian and Kurdish sovereignty.

As for the Arab provinces which British and France sought to control, Kemal renounced all claims. Still, two outstanding border disputes remained: the future of the Mosul province was not decided until 1926, when it was finally allocated to Iraq; and the province of Alexandretta, which had come under the French mandate for Syria, was conceded to Turkey in 1939 (a move that was met with strong protest from Damascus) in a bid to keep the Turks neutral in the coming Second World War.

Thus were created the borders of the newly constituted Republic of Turkey, with its new capital at Ankara. Headed by President Mustafa Kemal, who would eventually receive the honorific designation Atatürk, "Father of the Turks," Turkey was launched on the paradigmatic "Kemalist" project of authoritarian, secularizing nation-state-building. As the 1920s proceeded, Mustafa Kemal enforced a singular Turkish ethnonationalism through a growing number of measures (see Document 26). Emblematic among these were the deployment of military force against Kurdish rebellions; the closure of historic Sufi dervish lodges; the adoption of European-styled civil law; and the 1925 "Hat Law" banning the use of fezzes or turbans in public places. Just as these modes of dominating individuals' bodies were closely identified with discourses of wholesale Westernization, so too would Turkey's foreign policy be drawn into the Western camp (especially during the Cold War era).

Kemal's resistance to the sultan's humiliating subjugation to Western demands inspired supporting movements among Arabic-speaking peoples of the Ottoman Empire. Some even volunteered for Kemal's movement. Accordingly, it came as a huge disappointment to Arab leaders when Kemal finally accepted that the defensive lines he had held at the signing of the 1918 armistice should constitute the border of his new Turkish state and that his fellow Ottomans were now on their own.[22]

Iran

Although Iran declared neutrality during the war, foreign interference only deepened. Russian incursions in the north were matched by the strengthening of their cat's-paw Cossack Brigade, while in the south Britain bolstered its imperial presence around the oil-producing region of Abadan. These international interventions were largely responsible for the worsening economic context. Wartime trade disruptions (following from the closing of the Dardanelles and the collapse of the Russian economy) overlapped with bad harvests to bring some areas to the brink of famine. All of this was then exacerbated by what was, within Iran, the especially devastating spread of the 1918–1920 flu pandemic.

In the midst of this dislocation emerged an officer from the Cossack Brigade, Reza Khan. By 1921, he achieved dominance within the much-weakened governmental and military structures of the Qajar dynasty. A few years later, he achieved enough power to overthrow the Qajar and crown himself Reza Shah Pahlavi, the king of a self-styled Pahlavi dynasty (see Document 27). By evoking the power and splendor of the pre-Islamic, Sasanian-era Zoroastrian Persian Empire, both he and his son Mohammad Reza Pahlavi (1919–1980, r. 1941–1979) sought to outflank the power and influence of the Shi'i *ulema*.

Consciously emulating Iran's historic rival Turkey, Reza Shah patterned his forcible style of modernist nation-building after Atatürk. He sidelined

---

22. Provence, *Last Ottoman Generation*.

the influential Shi'i clerics in pursuit of a secularizing, ethno-nationalist Persian identity that left no room for competing ethnicities such as Kurds, Arabs, and Baluchis. By the 1930s, Reza Shah's arguably proto-fascist leanings resulted in an emerging alliance with the Nazi regime in Berlin that aided Adolf Hitler in his seeking to depict an Indo-European warrior race; influenced by Berlin, Reza Shah officially oversaw his country's official name change from Persia to Iran (evoking Aryan). In 1941, Reza Shah was overthrown by Britain and the Soviets, whose concerns over his closeness to Berlin led them to jointly occupy the country during World War II. As Reza Shah was sent into exile, his son Mohammad Reza Pahlavi was implanted by the Allies on the throne in Tehran, to begin what would prove to be another autocratic reign buffeted by British, Soviet, and US rivalries. This period would end with the 1979 revolution establishing the Islamic Republic of Iran. But the ongoing legacies of post-WWI developments—chief among them the centralizing power of an authoritarian system that so readily took root in the desperation of postwar chaos and relentless foreign interventions—continue to this day.

Egypt

Within days of the war's armistice being signed, on November 11, 1918, British high commissioner Reginald Wingate (1861–1953) was approached by an Egyptian delegation (*wafd* in Arabic, which would soon thereafter become the namesake of Egypt's preeminent political party). The group of public figures, led by Saad Zaghlul (1859–1927), informed Wingate that it wished to participate in the Paris Peace Conferences where they, like Faysal, could argue their case for self-determination (see Document 28). Not only was Zaghlul's request denied on the spot but, as popular support for the delegation gained momentum across Egypt, the British arrested him and his colleagues and deported them to Malta on March 8, 1919. The next day, a broad-based Egyptian revolt erupted. With Egyptians still reeling from the terrible legacy of heavy-handed wartime governance (especially the hundreds of thousands who were "volunteered" into the labor corps),[23] news of the political arrests

---

23. See Khaled Fahmy, "The Great Theft of History: The Egyptian Army in the First World War," November 11, 2019, https://khaledfahmy.org/en/2019/11/11/the-great-theft-of-history-the-egyptian-army-in-the-first-world-war/.

fomented a widespread uprising. Demonstrations spread from city to countryside and involved the full spectrum of society, including labor activists, judges, lawyers, transportation workers, and peasants. They paralyzed British economic interests in Egypt through such measures as work stoppages and the disruption of infrastructure like railways. Much of Egypt joined together, including women such as Hudá Sha'rāwi (1879–1947) and Safiyya Zaghlul (1876–1946), who emerged at this time as feminist nationalist organizers; the Zaghlul family house came to be known to as *bait al umma* ("house of the nation") (see Document 29).

The British responded in force. By the end of the first month, eight hundred civilians had been killed. But the revolt was not subdued until May 1919. By revealing the depths of discontent and anger, the Egyptian demonstrations (as elsewhere in the region) forced Britain into developing new strategies of control. By the terms of the ill-named 1922 Unilateral Declaration of Independence, Britain aimed to replace the protectorate established upon the outbreak of war in 1914 with a new arrangement setting up a nominally independent Egypt and acceding to some of the demands of nationalist protests. London's hope was that it could disentangle itself from day-to-day administrative duties of imperial rule, while safeguarding its so-called four Reserved Points: British control of imperial communications, defense, foreign interests, and Sudan.

From this turmoil, Egypt emerged as a constitutional monarchy, under the dynastic lineage first established by Muhammad Ali in 1805 and with a parliament dominated by the large landowning elite. Meanwhile, Zaghlul transformed his delegation into the political movement called the Wafd Party, which won the first elections held under the revised constitution. However, over the next two decades, the depths of differences between the larger population and this elite, who were regarded as ever more luxury-ridden and beholden to neocolonial interests, were gravely revealed. This ruling class would not be displaced until a military coup, led by Gamal Abdel Nasser (1918–1970, president 1954–1970) in 1952, brought historically marginalized groups to power. Still, the failures of the elite to address the deepening economic and social fissures in Egypt during the interwar period proved to be fertile ground for the emergence and growth of religious politics. The Muslim Brotherhood, a reformist educational and political organization, was established in 1928 by Egyptian schoolteacher Hassan al-Banna (1906–1949), who himself had participated in the 1919 anticolonial uprisings. Built on the belief that the reinvigoration of Muslim doctrine and practice was necessary

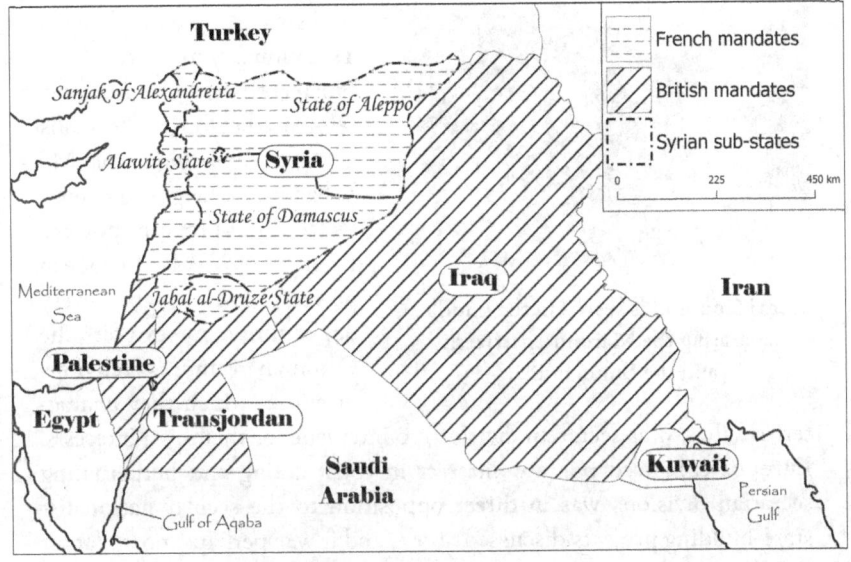

Middle East mandates post–World War I.

for overcoming the challenges of Western colonial influence and local corruption, the Muslim Brotherhood (branches of which would propagate in neighboring Arab countries) would prove to be one of the most enduringly significant religious movements in the making of the modern Middle East.

Lebanon

When France landed forces in Beirut in October 1918, it viewed Lebanon as a homeland for the Maronite population, long regarded as France's most loyal client force in the region. In September 1920, France declared the mandate of Greater Lebanon. This new state significantly expanded the borders of the prior Ottoman administrative district of Mt. Lebanon to incorporate both neighboring coastal towns, as well as the inland Beqaa Valley. In so doing, French imperial cartography both separated the Muslim inhabitants of these added-on territories from neighboring Syrian territory to which they had long felt connected and diluted the dominant Maronite demographic of the newly enlarged state.

Henri Gouraud is seated in the middle, separating the Maronite patriarch and the Sunni mufti.

As we glimpsed in Chapter 1's examination of the mid-nineteenth-century *Tanzimat* reform edicts, the Ottomans' governance systems for Mt. Lebanon had long been manipulated by European powers. Prior to WWI, European powers had sought every opportunity to exploit the Ottoman Empire's religious diversity (which they characteristically saw as sectarian division) to intervene for their own interests. Europe's enhanced postwar interest in constructing and perpetuating sectarian divisions was in direct opposition to the secular nationalist state-building projects discussed above, and it was perhaps most blatant in Lebanon.

In the newly established mandate of Greater Lebanon, Maronites now constituted a plurality rather than a majority. But France developed a particular system of proportional representation for the multi-sectarian population, by which the parliamentary system apportioned seats to specifically favor Maronites. The inequitable distribution of power and wealth would be one of the major reasons for the devastating civil war that eventually tore Lebanon apart from 1975 to 1990. But it is also important to note how the political system privileged a small, if fractious, elite consisting of the leaders of all religious communities. In this way, the French colonial system was responsible for creating a hierarchy of power that would benefit the interests of all elites in Lebanon, at the expense of the social and economic welfare of the vast majority of the population. This corrupt sectarian system continues to be manifested in endemic Lebanese political dysfunction. Together, sectarian leaders—particularly Sunni Muslims, Shi'i Muslims, and Maronite Christians, with the Shi'i-offshoot Druze branch also playing a role—control the levers of state, often as proxies for further international powers, in order to ensure that patronage reinforces the loyalties of their own constituencies. Though this colonial legacy has increasingly been condemned by the Lebanese people over the course of the twentieth and twenty-first centuries, the entrenched leadership forms a political class bent on maintaining the system that protects their own vested interests across all sectors of state administration and the economy.

Palestine

Colonial policies of divide and rule marked the British legacy in Palestine as well. In the previous chapter, we discussed Britain's various motivations in signing the 1917 Balfour Declaration promising support for a Jewish National Home in Palestine. Britain's patronage of Zionism promised to be an effective tool in forcing France to redraw the Sykes-Picot Agreement, and thereby supplant France's proclaimed interests in this strategic area near the Suez Canal. In the minds of some British officials at the time, the Zionist project also promised to be a much-appreciated source of investment and funds that could alleviate the administrative costs of ruling Palestine (see Document 30). They contended that Zionism's material benefits would ensure for all of Palestine "a flourishing community" built on the basis of "a spirit of cooperation upon which the future progress and prosperity of the Holy Land must largely depend."[24] However, as foreseen by the King-Crane Commission, enacting Zionism against the will of the overwhelming Arab majority could only be brought about by violence. For their own part, Palestinian leaders participated fully in the Syrian National Congress, and they effectively represented their visions of their own political future before the King-Crane Commission.

Palestine, like other Class A Mandates set up according to Article 22 of the League of Nations Covenant, was legally established as a provisionally independent nation. Yet the terms of the mandate itself were tailor-made for the Zionist project, even incorporating the whole text of the Balfour Declaration (see Document 31). As elsewhere throughout the region, violent opposition to foreign domination erupted immediately among Palestinians and mounted throughout the next two decades. In contrast to other colonial contexts—where violent opposition forced London, and Paris, to reconsider political strategies—Britain found it more difficult in Palestine to extricate itself from the internationally sanctioned terms of the Balfour promise without incurring significant costs, including the sacrifice of prestige and honor. Subject to the official mandate document, overseen by the Permanent Mandates Commission in Geneva, London feared there was no way of surrendering the British

---

24. "Statement of British Policy (Churchill Memorandum) on Palestine, 1 July 1922," in J. C. Hurewitz, ed., *The Middle East and North Africa in World Politics: A Documentary Record*, 2nd ed., Volume 2: *British-French Supremacy, 1914–1945* (New Haven, CT: Yale University Press, 1979), 301–5.

commitment toward building a Jewish national home without undermining the international legal basis of its control over this strategic territory. As cautioned by a British cabinet committee in 1923, there was "no way of reversing the policy without throwing up the mandate, and this might lead to the occupation of Palestine by France, Italy or Turkey."[25] Such a prospect was anathema to imperial strategists: in addition to the protective buffer Palestine provided to the vital Suez Canal zone, Palestine was increasingly the focus of key interests such as airports, seaports, and oil pipelines. In sum, although it was proved early on that there could in fact be no "flourishing community" between the competing territorial claims of Zionism and Palestinian nationalism, British officials struggled in vain for the next three decades trying to square the circle. Finally, they surrendered Palestine to its fractious fate in 1947–1948, figuratively leaving the key under the mat for the post-WWII United Nations (UN) to extract.[26]

Constitutional developments in Palestine were of particular importance for the interwar period. Unlike the political trajectory in neighboring mandates (and across the colonized world in general), Palestine was never permitted an elected legislative assembly. In its stead, imperial divide-and-rule policies were taken to an extreme as two parallel sets of institutions emerged, one for Zionists and another far less favorable one for Palestinians. On the one hand, London helped sponsor the growth of separate Zionist political, economic, educational, and even military institutions. Chief among them were the Jewish Agency (recognized as an elected public body to advise and cooperate with the British high commissioner in Jerusalem); the labor union known as Histadrut; and the Hebrew University in Jerusalem (founded in 1918), which demonstrated the vital role played by educational institutions in building Zionist predominance, not least by acculturating immigrant children through the new linguistic project of modernizing Hebrew. Militarily, the Zionist goal was to build what David Ben-Gurion's rival, Revisionist

---

25. Quoted in D. K. Fieldhouse, *Western Imperialism in the Middle East, 1914–1958* (Oxford: Oxford University Press, 2006), 199.

26. November 1947 is when the UN General Assembly voted in favor of partitioning Palestine into Zionist and Palestinian states. In May 1948, the State of Israel unilaterally declared its independence and the first Arab-Israeli War erupted, resulting in Israel's existence and the territorial dispossession of some 750,000 Palestinians (known to Palestinians as the *Nakba*, or catastrophe).

Zionist "Greater Israel" proponent Vladimir (Ze'ev) Jabotinsky (1880–1940), referred in 1923 as an "iron wall" against Palestinians:

> We cannot offer any adequate compensation to the Palestinian Arabs in return for Palestine. And therefore, there is no likelihood of any voluntary agreement being reached. So that all those who regard such an agreement as a condition sine qua non for Zionism may as well say "non" and withdraw from Zionism.
>
> *Zionist colonisation*... can proceed and develop only under the protection of a power that is independent of the native population—behind an iron wall, which the native population cannot breach.[27]

In the manifest absence of a legislative assembly, the British high commissioner ruled over the Arab community directly through notable elites (who, as we have seen, had been relied upon as intermediaries by the Ottomans and then deployed by all of the Ottomans' successor states). In Palestine, a dominant role would be achieved by Hajj Amin al-Husayni (1895–1974), appointed early on by the British to chair their newly created Supreme Muslim Council. From this religious post, which had not existed during Ottoman times, al-Husayni found himself in an advantageous position, vis-à-vis rival notable leaders, in bolstering his own personal leadership over the burgeoning Palestinian national movement. The position proved especially useful once political tensions became fused with religious matters following the 1929 conflict over holy sites in Jerusalem (often referred to as the Wailing Wall riots). But notable politics in Palestine, as elsewhere, was rife with internal divisions, and thus a poor substitute for the establishment of broader forms of political mobilization. Yet another revolt broke out in 1936 in response both to growing fears of Jewish immigration (which rose dramatically after the 1933 accession to rule by the Nazis in Germany) and to Britain's killing of Palestinian activist Izz ad-Din al-Qassam (1882–1935). Scared of possibly being left behind, the notables did finally come together at that point to form a national leadership body.

---

27. Vladimir Ze'ev Jabotinsky, "The Iron Wall," November 4, 1923, https://www.jewishvirtuallibrary.org/quot-the-iron-wall-quot. Italics in original.

Responses to Resistance

London responded to the 1936 demonstrations by launching a commission of enquiry. The publication in 1937 of the investigations of the Peel Commission changed the political landscape by concluding that the mandate was definitely unworkable and must come to an end. Chiding those who underestimated the difficulties confronting Britain's position, the Peel commission warned that continuing with the mandate meant only the worsening of "[a]n irrepressible conflict."[28] The commission's emphatic verdict to terminate the mandate was accompanied by a tentative and hurried plan of partition. But the proposal proved impossible to implement and withered under further inspection by yet more commissions.

With the renewal of Palestinian violence in what came to be known as the Great Revolt (1936–1939), the British engaged in brutal counterinsurgency methods. The besieged Zionists also responded by strengthening their own militias as well as their determination to become independent. But at the diplomatic level, the Great Revolt, including the high costs incurred by Britain in suppressing it, did bring about another dramatic change in British plans for governing Palestine. In early 1939, London issued a new white paper that declared limits on Jewish immigration (tragically curtailing Jewish immigration just months after Kristallnacht, the Nazi-sponsored anti-Semitic atrocity of November 1938). The white paper also restricted the continued purchase of land by Zionists to specific geographical zones and, most important, called for the establishment of a unitary Palestinian state in which Arabs (as the majority) and Jews (as a minority) would be forced to coexist. The document proposed a ten-year interim period within which to bring about an independent Palestinian state. But it was in this coming decade that Britain lost its dominant place in the world, as well as control of the situation in Palestine. Following the Second World War, Britain ignominiously surrendered the Palestine mandate back to an international community reeling from the shock of the revelations of the Holocaust.

---

28. "Text of the Peel Commission Report," July 1937, https://www.jewishvirtuallibrary.org/text-of-the-peel-commission-report.

Syria

France had worried that the Allied capture of and entry into Damascus in October 1918 would be understood as an Ottoman surrender to Faysal's Arab army. Much to the chagrin of Paris, Lord Allenby recognized the new Arab administration in Damascus as OETA East. When French troops disembarked in Beirut that month, it marked the start of a protracted struggle for control of Syria that Faysal, who in the end was abandoned by Britain to face France on his own, would ultimately lose.

Since the late nineteenth century, the cities of Damascus and Beirut had played prominent roles as centers of Arab proto-nationalist activity. For that matter, emboldened notions of Arab nationalism would remain at the heart of Syria's identity throughout the twentieth century. But, again, we must be careful not to read contemporary nationalist narratives back into history. What is clear is that Arab nationalist identity, if only gradually emerging prior to WWI, was greatly reinforced during the war. The experiences of shared suffering, both under Ottoman mobilization and during the subsequent animosity shown by rulers such as Cemal Pasha, had a profound impact. As Eugene Rogan observes, though Arab soldiers fought bravely for the Ottoman Empire, the terrible losses of the war would afterward be remembered "as someone else's war": "In the Arab world, the Great War left martyrs (especially Arab activists hanged in central squares of Beirut and Damascus that were subsequently renamed 'Martyrs' Square' in both cities) but no heroes."[29]

Following the war, many conflicting claims and aspirations competed for primacy among the Syrian population, but the nascent discourse of Arab nationalism would be thoroughly embedded into new state-making processes. Flying the flag of the WWI Arab revolt, Faysal set to work establishing new governing arrangements for an Arab kingdom that, from 1918 to 1920, drew in Arabs from throughout the region. For adherents of Faysal's Arab army, the actual administrative experience of setting up a new Arab government provided much inspiration for the elaboration of Arab nationalist ideologies. In contrast, many leading notable Ottoman families in Damascus and Aleppo felt different. Having worked hard over the previous century to preserve their own positions as political and economic

---

29. Eugene Rogan, *The Fall of the Ottomans: The Great War in the Middle East* (New York: Basic Books, 2015), xvi–xvii.

Arab forces enter Damascus, 1918.

intermediaries with Istanbul, they viewed Faysal's claims to leadership as those of a self-interested and autocratic Hejazi family who had betrayed the Ottoman Empire. Suspicious of Faysal and his supporters (many of whom came from Iraq), these notables resented the possibility that their own long-standing positions of authority might be eclipsed. Meanwhile, many Syrian soldiers of the Ottoman Army maintained an enduring loyalty to the sultan and focused their energies on resisting the localized impact of British and French military occupations. For a time, these soldiers continued to be inspired by, and even volunteer for, Mustafa Kemal's "defence of rights" committees. In the context of these anti-occupation struggles, some disparaged Faysal for relying too heavily on continued British subsidies.

At the same time, Britain increasingly pushed Faysal to reach an accommodation with France. London needed to reduce its ongoing military presence in the Middle East and, at the same time, manage simmering tensions with France. When Faysal traveled to the Paris Peace Conferences, he was extremely resentful to find that Arab claims were not to be treated on par with those of eastern Europeans. As Faysal struggled to reconcile with France, he felt he was being abandoned by Britain. In a personal note to T. E. Lawrence, he suggested sardonically that "the leading European statesmen be treated like a gallery of pictures—hung in a row and looked at from a distance."[30]

---

30. As recorded in Ernest Dowson, *Commonplace Book*. St. Antony's College, University of Oxford Middle East private papers collection.

Toward Syrian Independence and Revolt

Though Faysal remained conscious of the need to pursue diplomatic relations with France, political developments in Damascus increasingly reflected a more determined nationalist agenda. On March 8, 1920, the Syrian National Congress, first elected in June 1919, proclaimed Faysal king of a united Syria and unilaterally declared an independent Arab Kingdom of Syria. According to Elizabeth Thompson, the Islamic jurist and intellectual Rashid Rida described the moment as the "'Day of Resurrection' . . . the day Arabs truly arose as a nation from centuries of Turkish enslavement."[31] Arab activists in the region, led by Rida, drafted a new constitution for this objective. They aimed to draw autonomous Ottoman Syrian provinces (including what would become Lebanon, Palestine, and Transjordan) into a federal government centered at Damascus. In so doing, the constitution virtually disestablished the juridical force of Islam.

Thompson stresses the significance of Rida's seeking support from Wilson's reimagining of the postwar world: "In terms unimaginable a century later, the most famous Islamic scholar of the day praised a devout, Protestant American president as an instrument of God's will."[32]

These developments on the ground represented the Syrian National Congress's clear rejection of any potential dealmaking with France. Paris responded forcefully. It first sent Faysal an ultimatum demanding unconditional acceptance of the French mandate, and then it dropped leaflets from airplanes warning that "we now ask all of you to urge [Faysal] to leave your country at once lest his presence make it a bomb target."[33] Then, on July 24, 1920, the French military routed a small number of Arab defenders at the Battle of Maysalūn, following which it occupied Damascus (see Document 32). The first French high commissioner appointed to rule the French mandates of Syria and Lebanon was Henri Gouraud (1867–1946). Upon arriving in Damascus, Gouraud tellingly addressed not the occupied inhabitants, but the tomb of twelfth-century Muslim hero Saladin who had led armies against European Christian crusaders

---

31. Thompson, *How the West Stole Democracy from the Arabs*, 263.

32. Thompson, *How the West Stole Democracy from the Arabs*, 98.

33. Abū Khaldūn Sāti'al-Husrī, *The Day of Maysalūn: A Page from the Modern History of the Arabs*, trans. Sidney Glazer (Washington, DC: Middle East Institute, 1966), 79–82, 84.

(and was an ethnic Kurd, as it happens). The visit allowed Gouraud to declare publicly that "we have returned, and my presence here consecrates the victory of the Cross over the Crescent."[34]

Faysal's two-year Arab administration was quickly replaced by a highly interventionist form of French colonial control that divided Syria into separate statelets, all under the high commissioner's control from central offices in Beirut. These new entities were based on a highly sectarian reading of the region's demographics. One statelet was carved out for 'Alawis—a historically disadvantaged Shi'i offshoot community whose French-abetted rise to political dominance later manifested in the regimes of Hafez al-Assad (1930–2000, president 1971–2000) and his son Bashar. A separate statelet was also created for the Druze. Both of these remained in place until 1936. France's divide-and-rule tactics, predicated on supporting minority communities, greatly hampered the coalescence of a Syrian nationalist opposition to France.[35]

Despite French efforts, or perhaps because of them, a major anti-French uprising, known as the Great Syrian Revolt (as differentiated from that in 1930s Palestine) eventually erupted in 1925. Sparked by a rebellion among the Jabal Druze in August 1925, uprisings against foreign domination quickly spread across Syria. The revolt would not be suppressed until 1927, after much brutal destruction and loss of life. In broad regional terms, the Syrian revolt occurred in conjunction with the extraordinarily violent 1921–1926 Rif War pitting Moroccan nationalists against French (and Spanish) colonialism. In the central role it went on to play in future nationalist narratives, the Syrian revolt is comparable to 1920s uprisings in Iraq and the 1936–1939 revolt in Palestine. The French response inflicted great suffering on the Syrian population, but the growing burdens of suppressing the rebellion, and the increased international criticism France received for its responsibility for the Syrian mandate, forced Paris to reconsider its governance strategies. First, France began the amalgamation of microstates into a more viable unitary state.[36] Second, France crafted a new

---

34. Quoted in Provence, *Last Ottoman Generation*, 3.

35. See Nikolaos Van Dam, *The Struggle for Power in Syria* (London: I. B. Tauris, 2011).

36. This amalgamation eventually included all Syrian regions other than that around Antakya, known as Alexandretta, which, as previously indicated, was eventually ceded to Turkey in 1939.

administration that better represented the political and social power of the Ottoman notable class.

By this point, the notables had come together in a loose coalition known as the National Bloc. Fearful of losing the dominant role they had effectively maintained during centuries of Ottoman rule (and which first risked being displaced, as some notables had earlier feared, by Faysal's pan-Arab plans), and hopeful for a gradual relaxation of French control, notables under the National Bloc showed more willingness to collaborate with the French after 1927. Thus had Syrian politics transformed during this first postwar decade to the restoration of more traditional influence exercised by the notables within political circles defined by the borders of the new Syrian mandate. In the end, French rule effectively revitalized the quite traditional status quo that modern constitutional developments, as explored during both the *Tanzimat* and Faysal's brief kingdom, had sought to transform.

Iraq

As has been shown repeatedly in the region-by-region studies above, resistance movements emerged throughout the Middle East immediately after WWI. Broad-based rebellions were propelled by shared grievances against foreign occupation and the many serious social and economic injustices posed by the imposition of colonial rule. In Iraq, an uprising that began among southern Shi'i tribes in October 1920 quickly spread to many other rural areas, including Sunni populations. Yitzhak Nakash has underlined the prominent role that political poetry played in mobilizing a nationalist response (see Document 33).[37] Britain responded to this revolt in an especially violent way, including Royal Air Force bombardments and reported plans by Churchill (by now returned to British political life as a chief military and colonial official) to employ poison gas. For Iraqis, the revolt remains a signal moment in their prolonged struggle for national independence.

From Britain's perspective, the force of these anti-occupation uprisings exposed the vulnerability of Britain's position and the tenuousness of their postwar plans. Mounting Iraqi opposition forced Britain to focus

---

37. Yitzhak Nakash, *The Shi'is of Iraq*, 2nd ed. (Princeton, NJ: Princeton University Press, 2003), 68–70.

on achieving specific administrative goals at the lowest cost. This basic approach determined the formal political machinery that was crafted for the newly drawn Iraqi state. The authoritarian and divisive administrative structure Britain left behind is a legacy with which Iraqis have been forced to grapple ever since.[38]

Britain sought, as elsewhere, to rule indirectly through local leaders who could be won over to the goal of maintaining a conservative social and economic status quo. The classic colonial divide-and-rule dynamic was underwritten in Iraq by the decision to anoint King Faysal, recently expelled from Damascus by the French (but whose family was originally from the Hejaz), as a monarch in Baghdad. The March 1921 Cairo Conference promoted what is often referred to as a Hashemite "Sharifian solution": Faysal would rule the new state of Iraq while his older brother Abdullah (1882–1951, r. 1921–1951) would rule the newly carved-out state of Transjordan. As far as T. E. Lawrence was concerned, these arrangements "made straight the tangle" and allowed the British "to quit of the war-time Eastern adventure, with clean hands."[39] Most British officials, however, were simply attracted to the advantages of appointing someone who should prove pliable. In 1921, a hollow referendum was held which provided Britain with an opportunity to assert that 96 percent of the Iraqi population supported the new king—a specious move that only underscored what little heed was ever paid to Faysal's lack of legitimacy in the eyes of many Iraqis (especially those communities who had sacrificed the most in the 1920 uprisings). "[W]e've got our king crowned," crowed Gertrude Bell, the renowned archeologist and British civil servant (see Document 34).[40]

Faysal did go on to prove more independent-minded than Britain had supposed.[41] But he was clearly aware of the precarious tightrope he walked. At first, Faysal's most important supporters came from the small group of Sunni Ottoman military officers who had staffed his short-lived

---

38. See especially Charles Tripp, *A History of Iraq*, 3rd ed. (Cambridge: Cambridge University Press, 2007).

39. Quoted, and disparaged, in George Antonius, *The Arab Awakening: The Story of the Arab National Movement* (Safety Harbor, FL: Simon Publications, 2001 [1939]), 14.

40. Gertrude Bell to Sir Hugh Bell, August 28, 1921, https://gertrudebell.ncl.ac.uk/l/gb-1-1-2-1-17-29.

41. See Ali Allawi, *Faisal I of Iraq* (New Haven, CT: Yale University Press, 2014).

Coronation of King Faysal in Baghdad, 1921.

Damascus government. Now finding themselves unemployed, they accompanied Faysal to Baghdad. Once ensconced in Iraq, they made every effort to consolidate wealth and privilege in the developing new political order.

Perhaps understandably, given the alliance between these former Ottoman soldiers and British colonial officers, this new order placed a heavy emphasis on coercion and military force. But the new regime also sought to employ a broad patronage network to co-opt further support among local leaders for the emerging state. Thus, a second group through whom Britain, and the Sharifians, sought support in ruling Iraq consisted of the tribal shaykhs in the rural countryside. As this group consisted of both Sunni (Kurdish as well as Arab) and Shi'i leaders, the key cleavage for the imperial project to exploit in Iraq was between the landed elite and the vast majority of peasant tenants. The treasury's increasing oil revenues played a significant role in encouraging Iraq's landed rural elite to recognize Baghdad's newly centralized government. In addition to fueling such patronage networks, the Tribal Criminal and Civil Disputes Regulations comprised another key British instrument in this "indirect rule" arrangement. These policies empowered rural leaders with new legal and fiscal means to collect taxes and preserve stability. In fully understanding the significance of Britain's intervention in this regard, it is worth recalling the extent to which a shaykh's autonomy in Iraq had actually abated under the nineteenth-century Ottoman administrative and reform efforts. Hanna Batatu has concluded that "the semi-feudal shaikhly structure" nurtured under British rule "did not derive its strength from any inner vitality": rather, "life was pumped into it artificially by an outside force that had an interest in its perpetuation."[42] Charles Tripp elaborates by explaining how "in many cases, British policy was instrumental in shaping the very tribal hierarchies and units that, it was claimed, constituted the 'natural' order of society."[43] All in all, such policies threw into stark relief the purported mandate system that had patronizingly called upon European powers to help usher Arab communities into the modern world.

In the oil-rich north, Britain's hurried efforts to occupy the Ottoman vilayet of Mosul, after the Mudros Armistice had been signed, led to conflicting claims. These were not resolved until 1925, when a League of Nations commission recommended the province remain under the rule of Baghdad. These developments forced dominant Kurdish tribal leaders to reconsider the idea of an independent Kurdish state across the whole area that constituted their homeland (but was now divided among Syria and Iraq, as well as Turkey and Iran). That is, the new partitions of territory forced tribal leaders to recalibrate how best to secure their own positions of authority, together with the interests of their own clans and regions. In Iraq, some local leaders deepened their engagement with the central government in Baghdad, greatly sharpening the internal fault lines that had long divided Kurdish communities. As for those leaders who opposed Baghdad's co-optation strategies, and instead continued to seek greater independence from centralized control, they confronted increasingly violent military repression.

In these ways, Ottoman governance structures were replaced by a new state apparatus built by the British, together with the Hashemite monarchy. This apparatus was in large part crafted as a means for confirming power among a narrow circle of elites. These elites then

---

42. Hanna Batatu, *The Old Social Classes and the Revolutionary Movements of Iraq: A Study of Iraq's Old Landed and Commercial Classes and of Its Communists, Ba'athists, and Free Officers* (London: Saqi, 2004 [1978]), 99.

43. Charles Tripp, *A History of Iraq*, 3rd ed. (Cambridge: Cambridge University Press, 2007), 37.

found themselves in the privileged position of dispensing increasing oil profits to specific individuals who could be co-opted to accept the new status quo. To be sure, these co-optations and exclusions were to some degree based on sect and ethnicity, but they also significantly reinforced cross-cutting notions of status, class, and gender. In sum, by building this political machinery, Britain essentially launched Iraq into a cycle of authoritarian rule that long outlasted both the mandate (which ended in 1932, as Iraq became a nominally independent constitutional monarchy) and the Hashemite monarchy (bloodily deposed in a 1958 coup d'état led by Iraqi military officer and nationalist Abd al-Karim Qasim (1914–1963).

Kuwait

It is worth considering, if only briefly, Baghdad's contested claims on Kuwaiti territory. These claims were made repeatedly throughout the twentieth century and culminated in Saddam Hussein's (1937–2006, president 1979–2003) invasion in 1990. The broader context underpinning Iraq's demands involved the perceived need to expand its short low-lying coastline and build a deepwater port on the Persian Gulf. In justifying its claim to neighboring Kuwait's coastline, Iraq asserted that Kuwait had always been an Ottoman subdistrict ruled from Iraq.

As we saw in Chapter 1, Britain's security interests at the head of the Persian Gulf had made it increasingly wary of Germany's approaching railway infrastructure. Britain therefore took steps in the early twentieth century to sponsor the local al-Sabah family and support the quasi-independence of Kuwait as a separate protectorate. Istanbul insisted on its own continued sovereignty over this Ottoman administrative district. But the early launch of Britain's October 1914 offensive effectively sealed Kuwait's fate, and Britain declared it to be an independent principality under British protection.

From postwar Iraq's perspective, Britain's efforts to separate Kuwait from its administrative ties to the Ottoman Empire were part and parcel of illegitimate colonial designs to divide and weaken the Arab world. In this sense, Iraq's frustration can be likened to Syria's ongoing concern for the loss of the Ottoman province of Alexandretta. Yet the actual situation is more complicated than powerful anticolonial rhetoric allows. Baghdad's argument fails to recognize that in 1914 there was no political entity of Iraq from which Britain could have separated Kuwaiti territory. Whatever the actual legal basis for Iraq's persistent claim, the problem nonetheless sheds yet more light on the complex and fraught legacy of European boundary making—especially in remote desert areas lacking marked geographic features above ground, but endowed with oceans of oil below.

Transjordan

In sharp contrast to Britain's readily defined interests in what became Palestine and Iraq, London gave relatively little thought to the area lying in between. During late Ottoman times, this region achieved increased significance with the building of the Hejaz railway, which linked Aleppo with Mecca and Medina. Moreover, the area's inhabitants were equally subject to the centralizing administrative project undertaken by the Ottoman Empire. But the region itself held no administrative unity. The northern part belonged to what was known as Greater Syria, while the southern region was considered an extension of the Hejaz. Half-settled, half-nomadic, the communities in the western parts had stronger relations across the Jordan River into Palestine, while large tribal confederations in the east stretched across the desert areas to Iraq.

As far as European war aims were concerned, the Sykes-Picot Agreement had placed Transjordan within the British sphere as a presumed land bridge linking ports (especially Haifa) in the Mediterranean with those in the Persian Gulf. Yet, when in 1918 Lord Allenby mapped out his various military administrations under the postwar occupation, the area was placed in OETA East, and thus came under the rule of Damascus, where Faysal (much to the chagrin of France) established his Arab kingdom from 1918 to 1920. Subsequently, once France had completed its own conquest of Syria in 1920 and sent Faysal into exile, Transjordan was untethered from Damascus's rule.

Entering the scene at this point was Abdullah bin al-Husayn—Faysal's older brother who had played the key role in negotiating his family's wartime correspondence with Sir Henry McMahon (see Document 16). Abdullah had spent most of the war stuck in Medina, while Faysal attracted attention from London. Following his brother's defeat in Syria in 1920, however, and then his father's defeat to Ibn Saud, Abdullah sought to avenge his family's losses. At first, he positioned himself in Amman and built strong connections with local leaders. Though Abdullah's ambitions potentially posed a threat to European imperial projects, Britain was not then in a position (especially following the costly suppression of the Iraqi Revolt) to expend scarce resources. Accordingly, Britain experimented with the idea of building up Abdullah as a regional ally. Thus, as was decided at the Cairo Conference, British officials sought to deploy what legitimacy the Hashemite family could still muster as a cheap means for securing their own imperial needs in this frontier region.

From the evolving relationship between Britain and Abdullah eventually emerged the new state of Transjordan. Tellingly, Abdullah reported throughout the interwar period to the British high commissioner in Jerusalem. One should recall here the above-mentioned "Greater Israel" ambitions of Jabotinsky's Revisionist Zionist movement—an ideological forerunner of elements within today's Israeli settler movement that has appropriated territories conquered in the 1967 Six-Day War. From the outset, Revisionist Zionists sought Jewish settlement on the eastern as well as western sides of the River Jordan. As for Abdullah, his larger territorial ambitions chafed at the constraining puzzle-piece boundaries that were drawn for his landlocked desert kingdom. Still, Abdullah successfully built on these ad hoc circumstances to achieve independence in 1946 as the Hashemite Kingdom of Jordan, and of all the post-WWI creations, his regime also proved the most durable.

Saudi Arabia

Given Sharif Husayn's aspirations for his family to rule over an Arab kingdom, he cannot have felt anything but great resentment as he watched relations between his family and his erstwhile British patron deteriorate so badly in 1920. Husayn was barely able to secure his own rule in the Hejaz against the shifting balance of power in the Arabian Peninsula. When Mustafa Kemal extinguished the caliphate, a move that met with much worldwide consternation, Husayn (who, recall, had never shown much enthusiasm for the Ottomans' 1914 declaration of *jihād*) tried to claim the mantle of caliph. However, Sharif Husayn's capacity to rule even Arabia now faced the rival ambitions of Ibn Saud who, adding more to Husayn's deep sense of betrayal, was also supported by British weapons and subsidies.

Britain had established diplomatic relations with Ibn Saud during the war, in exchange for fighting against the al-Rashidi family, a faithful ally of the Ottomans in Ha'il. Following the war, Ibn Saud continued to expand his state, first launching attacks on Asir and Ha'il in 1920 and 1921, respectively, and then conquering the Hejaz and the holy places of Mecca and Medina in 1924. After forcing Sharif Husayn into exile, first to Transjordan and then Cyprus, Ibn Saud was proclaimed king of all the Arabian Peninsula in 1926 (apart from Aden, Yemen, and the British-protected shaykhdoms along the coast of the Persian Gulf). At first a poor and small administration, built on the primacy of personal relationships, Ibn Saud went on to establish a powerful oil-based alliance with the US (notwithstanding 1930s Soviet overtures to the Saudis). Ironically, this opened up the potential for a post-WWII rivalry between London and Washington for Middle East dominance.

CONCLUSION
Transformations, Directions, and Entanglements

In this book, we have sought to underscore the multiple ways in which the decision of the Ottoman Empire to side with Germany in World War I marked, in the words of Malcolm Yapp, "the single most important event" in the history of the modern Middle East.[1] In so doing, we have also sought to show how the four terrible years of WWI must be viewed in the context of a larger span of tumult, from the 1908–1909 Young Turk Revolution and 1912–1913 Balkan Wars (and for Iran, the revolutionary tumult of 1905–1911) to the early 1920s, when initial anticolonial resistance movements on the ground subsided and were replaced by new political developments within the bounds of externally imposed, European colonial state structures. Further, this tumult must be illuminated within the broader chronological reframing of the "modern Middle East" in the manner that we did by sketching within Chapter 1 the "long nineteenth century" of 1798–1914.[2] Crucially, "modern" is a deeply contested notion in need of continued critical reexamination. There exists no singular culture or ideology of Western modernity, least of all one that has been neatly grafted onto other societies through global processes of colonization. Rather, "multiple modernities" have arisen.[3] These include distinct formulations where non-Western (or partially Western, as the Eurasian Ottoman Empire, like its historical antagonist Russia, might be construed) societies have adapted and often transformed some modern Western ideas for their own aims. Moreover, all societies have come up with analogous ideas of their own, while rejecting others, or they have

---

1. Malcolm Yapp, *Making of the Modern Near East* (London: Longman, 1987), 266.

2. See Robin Wagner-Pacifici, *What Is an Event?* (Chicago: University of Chicago Press, 2017), on ways in which the concept of an "event," and various iterations of "events," are contingent on surrounding historical and interpretive contexts.

3. S. N. Eisenstadt, "Multiple Modernities," *Daedalus* 129, no. 1 (2000): 1–29.

carved out alternative visions of modern life in direct opposition to those sought to be imposed by the West.

This broader consideration of the prolonged modern transformations of the Middle East allows one to thoughtfully work through both the enduring legacies of Ottoman (and other, e.g., Persian/Iranian) patterns of rule and the enduring impact of their violent supplanting by Western, colonially dominated forms of rule. Chapter 1 examined Ottoman modernization across all realms of the state, including reforms to administration and education, the legal construction of citizenship and equal rights, and negotiations over constitutional checks and balances. In Chapter 2, we emphasized how the Ottoman WWI battlefronts witnessed Istanbul's marshaling of its modern powers of administrative and military prowess to fight the Allies to a standstill for almost four years. Chapter 3 threw into sharp relief the efforts of successor European colonial administrations to bring an end to, or even reverse, many of these important, if unfinished, processes of modernization. Specifically, where the late Ottoman Empire had managed to enhance the functioning of a geographically expansive, exceptionally multicommunal realm, its territories were ultimately divided by European empires, and by Atatürk-led 1920s Turkish nationalists, into state formations acting to inscribe intercommunal divides.

The Ottoman Empire's formidable war effort clearly belies facile portrayals of a "sick man of Europe" that were a staple of Orientalist consciousness foretelling the empire's imminent demise. Recent historiography, which we have sought to integrate throughout our account, offers vital correctives to the sick man narrative. Yet the image of the Ottoman Empire as a sick, dying man continues to mark popular perceptions. The persistence of that notion can be seen as a function of self-justifying, modernist discourses and narratives developed within the new entities that emerged from the ruins of the defeated Ottoman Empire. For European colonial administrators, the sick man image was a necessary foil to help justify and defend (if only to domestic constituencies) the extension of European imperial rule. As for the new independent Turkish Republic, we have seen how nationalist leaders of the postwar period, who only a few years earlier were hailed as Ottoman heroes loyally serving the sultan's army to which they pledged service, now disparaged and renounced as antiquated all vestiges of the empire's supposed, failed legacy. Arab leaders, too, would find reasons in the post-Ottoman period to celebrate what some then referred to as their liberation from

Conclusion: Transformations, Directions, and Entanglements   123

"the alien yoke."[4] The changes experienced by Arabic-speaking peoples of the Ottoman Empire during the 1839–1876 *Tanzimat* reforms resulted in the evolution of new forms of citizenship and identity. While these changes were vital to producing the continually shifting historical contours ever since—from nationalist identities and movements, to Islamic activism, to early twenty-first-century, neo-imperial Turkish state nostalgia for Ottomanism—the terrible suffering of wartime deprivations did produce a sharp rupture. As Salim Tamari has observed, the calamitous four years of *seferberlik*'s perpetual wartime footing "replaced four centuries of relative peace and dynamic activity, the Ottoman era, with what was known in Arabic discourse as 'the days of the Turks.'"[5] Arab leaders such as Sāti' al-Husrī, who had served a distinguished career in the Ottoman bureaucracy, now mobilized support for Arab nationalism.[6] None of this can be considered as preordained but must instead be seen as an integral part of the ongoing, modern nation-building projects upon which leaders were forced to embark in the postwar colonial period. Not least, Zionists in Palestine, buoyed by Britain's scattershot strategic decision in late 1917 to support Jewish nationhood with the Balfour Declaration, perceived themselves as a distinct outpost of enlightened, European modernity—a perspective that for a moment appeared useful to British colonial ambitions for the broader region. In Iran, new monarch Reza Shah's 1920s emulation of Atatürk saw the forcible superimposition of a European-inflected, modern Iranian national identity. Still further to the east in Afghanistan, Amanullah Khan's 1919 defeat of distracted British Indian forces allowed Afghans to shape their own vision of nationalist identity—a seemingly distant memory today, amid resurgent Taliban control of the country.

Britain and France played the dominant role in shaping the new state formations that replaced the Ottoman Empire. By endowing these new states with centralized and highly securitized administrations that paid undue attention to sectarian identities for the purpose of divide and rule,

---

4. George Antonius, *Arab Awakening: The Story of the Arab National Movement* (Safety Harbor, FL: Simon Publications, 2001 [1939]), 276.

5. Salim Tamari, *Year of the Locust: A Soldier's Diary and the Erasure of Palestine's Ottoman Past* (Berkeley: University of California Press, 2011), 5.

6. See William L. Cleveland, *The Making of an Arab Nationalist: Ottomanism and Arabism in the Life and Thought of Sāti' al-Husrī* (Princeton, NJ: Princeton University Press, 1972).

these strategies aimed at keeping nationalist opposition from coalescing. London and Paris came around quickly enough to accepting the mandate system of the post-WWI League of Nations, but only as a cover for the extension of traditional forms of colonial rule over the region's inhabitants, rather than a purported transition to the mandate's near-term independence. Thus, new state institutions were as much, or more, a product of European concerns with geostrategic balances of power than they were driven by emerging discourses around self-determination and democracy, that is, the imagined "spirit of the age" exemplified by US president Woodrow Wilson. Not surprisingly, the new states immediately witnessed a period of sustained conflict. At first, local leaders refused to accept the European effort to secure their spoils of war. Anticolonial revolts erupted throughout the region—from Libya, to Egypt, Iraq, Syria, Palestine, and beyond former Ottoman boundaries to Afghanistan and Morocco. Notably, in Syria, local constitutional efforts aimed at sorting out how inhabitants of a new state structure would live together were swiftly met and erased by a 1920 French invasion.[7]

Deploying, and experimenting with, counterinsurgency methods such as aerial bombardment, Britain and France were successful, at least in the short term, in imposing their rule and establishing new political regimes surrounded by the new international boundaries. Remarkably quickly, these regimes became the focus of all political activities. As a first step, local socially conservative forces—most commonly large landowners (i.e., landed "notables," those who had achieved elite positions under Ottoman rule)—pushed to remain relevant amid these convulsions. Within the colonial systems of indirect rule set up for the new centralized administrations, the notable class successfully maintained what influence and status they could as intermediaries. To be sure, there were important differences from one colonial structure to another, but more often than not, these elites gravitated to the new capital cities and opted to find ways to work within the British and French colonial structures. Thus, the new nationalizing state projects were largely led by conservative social forces whose own interests often overlapped with those of colonial powers, but which found little space for the peasantry and urban working classes. Some governments successfully negotiated terms of independence for

---

7. Elizabeth Thompson, *How the West Stole Democracy from the Arabs: The Syrian Arab Congress of 1920 and the Destruction of Its Historic Liberal-Islamic Alliance* (New York: Atlantic Monthly Press, 2020).

their emergent nations, even providing them with seats at the League of Nations. But it would not be until the post-WWII period that military revolutions would sweep through the Arab world to overthrow the systems of indirect rule set up by colonial powers. An emblematic instance would feature the rise in Egypt of Nasser (1918–1970), born at WWI's end to a Port Said postal worker, who by the 1950s became the preeminent regional as well as global standard-bearer of revolutionary socialist-inflected Arab nationalism. On the other hand, such seeming postcolonial restructurings would in key respects turn neocolonial; this, as Turkey, diverse Arab states, Israel, Iran, Afghanistan, and nation-state aspirants like the Palestinians and Kurds became entangled with the ideological and geostrategic dynamics of the late 1940s through the late 1980s/early 1990s global Cold War between the US and the Soviet Union. But that is another extraordinarily complex and still-resonating story for a different day.

All of this also prompts reflection on the illuminating possibilities posed by counterfactuals, or what-if historical questions.[8] For example, what if Sultan Abdülhamid II had persisted with the 1876 constitutional reforms that he had at first pledged to uphold? Would this have made the Ottoman Empire a more potent participant among the European concert of powers? For that matter, to pose the quintessential counterfactual that is pertinent here, what if the Austro-Hungarian Archduke Franz Ferdinand and Princess Sophie had not been assassinated in the first instance, or if the Ottoman Empire had allied, as it were, with the winning side? Would the Ottoman Empire have endured, and if so, in what form, and how resilient would it have remained to the specter of ongoing foreign interventions? In studying the end of the Ottoman Empire and the forging of the modern Middle East, we must guard against the problematic, characteristically modern conceit that history constitutes a forward-moving, linear trajectory at whose endpoint we reside.[9] If we are

---

8. Christopher Prendergast, *Counterfactuals: Paths of the Might Have Been* (London: Bloomsbury, 2019).

9. See James M. Banner Jr., *The Ever-Changing Past: Why All History Is Revisionist History* (New Haven, CT: Yale University Press, 2021); and François Hartog, *Regimes of Historicity: Presentism and Experiences of Time*, trans. Saskia Brown (New York: Columbia University Press, 2017). Hartog is known for critiquing the modern tendency toward "presentism," that is, regarding the past through the distorting lens of the present (a perspective which also, as it happens, hinders our ability to look toward the future).

126 Conclusion: Transformations, Directions, and Entanglements

Screenshot that was originally posted to social media
by ISIS, when declaring an end to Sykes-Picot.

to learn from history, and how it continually reshapes our ever-developing world, we cannot avoid importing a present-day perspective into our assessments of the past. Nonetheless, we do need to guard against presentism. In place of teleological narratives—which, ironically, are backward-looking rather than progressive, with their presupposition that present or future ideals can be justified by how the past is framed—it is pivotal to maintain an awareness of the constantly fluctuating role played by chance and contingency.

All of which brings us to the immediate, unfolding historical moment during which you happen to be reading this book. Perhaps you picked up the book, or registered for the course in which it is assigned, because you are interested in better understanding some among the myriad twenty-first-century events whose genealogies are linked to the era we have explored here: for example, the protracted and destructive Afghanistan and Iraq Wars that followed from the Al-Qaeda attacks of September 11, 2001; apparently unending conflict between Israelis and Palestinians, seeming ever more intractable since Hamas's October 7, 2023, attack on Israel, followed by Israel's massive military response; the region-wide Arab uprisings against highly centralized and securitized states that ignited in 2010. As to the latter, in particular, the Arab uprisings' chaotic outflows were numerous and highly pertinent to the central themes of this book. These outflows include dimensions like the Syrian, Libyan,

Conclusion: Transformations, Directions, and Entanglements

and Yemeni civil wars and regional/global proxy conflicts (which have been stoked anew amid the most recent war between Israel and Hamas) and the brief rise to territorial dominance of the self-proclaimed Islamic State (best known as ISIS), which held aloft its black banner for the supposed, reembodied caliphate supplanting illegitimate, European colonial Sykes-Picot boundaries. A further recent illustration is the one hundredth anniversary, in 2023, of the Treaty of Lausanne that demarcated the new Turkish Republic emerging from Ottoman ashes.

Each of these, and countless others, is an "event" whose underlying sediments of history we hope we have helped to reveal a bit. However, there is no necessary predetermination of these events arising as they have, nor can we any better predict the future. Please recall the absence of foresight shared by both the imagined Jewish civil servant and port laborer, from pre-WWI Salonica, whom we met in the Preface. The universe is a complex and chaotic place. But at the least, studying history is an invaluable means by which we can seek to glimpse something of a (or our own) tiny corner and moment in time, without knowing where we are headed.

DOCUMENTS

Document 1

Abd al-Rahman Al-Jabartī's 1798 Condemnation of Egypt's French Occupiers[1]

Egyptian scholar and cleric 'Abd al-Rahman al-Jabartī (1753–1825) was a firsthand witness to Napoleon Bonaparte's invasion and occupation of Egypt (1798–1801). His chronicle represents a crucial point of view on a historical episode that has usually been studied solely through European sources. Despite acknowledging some European technological achievements, al-Jabartī fiercely denounced the French presence in Egypt, characterized by France's divide-and-rule approach favoring Coptic Christians over Muslims. Thereafter, al-Jabartī speaks of the brutality with which Napoleon's forces sought to crush an October 1798 rebellion in Cairo.

For further discussion: *How do al-Jabartī's perspectives further our understandings of both Napoleon's military expeditions themselves and historians' notion that the French invasion of Egypt marked the beginning of a new historical era characterizable as "the modern Middle East"? How and when does a historian judge an event to be a "watershed moment"?*

The French prescribed the organization of a new *dīwān* which was called *mahkamat al-qadāyā* (court of legal cases). They wrote up a document for this purpose and set down all the stipulations. They appointed six Copts to it and six Muslim merchants; they nominated Maltī, the Copt, who

---

1. 'Abd al-Rahmān al-Jabartī, *'Abd al-Rahmān al-Jabartī's History of Egypt, Volumes III & IV*, trans. Thomas Philipp and Moshe Perlmann (Stuttgart: Franz Steiner Verlag, 1994), 31, 42–44.

Document 1. Abd al-Rahman Al-Jabartī's 1798 Condemnation

was the secretary of 'Ayyūb Bey al-Daftardār to serve as the chief *qādī* [i.e., a judge]. They authorized this court to deal with commercial and civil affairs, legacies, and law suits. They laid down for this *dīwān* evil, heretical rules and principles. They made many copies of this document, sent them to the dignitaries, posted copies at the intersections, alley entrances, and the gates of the mosques. They set stipulations within stipulations in incomprehensible phrases, the intention of which could be understood only after much reflection because of their ignorance of the rules of Arabic syntax. The purpose of it was trickery to exact money.

. . . After nightfall, the French entered the city like a torrent. They passed through the alleys and streets without encountering resistance— just as if they were devils or Satan's troops. They tore down all the barricades they found. One group entered from Bāb al-Barqīya and marched to al-Ghawrīya. They patrolled it constantly, never closing an eye. Thus they knew for sure that there was no move against them and no ambush prepared. They kept in contact with each other by dispatching messengers on horse or foot. Then they entered al-Azhar Mosque on horseback with some infantry among them—like wild goats! They spread in its courtyard and the ruler's enclosure and tied their horses to the *qibla*. They created havoc in the *riwāqs* and sections, smashing the lamps and the night lights, breaking open the bookcases of the students living inside and outside of al-Azhar and of the scribes. They plundered all possessions they found: furniture, vessels, copper kettles, deposits of valuables and hidden treasures in lockers and coffers. They threw books and copies of the Koran as refuse on the ground, trampling on them with their feet and shoes. They defecated and pissed on them and blew their noses over them. They drank wine and broke the containers and threw them in the courtyard corners. They ripped off the clothes of everybody they encountered there. . . .

Afterwards, they patrolled the streets, taking up positions in lines of hundreds and thousands. If anybody passed them, they would search him, take his belongings, and sometimes even kill him. They removed the bodies of slain Muslims and French from the ground and cleared the barricades by removing all the piled up stones and earth and putting them aside, so that the road would be clear for traffic. The Syrian Christians and also a group of Greek Orthodox whose houses had been looted in al-Jawānīya Quarter joined forces to complain to the chief of the French about the calamity that had afflicted them. They availed themselves of this opportunity to deal the Muslims a heavy blow, showing what was hidden in their hearts, as if they had shared in the vicissitudes of the French. But the Muslims had gone after them and plundered them only because of their connections with the French. Besides, even the Muslims living close to them had been plundered by the mob, just as the famous Khān al-Milāyāt next to the gate of the Greek Quarter. There were goods belonging to Muslims in it and deposits left by travelers—but the injured parties were silent about their agony, asking God for compensation in this matter, for even if they had spoken out, their complaint would not have been heard and no attention would have been paid to their grievance....

They slew many people and threw them into the Nile. During these two days and the following, many people perished—only God knows their number. The injustice and obdurancy [sic] of the infidels continued, and they wreaked their vengeance on the Muslims.

Document 2
1839 Edict of Gülhane[2]

The 1839 Edict of Gülhane was proclaimed by Sultan Abdülmecid I (1823–1861, r. 1839–1861) at the behest of his reform-minded grand vizier, Mustafa Reşid Pasha (1800–1858). It represented a series of promises on forthcoming reforms centered around issues of legal equality, fair taxation, and regularized military service. Aimed specifically at "the benefit of a good administration," the edict initiated a new era of Ottoman history known as the Tanzimat *(meaning "reordering").*

For further discussion: *In which ways, and to what extent, did the* Tanzimat *reforms transform relationships between identity groups across the Ottoman Empire? How did some groups stand to benefit from such promised reforms, and why might others have felt threatened?*

---

2. "The Rescript of Gülhane—Gülhane Hatt-ı Hümayunu (3 November 1839)," https://www.anayasa.gen.tr/gulhane.htm.

Document 2. 1839 Edict of Gülhane

All the world knows that in the first days of the Ottoman monarchy, the glorious precepts of the Kuran and the laws of the empire were always honored.

The empire in consequence increased in strength and greatness, and all its subjects, without exception, had risen in the highest degree to ease and prosperity. In the last one hundred and fifty years a succession of accidents and divers causes have arisen which have brought about a disregard for the sacred code of laws and the regulations flowing therefrom, and the former strength and prosperity have changed into weakness and poverty; an empire in fact loses all its stability so soon as it ceases to observe its laws.

These considerations are ever present to our mind, and ever since the day of our advent to the throne the thought of the public weal, of the improvement of the state of the provinces, and of relief to the (subject) peoples, has not ceased to engage it. If, therefore, the geographical position of the Ottoman provinces, the fertility of the soil, the aptitude and intelligence of the inhabitants are considered, the conviction will remain that by striving to find efficacious means, the result, which by the help of God we hope to attain, can be obtained within a few years. Full of confidence, therefore, in the help of the Most High, and certain of the support of our Prophet, we deem it right to seek by new institutions to give to the provinces composing the Ottoman Empire the benefit of a good administration.

These institutions must be principally carried out under three heads, which are:

1. The guarantees insuring to our subjects perfect security for life, honor, and fortune.

2. A regular system of assessing and levying taxes.

3. An equally regular system for the levying of troops and the duration of their service....

If there is an absence of security as to one's fortune, everyone remains insensible to the voice of the Prince and the country; no one interests himself in the progress of public good, absorbed as he is in his own troubles. If, on the contrary, the citizen keeps possession in all confidence of all his goods, then, full of ardor in his affairs, which he seeks to enlarge in order to increase his comforts, he feels daily growing and bubbling in his heart not only his love for the Prince and country, but also his devotion to his native land.

These feelings become in him the source of the most praiseworthy actions.

Document 3
1856 Reform Edict[3]

Following on the earlier Gülhane Edict of 1839, and coming right after the end of the Crimean War, this imperial reform offered further promises on behalf of the sultan for the reorganization and improvement of the Ottoman Empire. Proclaimed during the height of the Tanzimat era, this edict focused on equal access to education and government appointments, as well as the equal administration of justice regardless of one's class or religious creed.

For further discussion: *Some Western observers have dismissed such reforms as window dressing in the face of growing European pressure. Does the contested practical significance of the edict detract from the overall significance of the empire's attempt to reform itself?*

The guarantees promised on our part by the Hatt-ı Hümayun of Gülhane, and in conformity with the Tanzimat, to all the subjects of my Empire, without distinction of classes or of religion, for the security of their persons and property and the preservation of their honour, are today confirmed and consolidated, and efficacious measures shall be taken in order that they may have their full and entire effect.

All the privileges and spiritual immunities granted by my ancestors *ab antiquo*, and at subsequent dates, to all Christian communities or other non-Muslim persuasions established in my empire under my protection, shall be confirmed and maintained.

Each sect, in localities where there are not other religious denominations, shall be free from every species of restraint as regards the public exercise of its religion. . . .

---

3. "Rescript of Reform—Islahat Fermanı (18 February 1856)," https://www.anayasa .gen.tr/reform.htm.

Document 3. 1856 Reform Edict

Every distinction or designation tending to make any class whatever of the subjects of my Empire inferior to another class, on account of their religion, language, or race, shall be for ever effaced from the Administrative Protocol. The laws shall be put in force against the use of any injurious or offensive term, either among private individuals or on the part of the authorities.

As all forms of religion are and shall be freely professed in my dominions, no subject of my Empire shall be hindered in the exercise of the religion that he professes, nor shall be in any way annoyed on this account. No one shall be compelled to change their religion....

[A]ll the subjects of my Empire, without distinction of nationality, shall be admissible to public employments, and qualified to fill them according to their capacity and merit, and conformably with rules to be generally applied.

All the subjects of my Empire, without distinction, shall be received into the Civil and Military Schools of the Government if they otherwise satisfy the conditions as to age and examination which are specified in the organic regulations of the said schools. Moreover, every community is authorized to establish Public Schools of Science, Art, and Industry. Only the method of instruction and the choice of professors in schools of this class shall be under the control of a Mixed Council of Public Insturiction [sic], the members of which shall be named by my Sovereign command....

The equality of taxes entitling equality of burdens, as equality of duties entails that of rights, Christian subject and those of other non-Muslim sects, as it has been already decided, shall, as well as Muslim, be subject to the obligations of the Law of Recruitment. The principle of obtaining substitutes, or of purchasing exemption, shall be admitted. A complete law shall be published, with as little delay as possible, respecting the admission into and service in the army of Christian and other non-Muslim subjects....

As the laws regulating the purchase[,] sale, and disposal of real property are common to all the subjects of [my] empire, it shall be lawful for foreigners to possess landed property in my dominions, conforming themselves to the laws and police regulations, and bearing the same charges as the native inhabitants, and after arrangements have been come to with foreign powers.

The taxes are to be levied under the same denomination from all the subjects of my empire, without distinction of class or of religion....

Steps shall also be taken for the formation of roads and canals to increase the facilities of communication and increase the sources of the wealth of the country. Everything that can impede commerce or agriculture shall be abolished. To accomplish these objects means shall be sought to profit by the science, the art, and the funds of Europe, and thus gradually to execute them. . . .

Document 4
1876 Ottoman Constitution[4]

Proclaimed during Sultan Abdülhamid II's (1842–1918, r. 1876–1909) first year on the throne, the 1876 Ottoman constitution was seen by some as the culmination of the Tanzimat era, fulfilling the long-held dream of secular, modern, and systematic reformers. Written by members of the Young Ottomans (a society of radical pro-reformists established in 1865), it borrowed heavily from the 1831 Belgian constitution and the 1850 Prussian constitution. This document sought to establish parliamentary rule within a strong constitutional monarchy, manage the legal and social relationships between distinct religious and national subgroups, and legitimize the Ottoman government in the eyes of Europeans.

For further discussion: *Why was this first Ottoman constitution revoked so unceremoniously by Sultan Abdülhamid II within just two years, and what did this revocation mean for the broader push for reforms?*

Art. 1. The Ottoman Empire comprises present territory and possessions, and semi-dependent provinces. It forms an indivisible whole, from which no portion can be detached under any pretext whatever.

Art. 2. Istanbul is the capital of the Ottoman Empire. This city possesses no pr[i]vilege or immunity peculiar to itself over the other towns of the empire.

---

4. "The Ottoman Constitution (23 December 1876)," https://iow.eui.eu/wp-content/uploads/sites/18/2014/05/Brown-01-Ottoman-Constitution.pdf.

Art. 3. The Ottoman sovereignty, [which] includes in the person of the Sovereign the Supreme Caliphat[e] of Islam, belongs to the eldest Prince of the House of Osman, in acc[or]dance with the rules established ab antiquo.

Art. 4. His Majesty the Sultan, under the title of "Supreme Caliph," is the protector of the Muslim religion. He is the sovereign and padişah (emperor) of all Ottomans. . . .

Art. 8. All subjects of the empire are called Ottomans, without distinction whatever faith they profess; the status of an Ottoman is acquired and lost according to conditions specific by law.

Art. 9. Every Ottoman enjoys personal liberty on condition of non interfering [sic] with the liberty of others. . . .

Art. 10. Personal liberty is wholly inviolable. No one can suffer punishment, under any pretext whatsoever, except in cases determined by law, and according to the forms prescribed by it.

Art. 11. Islam is the state religion. But, while maintaining this principle, the state will protect the free exercise of faiths professed in the Empire, and uphold the religious privileges granted to various bodies, on condition of public order and morality not being interfered with. . . .

Art. 14. One or more persons of [O]ttoman nationality have the right of presenting petitions in the proper quarter relating to the breaking of law and regulation, done either to their own or public detriment, and may likewise present in protest signed petitions to the General Ottoman Assembly, complaining of the conduct of state servants and functionaries.

Art. 15. Education is free. Every Ottoman can attend public or private instructions on condition of conforming to the law. . . .

Art. 17. All Ottomans are equal in the eyes of the law. They have the same rights, and owe the same duties towards their country, without prejudice to religion. . . .

Art. 42. The General Assembly is composed of two chambers: the Chamber of Notables or Senate, and the Chamber of Deputies.

Art. 43. The two chambers will meet on the 1st of November of each year, the opening to take place by imperial decree (irade), the closing, fixed for the following 1st March, also to take place following an imperial decree. Neither of the two chambers can meet while the other chamber is not sitting.

Art. 44. His Majesty the Sultan according to the exigencies of circumstances, may anticipate the date of the opening or may abridge or prolong the session. . . .

Art. 47. Members of the General Assembly are free to express their opinions and to vote as they like. . . .

Art. 108. The administration of provinces shall be based on the principles of decentralization. . . .

Art. 109. A special law will settle on wider bases the election of the administrative councils of provinces (vilayet), districts (sancak), and cantons (kaza), as also of the Council General, which meets annually in the chief town of each province. . . .

Art. 110. The functions of the Provincial Council General shall be fixed by the same special law, and shall comprise:

> The right of deliberating on matters of public utility, such as the establishment of means of communication, the organization of "caisses de crédit agricole," the development of manufactures, commerce, and agriculture, and the diffusion of education.
>
> The right of applying to the competent authorities for the redress of acts committed in contravention of the laws and regulations as regards assessment or collection of taxes or any other matter. . . .

Art. 114. Primary education will be obligatory on all Ottomans. The details of application will be fixed by a special law.

Document 5
1901 D'Arcy Concession[5]

The D'Arcy Concession was an agreement between the imperial Qajar Persian government of Mozaffar ad-Dīn Shah (1853–1907, r. 1896–1907) and William Knox D'Arcy (1849–1917), a private British citizen and businessman. At the time, it was unclear whether commercially

---

5. "The William Knox D'Arcy Oil Concession in Persia, 29 May 1901," in J. C. Hurewitz, ed., *The Middle East and North Africa in World Politics: A Documentary Record*, 2nd ed., Volume 1: *European Expansion, 1535–1914* (New Haven, CT: Yale University Press, 1975), 482–84.

viable quantities of oil existed in Iran. But after seven years, the discovery of a large oil field at Masjed Soleymen laid the foundation for the establishment of the Anglo-Persian Oil Company (over which the British government gained a controlling number of shares in 1914).

For further discussion: *In what ways did the discovery of oil in southwest Iran prove a turning point in British meddling within Iran, and in the evolution of rival great power interventions throughout the Middle East?*

Between the Government of His Imperial Majesty the Shah of Persia, of the one part, and William Knox d'Arcy, of independent means, residing in London ... (hereinafter called 'the Concessionnaire")....

ART. 1. The Government of His Imperial Majesty the Shah grants to the concessionnaire by these presents a special and exclusive privilege to search for, obtain, exploit, develop, render suitable for trade, carry away and sell natural gas petroleum, asphalt and ozokerite throughout the whole extent of the Persian Empire for a term of sixty years as from the date of these presents....

ART. 3. The Imperial Persian Government grants gratuitously to the concessionaire all uncultivated lands belonging to the State which the concessionaire's engineers may deem necessary for the construction of the whole or any part of the above-mentioned works. As for cultivated lands belonging to the State, the concessionnaire must purchase them at the fair and current price of the province.

The Government also grants to the concessionnaire the right of acquiring all and any other lands or buildings necessary for the said purpose, with the consent of the proprietors, on such conditions as may be arranged between him and them without their being allowed to make demands of a nature to surcharge the prices ordinarily current for lands situate in their respective localities.

Holy places with all their dependencies within a radius of 200 Persian archines are formally excluded....

ART. 8. The concessionaire shall immediately send out to Persia and at his own cost one or several experts with a view to their exploring the region in which there exist, as he believes, the said products, and in the event of the report of the expert being in the opinion of the concessionnaire of a satisfactory nature, the latter shall immediately send to Persia and at his own cost all the technical staff necessary, with the working plant and machinery required for boring and sinking wells and ascertaining the value of the property. . . .

ART. 10. It shall be stipulated in the contract between the concessionnaire, of the one part, and the company, of the other part, that the latter is, within the term of one month as from the date of the formation of the first exploitation company, to pay the Imperial Persian Government the sum of £20,000 sterling in cash, and an additional sum of £20,000 sterling in paid-up shares of the first company founded by virtue of the foregoing article. It shall also pay the said Government annually a sum equal to 16 per cent of the annual net profits of any company or companies that may be formed in according with the said article.

ART. 11. The said government shall be free to appoint an Imperial Commissioner, who shall be consulted by the concessionaire and the directors of the companies to be formed. He shall supply all and any useful information at his disposal, and he shall inform them of the best course to be adopted in the interest of the undertaking. He shall establish, by agreement with the concessionaire, such supervision as he may deem expedient to safeguard the interests of the Imperial Government.

The aforesaid powers of the Imperial Commissioner shall be set forth in the "statutes" of the companies to be created. The concessionaire shall pay the Commissioner thus appointed an annual sum of £1,000 sterling for his services as from the date of the formation of the first company. . . .

ART. 12. The workmen employed in the service of the company shall be subject to His Imperial Majesty the Shah, except the technical staff, such as the managers, engineers, borers and foremen. . . .

Document 6
Iran's 1906 Constitution and Supplementary Fundamental Laws of 1907[6]

In the late nineteenth and early twentieth centuries, the Iranian public was increasingly resentful of the incompetence and lavishness of the

---

6. "Iran's 1906 Constitution: Constitution and Its Supplement [the Supplementary Fundamental Laws of October 7, 1907]," https://fis-iran.org/document/iran-1906-constitution/.

autocratic Qajar government. This frustration fueled a burgeoning constitutionalist movement aimed at limiting the power of the shah. In August 1906, after a period of widespread protests and sporadic violence, the shah finally agreed to call for a National Assembly, and on December 30 he signed the country's first constitution.

For further discussion: *To what extent did similar intellectual trends and politico-economic circumstances influence both the Iranian Constitutional Revolution and the Young Turk Revolution? Compare the challenges that subsequently confronted both constitutional movements.*

In the name of God, the Merciful, the Forgiving

Whereas in accordance with the Imperial Farman dated the fourteenth of Jumada the Second, A.H. 1324 (August 5, 1906), a command was issued for the establishment of a National Council, to promote the progress and happiness of our Kingdom and people, strengthen the foundations of our Government, and give effect to the enactments of the Sacred Law of His Holiness the Prophet....

Art. 2. The National Consultative Assembly represents the whole of the people of Persia, who [thus] participate in the economic and political affairs of the country....

Art. 5. The Members shall be elected for two whole years. This period shall begin on the day when all the representatives from the provinces shall have arrived in Tihran. On the conclusion of this period of two years, fresh representatives shall be elected, but the people shall have the option of re-electing any of their former representatives whom they wish and with whom they are satisfied....

Art. 10. On the opening of the Assembly, an Address shall be presented by it to His Imperial Majesty, and it shall afterwards have the honour of receiving an answer from that Royal and August quarter.

Art. 11. Members of the Assembly, on taking their seats, shall take and subscribe to the following form of oath:

"We the undersigned take God to witness, and swear on the Qur'an, that, so long as the rights of the Assembly and its Members are observed and respected, in conformity with these Regulations, we will, so far as possible, discharge, with the utmost truth, uprightness, diligence and endeavour, the duties confided to us; that we will act loyally and truthfully towards our just and honoured Sovereign, commit no treason in respect of either the foundations of the Throne or the Rights of the People, and will consider only the advantage and well-being of Persia." . . .

Art. 15. The National Consultative Assembly has the right in all questions to propose any measure which it regards as conducive to well-being of the Government and the People, after due discussion and deliberation thereof in all sincerity and truth; and, having due regard to the majority of votes, to submit such measure, in complete confidence and security, after it has received the approval of the Senate, by means of the First Minister of the State, so that may receive the Royal Approval and be duly carried out.

Art. 16. All laws necessary to strengthen the foundations of the State and Throne and set in order the affairs of the Realm and the establishment of the Ministries, must be submitted for approval to the National Consultative Assembly.

Art. 17. The National Consultative Assembly shall, when occasion arises, bring forward such measures as shall be necessary for the creation, modification, completion or abrogation of any Law, and, subject to the approval of the Senate, shall submit it for the Royal Sanction, so that due effect may thereafter be given to it.

Art. 18. The regulation of all financial matters, the construction and regulation of the Budget, all changes in fiscal arrangements, the acceptance or rejection of all incidental and subordinate expenditure, as also the new Inspectorships [of Finance] which will be founded by the Government, shall be subject to the approval of the Assembly. . . .

Art. 22. Any proposal to transfer or sell any portion of the [National] resources, or of the control exercised by the Government or the Throne, or to effect any change in the boundaries and frontiers of the Kingdom, shall be subject to the approval of the National Consultative Assembly.

Art. 23. Without the approval of the National Council, no concession for the formation of any public Company of any sort shall, under any plea soever, be granted by the State.

Art. 24. The conclusion of treaties and covenants, the granting of commercial, industrial, agricultural and other concessions, irrespective of whether they be to Persian or foreign subjects, shall be subject to the approval of the National Consultative Assembly, with the exception of treaties which, for reasons of State and the public advantage, must be kept secret. . . .

THE SUPPLEMENTARY FUNDAMENTAL LAWS OF OCTOBER 7, 1907....

In the Name of God the Merciful the Forgiving

The Articles added to complete the Fundamental Laws of the Persian Constitution ratified by the late Shahinshah of blessed memory, Muzaffaru'd-Din Shah Qajar (may God illuminate his resting-place!) are as follows.

General Dispositions

Art. 1. The official religion of Persia is Islam, according to the orthodox Ja'fari doctrine of the Ithna 'Ashariyya (Twelve Imams), which faith the Shah of Persia must profess and promote.

Art. 2. At no time must any legal enactment of the Sacred National Consultative Assembly, established by the favour and assistance of His Holiness the Imama of the Age (may God Hasten his glad Advent!), the favour of His Majesty the Shahinshah, of Islam (may God multiply the like them!), and the whole people of the Persian Nation, be at variance with the sacred rules of Islam or the laws established by His Holiness the Best of Mankind (on whom and on whose household be the Blessings of God and His Peace).

It is hereby declared that, it is for the learned doctors of theology (the 'ulama)—may God prolong the blessing of their existence!—to determine whether such laws as may be proposed are or are not conformable to the rules of Islam.... In such matters the decision of this ecclesiastical committee shall be followed and obeyed and this article shall continue unchanged until the appearance of His Holiness the Proof of the Age (may God hasten his glad Advent!)....

Art. 6. The lives and property of foreign subjects residing on Persian soil are guaranteed and protected, save in such contingencies as the laws of the land except.

Art. 7. The principles of the Constitution cannot be suspended either wholly or in part.

Rights of the Persian Nation

Art. 8. The people of the Persian Empire are to enjoy equal rights before the Law.

Art. 9. All individuals are protected and safeguarded in respect to their lives, property, homes, and honour, from every kind of interferences, and none shall molest them save in such case and in such way as the laws of the land shall determine.

Art. 10. No one can be summarily arrested, save flagrante delicto in the commission of some crime or misdemeanour, except on the written authority of the President of the Tribunal of Justice, given in conformity with the Law. Even in such case the accused must immediately, or at latest in the course of the next twenty-four hours, be informed and notified of the nature of his offence....

Art. 12. No punishment can be decreed or executed save in conformity with the Law.

Art. 13. Every person's house and dwelling is protected and safeguarded, and no dwelling-place may be entered save in such case and in such way as the Law has decreed....

Art. 16. The confiscation of the property or possessions of any person under the title of punishment or retribution is forbidden, save in conformity with the Law.

Art. 17. To deprive owners or possessors of the properties or possessions controlled by them on any pretext whatever is forbidden, save in conformity with the Law.

Art. 18. The acquisition and study of all sciences, arts and crafts is free, save in the case of such as may be forbidden by the ecclesiastical law.

Art. 19. The foundation of schools at the expense of the government and the nation, and compulsory instruction, must be regulated by the Ministry of Sciences and Arts, and all schools and colleges must be under the supreme control and supervision of that Ministry.

Art. 20. All publications, except heretical books and matters hurtful to the perspicuous religion [of Islam] are free, and are exempt from the censorship....

Art. 30. The deputies of the National Consultative Assembly and the Senate represent the whole nation, and not only the particular classes, provinces, departments or districts which have elected them....

Art. 35. The sovereignty is a trust confided (as a Divine gift) by the people to the person of the King.

Art. 36. The constitutional monarchy of Persia is vested in the person of His Imperial Majesty Sultan Muhammad 'Ali Shah Qajar (may God prolong his sovereignty!) and in his heirs, generation after generation.

Art. 58. No one can attain the rank of Minister unless he be a Musulman by religion, a Persian by birth, and a Persian subject....

Document 7
Jamāl ad-Dīn Al-Afghānī's Late-1870s Letter to Abdülhamid II[7]

One of the most influential Islamic scholars and political activists of the nineteenth century, Sayyid Jamāl ad-Dīn al-Afghāni (c. 1839–1897) was a relentless critic of Western imperialism and promoter of Islamic unity. In this excerpted letter, written in Persian, he submits a plan to Abdülhamid II on how to secure the cooperation and unity of Muslims outside the Ottoman domain. A concise and forceful expression of al-Afghāni's political and religious views, the document also underscores a strong sense of societal self-confidence and desire for autonomy.

For further discussion: *In what ways does al-Afghāni, like Tahtawi, provide a compelling example of how people in the Middle East were aware of, and tried to respond to, European intellectual trends, social changes, and encroaching European imperialism?*

To the Firm Pillar of the Kingdom and the People and the Impregnable Fortress of the Eternal Lofty Government, the Glory of the Ottoman Race and Soul of the Body of All the Muslims, the Pivot of the State and the Glorious One:
I respectfully submit:
[W]hen I looked at the state of the lofty Ottoman Government in this age, and when I considered the condition of the Islamic nation (*millat-i islāmiyyeh*) it rent the shirt of my patience and I was overcome by fearful thoughts and visions from every side. Like a fearfully obsessed man day and night, from beginning to end, I have thought of this affair and have

---

7. Sayyid Jamāl ad-Dīn al-Afghāni, letter to an Ottoman official, in Nikki R. Keddie, *Sayyid Jamāl ad-Dīn "al-Afghānī": A Political Biography* (Berkeley: University of California Press, 1972), 133–38.

made the means of reform and salvation of this *milla* my profession and incantation....

FIRST: Since the Muslims of India, with their great numbers and mostly holders of property and wealth, and are extremely firm in Islam and are devoted in the defence of the faith and the *milla*, despite the frailty of their bodies... nevertheless they have slept the sleep of neglect and reposed on the bed of ignorance; and they have not understood the benefits of unity and harmony and they do not perceive the harm of division and discord. Therefore, this humble one [i.e., I] desires for the love of the community (or patriotically—Arabic, *ḥubban fī al-milla*) to proceed to that kingdom and to meet with all the *navvābs* and princes and ulama and grandees of that land and explain to them one by one the results that are manifested from unity and solidarity in the whole world and the injuries that have appeared from division and disunity ... and to breathe into them *the new spirit of love of nationality* [*rūḥ-i jadīd-i hubb-i milliyat*—an indication that al-Afghānī recognized the novelty of this spirit] and to rend the curtains of their neglect; to explain to them the place of the luminous Sultanate in the world of Islam; and to reveal and make manifest to this group the fact that the perpetuation of religion depends on the perpetuation of this government....

SECOND: I wish that after the completion of the Indian fair to go to Afghanistan and invite the people of that land, who like a wild lion have no fear of bloodshed and do not admit hesitation in war, especially in religious war, to a religious struggle and a national endeavour [*muḥārabeh-yi dīniyyeh va mujāhadeh-yi milliyeh*].[8] I shall emphasize Russia's aims and convey with an eloquent tongue that if, God forbid, a calamity befalls the Ottoman Government, neither will permanence remains to Mecca, nor majesty to Medina, and not even the name of Islam or a rite of faith with survive. And that afterward they will neither hear the voice of the *mu'azzin* nor see the Koran reader. ... I shall strike the call, "Arise to battle," and raise the sound, "O, sacrifice for Islam." And I shall send the good eloquent ulama to all the people, to the valleys and the mountains, and I shall sponsor alliances with the princes and nobles and warriors and khans....

---

8. This phrase is an interesting indication of the admixture of the secular and religious "nationalism" in al-Afghānī; the secular word for war is modified by "religious" while the "holy war" is defined as "national," though at this time *milliyeh* could still also have a religious meaning. Both meanings were probably intermixed in al-Afghānī.

And after finishing the call in Afghanistan I will go to Baluchistan... And I will head to the Turkomans... and I will call them to revenge and incite the pride of their Turkish race [*jinsiyyat-i turkiyyeh*—another modern thought] and carry the banner of Unity of Islam (*ittihād-islāmiyyeh*) on my shoulder into those regions also and call to religious war....

Document 8
Theodor Herzl's 1896 Pamphlet "The Jewish State"[9]

In 1896, Theodor Herzl (1860–1904), the renowned Jewish nationalist, political activist, and writer, published a pamphlet entitled "Der Judenstaat," or "The Jewish State." In this excerpt, Herzl attempts to address Europe's "Jewish question," which was, in his words: "Are [the Jewish people] to 'get out' now and where to? Or, may we yet remain?" After a brief review of the causes and effects of antisemitism, Herzl strongly endorses the creation of a fully sovereign Jewish nation-state, preferably within the Ottoman lands of Palestine. The pamphlet is arguably the most famous expression of Zionism, which is a continually unfolding nationalist movement in support of a political homeland for the Jewish people.

For further discussion: *By embracing dominant ethno-nationalist discourses of the nineteenth century, how does Herzl position the Zionist homeland in Palestine in relation both to Europe, and to the native Palestinian population?*

... The Jewish Question

No one can deny the gravity of the situation of the Jews. Wherever they live in perceptible numbers, they are more or less persecuted. Their equality before the law, granted by statute, has become practically a dead letter. They are debarred from filling even moderately high positions, either in

---

9. Theodor Herzl, "The Jewish State," 1896, https://www.jewishvirtuallibrary.org/quot-the-jewish-state-quot-theodor-herzl.

the army, or in any public or private capacity. And attempts are made to thrust them out of business also: "Don't buy from Jews!"...

I do not intend to arouse sympathetic emotions on our behalf. That would be foolish, futile, and undignified proceeding. I shall content myself with putting the following questions to the Jews: Is it not true that, in countries where we live in perceptible numbers, the position of Jewish lawyers, doctors, technicians, teachers, and employees of all descriptions becomes daily more intolerable? Is it not true, that the Jewish middle classes are seriously threatened? Is it not true, that the passions of the mob are incited against our wealthy people? Is it not true, that our poor endure greater sufferings than any other proletariat?...

I shall now put the Question in the briefest possible form: Are we to "get out" now and where to?

Or, may we yet remain? And, how long?...

THE PLAN

The whole plan is in its essence perfectly simple, as it must necessarily be if it is to come within the comprehension of all.

Let the sovereignty be granted us over a portion of the globe large enough to satisfy the rightful requirements of a nation; the rest we shall manage for ourselves.

The creation of a new State is neither ridiculous nor impossible. We have in our day witnessed the process in connection with nations which were not largely members of the middle class, but poorer, less educated, and consequently weaker than ourselves. The Governments of all countries scourged by Anti-Semitism will be keenly interested in assisting us to obtain the sovereignty we want....

We must not imagine the departure of the Jews to be a sudden one. It will be gradual, continuous, and will cover many decades. The poorest will go first to cultivate the soil. In accordance with a preconceived plan, they will construct roads, bridges, railways and telegraph installations; regulate rivers; and build their own dwellings; their labor will create trade, trade will create markets and markets will attract new settlers, for every man will go voluntarily, at his own expense and his own risk. The labor expended on the land will enhance its value, and the Jews will soon perceive that a new and permanent sphere of operation is opening here for that spirit of enterprise which has heretofore met only with hatred and obloquy....

Let all who are willing to join us, fall in behind our banner and fight for our cause with voice and pen and deed.

Those Jews who agree with our idea of a State will attach themselves to the Society [i.e., the Society of Jews, a precursor to the Jewish Agency in post-WWI Palestine], which will thereby be authorized to confer and treat with Governments in the name of our people. The Society will thus be acknowledged in its relations with Governments as a State-creating power. This acknowledgment will practically create the State.

Should the Powers declare themselves willing to admit our sovereignty over a neutral piece of land, then the Society will enter into negotiations for the possession of this land. Here two territories come under consideration, Palestine and Argentine. In both countries important experiments in colonization have been made, though on the mistaken principle of a gradual infiltration of Jews. An infiltration is bound to end badly. It continues till the inevitable moment when the native population feels itself threatened, and forces the Government to stop a further influx of Jews. Immigration is consequently futile unless we have the sovereign right to continue such immigration.

The Society of Jews will treat with the present masters of the land, putting itself under the protectorate of the European Powers, if they prove friendly to the plan. We could offer the present possessors of the land enormous advantages, assume part of the public debt, build new roads for traffic, which our presence in the country would render necessary, and do many other things. The creation of our State would be beneficial to adjacent countries, because the cultivation of a strip of land increases the value of its surrounding districts in innumerable ways.

PALESTINE OR ARGENTINE?

Shall we choose Palestine or Argentine? We shall take what is given us, and what is selected by Jewish public opinion. The Society will determine both these points.

Argentine is one of the most fertile countries in the world, extends over a vast area, has a sparse population and a mild climate. The Argentine Republic would derive considerable profit from the cession of a portion of its territory to us. The present infiltration of Jews has certainly produced some discontent, and it would be necessary to enlighten the Republic on the intrinsic difference of our new movement.

Palestine is our ever-memorable historic home. The very name of Palestine would attract our people with a force of marvellous potency. If His Majesty the Sultan were to give us Palestine, we could in return undertake to regulate the whole finances of Turkey. We should there form a portion of a rampart of Europe against Asia, an outpost of civilization as opposed to barbarism. We should as a neutral State remain in contact with all Europe, which would have to guarantee our existence. The sanctuaries of Christendom would be safeguarded by assigning to them an extra-territorial status such as is well-known to the law of nations. We should form a guard of honor about these sanctuaries, answering for the fulfillment of this duty with our existence. This guard of honor would be the great symbol of the solution of the Jewish question after eighteen centuries of Jewish suffering. . . .

Document 9
Halide Edib's 1908 Recounting of the Young Turk Revolution[10]

This source provides a rare and detailed firsthand account of the events of July 1908, when Sultan Abdülhamid II reinstated the Ottoman Constitution of 1876 and recalled the empire's Parliament. It was written by Halide Edib (1884–1964), a Turkish novelist and women's rights activist. Living in Istanbul at the time, Edib describes a scene of widespread euphoria and social solidarity.

For further discussion: *As a primary source, how can the subjective account presented by Edib's memoir contribute to a later observer's understanding of the historical context within which she lived?*

What was the effect of this thunderbolt in the city of Istamboul? How would the city act, or how had it already acted? These were the enigmas we tried to solve that morning.

---

10. Halide Edib Adīvar, *Memoirs of Halidé Edib* (New York: Century Co., [n.d.] [1926]), 252–60.

Document 9. Halide Edib's 1908 Recounting of the Young Turk Revolution   149

It was Hussein Jahid who brought us the news in the evening. The city had looked hesitantly at the constitution so suddenly and simply announced. The people gathered at street corners and tried to talk in undertones, but there was a feeling of uncertainty, even of distrust, a vague questioning as to the meaning of this sudden change; some went so far as to take it for a trap in which to catch the people of Istamboul.... Something invisible and new in the air haunted us. We had queer dreams and visions about the terror and blood which accompany revolutions, but we did not allow them utterance.

The words "equality, liberty, justice, and fraternity" sounded most strange. Fraternity was added on account of the Christians. The great ideals of Tanzimat, expressed as the Union of the Elements, had taken this familiar form. There had never been a more passionate desire in the people of Turkey to love each other, to work for the realization of this new Turkey, where a free government and a free life was to start.

Poor granny was restless. "No good comes out of new things. What you call constitution was given at the time of Midhat Pasha, and he lost his head for it," she said....

The papers might have been printed on gold-leaf, so high were the prices paid for them. People were embracing each other in the streets in mad rejoicing....

The next day I went down to see Istamboul. The scene on the bridge caught me at once. There was a sea of men and women all cockaded in red and white, flowing like a vast human tide from one side to the other. The tradition of centuries seemed to have lost its effect. There was no such thing as sex or personal feeling. Men and women in a common wave of enthusiasm moved on, radiating something extraordinary, laughing, weeping in such intense emotion that human deficiency and ugliness were for a time completely obliterated. Thousands swayed and moved on. Before each official building there was an enormous crowd calling to the minister to come out and take the oath of allegiance to the new régime....

In three days the whole empire had caught the fever of ecstasy. No one seemed clear about its meaning. The news of the change had come from Saloniki through several young officers whose names were shouted as its symbol. To the crowd the change in its clearest sense spelled the pulling down of a régime which meant oppression, corruption, and tyranny, while the new, whatever it was, spelled happiness and freedom....

In the general enthusiasm and rebirth I became a writer. Istamboul in the enchantment and beauty of the first days reminded me of a line of Tewfik Fikret, from his "Mist." He had written it in secret, and it had circulated from hand to hand in the old days. The poet, looking through the enchanted mist of Istamboul, had seen all that was incurable, unclean, and evil in the hearts and lives of its dwellers, and painting it in lurid word-coloring, he had asked, "Among the millions who live in thy heart, how many spirits will rise pure and luminous?"

The mist with all the vile and unclean spirit had dispersed, and the people were in the throes of a marvelous spiritual rebirth.

Document 10
1913 Resolution of the Arab-Syrian Congress[11]

After years of revolutionary politics and war, the Ottoman Empire in 1913 was in a state of tumult, straining its institutional and social bonds. Within this climate, a group of reform-minded Arabs living in Paris called for an "Arab-Syrian Congress" to discuss the place of Arabs within the larger imperial apparatus. This resolution, produced after five days of discussion, set forth a list of priorities and demands aimed at ensuring continued harmony between Istanbul and its Arab subjects.

For further discussion: *Should this document be seen as an example of nascent Arab nationalism, or do the authors remain deeply Ottoman in their outlook? With which other forms of belonging and community did proto-nationalists contend at this time?*

1. Radical and urgent reforms are needed in the Ottoman Empire.

2. It is important to guarantee the Ottoman Arabs the exercise of their political rights by making effective their participation in the central administration of the Empire.

---

11. "Resolution of the Arab-Syrian Congress at Paris, 21 June 1913," in J. C. Hurewitz, ed., *The Middle East and North Africa in World Politics: A Documentary Record*, 2nd ed., Volume 1: *European Expansion, 1535–1914* (New Haven, CT: Yale University Press, 1975), 566–67.

3. It is important to establish in each of the Syrian and Arab *vilâyets* a decentralized regime suitable to their needs and aptitudes.

4. The vilayet of Bayrut having formulated its claims in a special project adopted on 31 January 1913 by an ad hoc General Assembly and based on the double principle of the extension of the powers of the general council of the vilayet and the nomination of foreign councillors, the Congress requests the execution of the above project.

5. The Arabic language must be recognized in the Ottoman Parliament and considered as an official language in Syrian and Arab countries.

6. Military service shall be regional in Syrian and Arab vilayets, except in case of extreme necessity.

7. The Congress expresses the wish that the Ottoman Imperial Government provide the *mutasarriflık* (autonomous provincial district) of Lebanon with the means of improving its financial situation.

8. The Congress affirms that it favors the reformist and decentralizing demands of the Armenian Ottomans.

9. The present resolution shall be communicated to the Ottoman Imperial Government.

10. These resolutions shall also be communicated to the Powers friendly to the Ottoman Empire.

11. The Congress conveys its grateful thanks to the Government of the [French] Republic for its generous hospitality.

Document 11
Mehmed V's 1914 Call to *Jihād*[12]

When war broke out in Europe in early August 1914, it prompted much debate in Istanbul. It was unclear whether the empire should enter the war—or which side it should potentially join. Pushed on by his

---

12. From Charles F. Horne and Walter F. Austin, eds., *Source Records of the Great War*, Vol. II (USA: National Alumni, 1923), 400.

eventual German allies, Ottoman Sultan Mehmed V (1844–1918, r. 1909–1918) issued a call for jihād in November 1914, exhorting the world's Muslims to join in the conflict against the Allied powers.

For further discussion: Consider the multiple audiences (national, regional, international) at whom the sultan's declaration of jihād was directed.

Sultan Mehmet Reshad "To my army! To my navy"

My heroes! My soldiers! In this sacred war and struggle, which we began against the enemies who have undermined our religion and our holy fatherland, never for a single moment cease from strenuous effort and from self-abnegation.

Throw yourselves against the enemy as lions, bearing in mind that the very existence of our empire, and of 300,000,000 Moslems whom I have summoned by sacred Fetva to a supreme struggle, depend on your victory....

My children! My soldiers! No army in the history of the world was ever honored with a duty as sacred and as great as is yours. By fulfilling it, show that you are the worthy descendants of the Ottoman Armies that in the past made the world tremble, and make it impossible for any foe of our faith and country to tread on our ground, and disturb the peace of the sacred soil of Yemen, where the inspiring tomb of our Prophet lies. Prove beyond doubt to the enemies of our country that there exist an Ottoman army and navy which know how to defend their faith, their country and their military honor, and how to defy death for their sovereign!

Right and loyalty are on our side, and hatred and tyranny on the side of our enemies, and therefore there is no doubt that the Divine help and assistance of the just God and the moral support of our glorious Prophet will be on our side to encourage us. I feel convinced that from this struggle we shall emerge as an empire that has made good the losses of the past and is once more glorious and powerful.

Do not forget that you are brothers in arms of the strongest and bravest armies of the world, with whom we are now fighting shoulder to shoulder. Let those of you who are to die a martyr's death be messengers of victory to those who have gone before us, and let the victory be sacred and the sword be sharp of those of you who are to remain in life.

Document 12
John Buchan's 1916 Novel *Greenmantle*[13]

Given that the British and French Empires contained millions of Muslim subjects, London and Paris took the threat of Muslim revolts seriously. Such fears of jihād *were stoked by Allied writers and propagandists, such as renowned novelist John Buchan (1875–1940), who at the time worked for the British War Propaganda Bureau. In this excerpt from a popular 1916 novel, Buchan conjures up a British Foreign Office conversation proposing a new mission to the Middle East, and weaving together a combination of stereotypes and imperial tropes to capture the fear that "Islam is a fighting creed."*

For further discussion: *Compare Allied perceptions of the threat posed by the Ottoman call to* jihād *with the actual success of that appeal among colonized Muslims. How can such a discussion help us understand the contemporary uses to which contentious terms such as* jihād *are put and the challenges of interpreting them correctly?*

Sir Walter lay back in an arm-chair and spoke to the ceiling. It was the best story, the clearest and the fullest, I had ever got of any bit of the war. He told me just how and why and when Turkey had left the rails. I heard about her grievances over our seizure of her ironclads, of the mischief the coming of the *Goeben* had wrought, of Enver and his precious Committee and the way they had got a cinch on the old Turk. When he had spoken for a bit, he began to question me.

"You are an intelligent fellow, and you will ask how a Polish adventurer, meaning Enver, and a collection of Jews and gipsies should have got control of a proud race. The ordinary man will tell you that it was German organisation backed up with German money and German arms. You will inquire again how, since Turkey is primarily a religious power, Islam has played so small a part in it all. The Sheikh-ul-Islam is neglected, and though the Kaiser proclaims a Holy War and calls himself Hadji Mohammed Guilliamo, and says the Hohenzollerns are descended from the Prophet, that seems to have fallen pretty flat. The ordinary man again will answer that Islam in Turkey is becoming a back number, and that

---
13. John Buchan, *Greenmantle* (London: Hodder & Stoughton, 1916), 1–10.

Krupp guns are the new gods. Yet—I don't know. I do not quite believe in Islam becoming a back number."

"Look at it in another way," he went on. "If it were Enver and Germany alone dragging Turkey into a European war for purposes that no Turk cared a rush about, we might expect to find the regular army obedient, and Constantinople. But in the provinces, where Islam is strong, there would be trouble. Many of us counted on that. But we have been disappointed. The Syrian army is as fanatical as the hordes of the Mahdi. The Senussi have taken a hand in the game. The Persian Moslems are threatening trouble. There is a dry wind blowing through the East, and the parched grasses wait the spark. And the wind is blowing towards the Indian border. Whence comes that wind, think you?" . . .

"Have you an explanation, Hannay?" he asked again.

"It looks as if Islam had a bigger hand in the thing than we thought," I said. "I fancy religion is the only thing to knit up such a scattered empire."

"You are right," he said. "You must be right. We have laughed at the Holy War, the Jehad that old Von der Goltz prophesied. But I believe that stupid old man with the big spectacles was right. There is a Jehad preparing. The question is, How?" . . .

"They are not fools, however much we try to persuade ourselves of the contrary. But supposing they had got some tremendous sacred sanction—some holy thing, some book or gospel or some new prophet from the desert, something which would cast over the whole ugly mechanism of German war the glamour of the old torrential raids which crumpled the Byzantine Empire and shook the walls of Vienna? Islam is a fighting creed, and the mullah still stands in the pulpit with the Koran in one hand and a drawn sword in the other. Supposing there is some Ark of the Covenant which will madden the remotest Moslem peasant with dreams of Paradise? What then, my friend?"

"Then there will be hell let loose in those parts pretty soon. . . ."

"One last question. You say it is important. Tell me just how important."

"It is life and death," he said solemnly. "I can put it no higher and no lower. Once we know what is the menace we can meet it. As long as we are in the dark it works unchecked and we may be too late. The war must be won or lost in Europe. Yes; but if the East blazes up, our effort will be distracted from Europe and the great *coup* may fail. The stakes are no less than victory and defeat. . . ."

Document 13
Britain's 1914 Establishment of a Protectorate over Egypt[14]

By 1914, Egyptians had been under Britain's de facto control for over three decades, though Egypt was still technically within the Ottoman sultan's domain. However, with the Ottoman entry into World War I, Britain decided to put an end to the muddled sovereignty and declare Egypt a protectorate. London installed Hussein Kamil (1853–1917), who was regarded as more supportive of British interests, as the new sultan of Egypt.

For further discussion: *What overriding concerns motivated London's assurances to Hussein Kamil that Britain would take on the fullest responsibility for the defense of the country?*

Note on the Protectorate by Acting High Commissioner Milne Cheetham to Sultan Hussein Kamil, 19 December 1914

I am instructed by His Majesty's Principal Secretary of State for Foreign Affairs to bring to the notice of your Highness the circumstances preceding the outbreak of war between His Britannic Majesty and the Sultan of Turkey and the changes which the war entails in the status of Egypt.

In the Ottoman cabinet there were two parties. On the one side was a Moderate Party, mindful of the sympathy extended by Great Britain to every effort towards reform in Turkey, who recognized that in the war in which His Majesty was already engaged no Turkish interests were concerned, and welcomed the assurance of His Majesty and his Allies that neither in Egypt nor elsewhere would war be used as a pretext for any action injurious to Ottoman interests. On the other side a band of unscrupulous military adventurers looked to find in a war of aggression, waged in concert with His Majesty's enemies, the means of retrieving the disasters, military, financial, and economic, into which they had already

---

14. "Establishment of the British Protectorate over Egypt, 18–19 December 1914," in J. C. Hurewitz, ed., *The Middle East and North Africa in World Politics: A Documentary Record*, 2nd ed., *Volume 2: British-French Supremacy, 1914–1945* (New Haven, CT: Yale University Press, 1979), 12–14.

plunged their country. Hoping to the last that wiser counsels might prevail, His Majesty and his Allies, in spite of repeated violations of their rights, abstained from retaliatory action until compelled thereto by the crossing of the Egyptian frontier by armed bands and unprovoked attacks on Russian open ports by the Turkish naval forces under German officers....

Of the rights thus accruing to His Majesty, no less than those exercised in Egypt during his last thirty years of reform, His Majesty's Government regard themselves as trustees for the inhabitants of Egypt. And His Majesty's Government have decided that Great Britain can best fulfil the responsibilities she has incurred toward Egypt by the formal declaration of a British Protectorate, and by the government of the country under such Protectorate by a Prince of the Khedival family....

I am to give you the formal assurance that Great Britain accepts the fullest responsibility for the defence of the territories under your Highness against all aggression whencesoever coming; and His Majesty's Government authorize me to declare that under the establishment of the British Protectorate now announced all Egyptian subjects wherever they may be will be entitled to receive protection of His Majesty's Government....

As regards foreign relations, His Majesty's Government deem it most consistent with the new responsibilities assumed by Great Britain that the relations between your Highness's Government and the representatives of foreign Powers should henceforth be conducted through His Majesty's representative in Cairo.

His Majesty's Government have repeatedly placed on record that the system of treaties, known as the Capitulations, by which your Highness's Government is bound, are no longer in harmony with the development of the country; but, in the opinion of His Majesty's Government, the revision of those treaties may most conveniently be postponed until the end of the present war....

The religious convictions of the Egyptian subjects will be scrupulously respected as are those of His Majesty's own subjects, whatever their creed. Nor need I affirm to your Highness that, in declaring Egypt free from any duty of obedience to those who have usurped political power at Constantinople, His Majesty's Government are animated by no hostility towards the Caliphate. The past history of Egypt shows, indeed, that the loyalty of Egyptian Mahommedans towards the Caliphate is independent of any political bonds between Egypt and Constantinople.

The strengthening and progress of Mahommedan institutions in Egypt is naturally a matter in which His Majesty's Government take a deep interest and with which your Highness will be specially concerned, and in carrying out such reforms as may be considered necessary, your Highness may count upon the sympathetic support of His Majesty's Government....

Document 14
Henry Morgenthau on the "Murder of a Nation," 1918[15]

Henry Morgenthau (1856–1946) was US ambassador to the Ottoman Empire from 1913 to 1916, a time when Allied ambassadors had been withdrawn; note that the US was still neutral in WWI at this time. Concerned with the increasing violence targeting the empire's Armenian community, Morgenthau was one of the earliest international observers to describe Ottoman actions as what would now be labeled a genocide (though the term itself had not yet been coined).

For further discussion: *Consider the context within which Henry Morgenthau wrote his memoirs, and try to distinguish between the observations that are informed by an eyewitness account and those fueled by the intense passions of the time.*

CHAPTER XXV: TALAAT TELLS WHY HE "DEPORTS" THE ARMENIANS

Every morning all uncoded cablegrams received in Constantinople were forwarded to Talaat, who read them.... Even the cablegrams of the ambassadors were apparently not exempt, though, of course, the ciphered messages were not interfered with. Ordinarily I might have protested against this infringement of my rights, but Talaat's engaging frankness

---

15. Henry Morgenthau, *Ambassador Morgenthau's Story* (Garden City, NY: Doubleday, Page, 1918), 332–38.

about pilfering my correspondence and in even waving my own cablegrams in my face gave me an excellent opening to introduce the forbidden subject....

Talaat was evasive and non-committal and showed much hostility to the interest which the American people were manifesting in the Armenians. He explained his policy on the ground that the Armenians were in constant correspondence with the Russians. The definite conviction which these conversations left upon my mind was that Talaat was the most implacable enemy of this persecuted race....

"Why are you so interested in the Armenians, anyway?" he said, on another occasion. "You are a Jew; these people are Christians. The Mohammedans and the Jews always get on harmoniously. We are treating the Jews here all right. What have you to complain of? Why can't you let us do with these Christians as we please?"

I had frequently remarked that the Turks look upon practically every question as a personal matter, yet this point of view rather stunned me. However, it was a complete revelation of Turkish mentality; the fact that, above all considerations of race and religion, there are such things as humanity and civilization, never for a moment enters their mind. They can understand a Christian fighting for a Christian and a Jew fighting for a Jew, but such abstractions as justice and decency form no part of their conception of things.

"You don't seem to realize," I replied, "that I am not here as a Jew but as American Ambassador. My country contains something more than 97,000,000 Christians and something less than 3,000,000 Jews. So, at least in my ambassadorial capacity, I am 97 per cent Christian. But after all, that is not the point. I do not appeal to you in the name of any race or any religion, but merely as a human being. You have told me many times that you want to make Turkey a part of the modern progressive world. The way you are treating the Armenians will not help you to realize that ambition; it puts you in the class of backward, reactionary peoples....

"And you should understand the great changes that are taking place among Christians all over the world. They are forgetting their differences and all sects are coming together as one. You look down on American missionaries, but don't forget that it is the best element in America that supports their religious work, as well as their educational institutions. Americans are not mere materialists, always chasing money—they are broadly humanitarian, and interested in the spread of justice and civilization throughout the world. After this war is over you will face a new situation. You say that, if victorious, you can defy the world, but you are wrong. You will have to meet public opinion everywhere, especially in the United States. Our people will never forget these massacres. They will always resent the wholesale destruction of Christians in Turkey. They will look upon it as nothing but wilful murder and will seriously condemn all the men who are responsible for it. You will not be able to protect yourself under your political status and say that you acted as Minister of the Interior and not as Talaat. You are defying all ideas of justice as we understand the term in our country."

Strangely enough, these remarks did not offend Talaat, but they did not shake his determination. I might as well have been talking to a stone wall. From my abstractions he immediately came down to something definite.

"These people," he said, "refused to disarm when we told them to. They opposed us at Van and at Zeitoun, and they helped the Russians. There is only one way in which we can defend ourselves against them in the future, and that is just to deport them."

"Suppose a few Armenians did betray you," I said. "Is that a reason for destroying a whole race? Is that an excuse for making innocent women and children suffer?"

"Those things are inevitable," he replied.

This remark to me was not quite so illuminating as one which Talaat made subsequently to a reporter of the *Berliner Tageblatt*, who asked him the same question. "We have been reproached," he said, according to this interviewer, "for making no distinction between the innocent Armenians and the guilty; but that was utterly impossible, in view of the fact that those who were innocent to-day might be guilty to-morrow"!

One reason why Talaat could not discuss this matter with me freely, was because the member of the embassy staff who did the interpreting was himself an Armenian. In the early part of August, therefore, he sent a personal messenger to me, asking if I could not see him alone—he said that he himself would provide the interpreter. This was the first time that Talaat had admitted that his treatment of the Armenians was a matter with which I had any concern....

"I have asked you to come to-day," began Talaat, "so that I can explain our position on the whole Armenian subject. We base our objections to the Armenians on three distinct grounds. In the first place, they have enriched themselves at the expense of the Turks. In the second place, they are determined to domineer over us and to establish a separate state. In the third place, they have openly encouraged our enemies. They have assisted the Russians in the Caucasus and our failure there is largely explained by their actions. We have therefore come to the irrevocable decision that we shall make them powerless before this war is ended."

On every one of these points I had plenty of arguments in rebuttal. Talaat's first objection was merely an admission that the Armenians were more industrious and more able than the dull-witted and lazy Turks. Massacre as a means of destroying business competition was certainly an original conception! His general charge that the Armenians were "conspiring" against Turkey and that they openly sympathized with Turkey's enemies merely meant, when reduced to its original elements, that the Armenians were constantly appealing to the European Powers to protect them against robbery, murder, and outrage. The Armenian problem, like most race problems, was the result of centuries of ill-treatment and injustice. There could be only one solution for it, the creation of an orderly system of government, in which all citizens were to be treated upon an equality, and in which all offenses were to be punished as the acts of individuals and not as of peoples. I argued for a long time along these and similar lines.

"It is no use for you to argue," Talaat answered, "we have already disposed of three quarters of the Armenians; there are none at all left in Bitlis, Van, and Erzeroum. The hatred between the Turks and the Armenians is now so intense that we have got to finish with them. If we don't, they will plan their revenge."

"If you are not influenced by humane considerations," I replied, "think of the material loss. These people are your businessmen. They control many of your industries. They are very large tax-payers. What would become of you commercially without them?"

"We care nothing about the commercial loss," replied Talaat. "We have figured all that out and we know that it will not exceed five million pounds. We don't worry about that. I have asked you to come here so as to let you know that our Armenian policy is absolutely fixed and that nothing can change it. We will not have the Armenians anywhere in Anatolia. They can live in the desert but nowhere else."

Document 15
1915 Constantinople Agreement[16]

In early 1915, the planned Gallipoli operation forced the Allies to grapple with "the question of Constantinople and of the Straits." Russia's primary war aim was to secure the city and its strategic waterways linking the Black Sea with the Mediterranean. The British and French were now willing to accept this in order to keep Russia happy, but pressed for their own corresponding territorial gains. Such secret agreements would be perceived by US president Woodrow Wilson (1856–1924) as an underlying cause of global conflict and were decried in his 1918 Fourteen Points.

For further discussion: *What can the description of the straits as "the richest prize of the war" tell us about the importance of the Middle Eastern theater of war and the nature of the concessions Britain and France were suddenly prepared to make to Russia?*

1. *Aide-Mémoire* from Russian Foreign Minister to British and French Ambassadors at Petrograd, 19 February/4 March 1915

The course of recent events leads His Majesty Emperor Nicholas to think that the question of Constantinople and of the Straits must be definitively solved, and according to the time-honored aspirations of Russia.

Every solution will be inadequate and precarious if the city of Constantinople, the western bank of the Bosphorus, of the Sea of Marmara and of the Dardanelles, as well as southern Thrace and into the Enez-Midye line, should henceforth not be incorporated into the Russian Empire.

Similarly, and by strategic necessity, that part of the Asiatic shore that lies between the Bosphorus, the Sakarya River and a point to be determined on the Gulf of Izmit, and the islands of the Sea of Marmara, the

---

16. "The Constantinople Agreement, 4 March–10 April 1915," in J. C. Hurewitz, ed., *The Middle East and North Africa in World Politics: A Documentary Record*, 2nd ed., Volume 2: *British-French Supremacy, 1914–1945* (New Haven, CT: Yale University Press, 1979), 16–21.

Imbros Islands and the Tenedos Islands must be incorporated into the (Russian) Empire.

The special interests of France and of Great Britain in the above region will be scrupulously respected....

3. British Memorandum to the Russian Government, 27 February/12 March 1915 ...

The claim made by the Imperial Government in their *aide-mémoire* of February 19/March 4, 1915, considerably exceeds the desiderata which were foreshadowed by M. Sazonof as probable a few weeks ago. Before His Majesty's Government have had time to take into consideration what their own desiderata elsewhere would be in the final terms of peace, Russia is asking for a definite promise that her wishes shall be satisfied with regard to what is in fact the richest prize of the entire war....

In view of the fact that Constantinople will always remain a trade *entrepôt* for South-Eastern Europe and Asia Minor, His Majesty's Government will ask that Russia shall, when she comes into possession of it, arrange for a free port for the goods in transit to and from non-Russian territory. His Majesty's Government will also ask that there shall be commercial freedom for merchant-ships passing through the straits.

Sir E. Grey points out that it will obviously be necessary to take into consideration the whole question of the future interests of France and Great Britain in what is now Asiatic Turkey; and, in formulating the desiderata of His Majesty's Government with regard to the Ottoman Empire, he should consult the French as well as the Russian Government. As soon, however, as it becomes known that Russia is to have Constantinople at the conclusion of the war, Sir E. Grey will wish to state that throughout negotiations, His Majesty's Government have stipulated that the Mussulman Holy places and Arabia shall under all circumstances remain under independent Mussulman dominion....

4. French Ambassador in Petrograd to Russian Foreign Minister, 1/14 March 1915

[T]he French Republic, having studied the conditions of the peace to be imposed on Turkey, would like to annex Syria together with the region of the Gulf of Alexandretta and Cilicia up to the Taurus [mountain] range. I should be happy to inform my government, without delay, of the Imperial Government's consent....

6. Russian Foreign Minister to Russian Ambassador in Paris, 3/16 March 1915

[T]he French Government refers also to Palestine when speaking of Syria. However, since in this telegram there is no question of Palestine, it would be desirable to elucidate whether the explanation of the Ambassador really corresponds to the view of the French government. This question appears important to us; for, if the Imperial Government should be prepared largely to satisfy France's desires concerning Syria and Cilicia proper, it is indispensable to study the question with closer attention, if the Holy Places are involved....

Document 16
1915–1916 Husayn-McMahon Correspondence[17]

The Husayn-McMahon correspondence is a series of letters exchanged between Husayn bin Ali (1853–1931), sharif of Mecca, and Sir Henry McMahon (1862–1949), the British high commissioner in Egypt. Written from July 1915 to March 1916, the correspondence established an alliance between the British government and the Hejaz Arabs ruled by Husayn. In return for British recognition of a large and independent Arab state after the war, Husayn promised an Arab revolt against the Ottomans.

For further discussion: *How compatible, or incompatible, was the Husayn-McMahon correspondence with competing agreements among the Allied powers?*

---

17. "The Husayn-McMahon Correspondence, 14 July 1915–10 March 1916," in J. C. Hurewitz, ed., *The Middle East and North Africa in World Politics: A Documentary Record*, 2nd ed., Volume 2: *British-French Supremacy, 1914–1945* (New Haven, CT: Yale University Press, 1979), 46–56.

1. From Amir 'Abdallah to Ronald Storrs, 14 July 1915

Whereas the whole of the Arab nation without any exception have decided in these last years to live, and to accomplish their freedom, and grasp the reins of their administration both in theory and practice; and whereas they have found and felt that it is to the interest of the Government of Great Britain to support them and aid them to the attainment of their firm and lawful intentions (which are based upon the maintenance of the honour and dignity of their life) without any ulterior motives whatsoever...

And whereas it is to their (the Arabs') interest also to prefer the assistance of the Government of Great Britain in consideration of their geographical position and economic interests, and also of the attitude of the above-mentioned Government, which is known to both nations and therefore need not be emphasised;

For these reasons the Arab nation see fit to limit themselves, as time is short, to asking the Government of Great Britain, if it should think fit, for the approval, through her deputy or representative, of the following fundamental propositions . . . : –

Firstly.–England to acknowledge the independence of the Arab countries, bounded on the north by Mersina and Adana up to the 37° of latitude . . . up to the border of Persia; on the east by the borders of Persia up to the Gulf of Basra; on the south by the Indian Ocean, with the exception of the position of Aden to remain as it is; on the west by the Red Sea, the Mediterranean Sea up to Mersina. England to approve of the proclamation of an Arab Khalifate of Islam....

2. From Sir Henry McMahon to Sharif Husayn, 30 August 1915

We have the honour to thank you for your frank expression of the sincerity of your feeling towards England. We rejoice, moreover, that your Highness and your people are of one opinion—that Arab interests are English interests and English Arab. To this intent we confirm to you the terms of Lord Kitchener's message, which reached you by the hand of Ali Effendi, and in which was stated clearly our desire for the independence of Arabia and its inhabitants, together with our approval of the Arab Khalifate when it should be proclaimed.... With regard to the questions of limits and boundaries, it would appear to be premature to consume our time in discussing such details in the heat of war, and while, in many portions of them, the Turk is up to now in effective occupation; especially as we have learned, with surprise and regret, that some of the Arabs in those very parts, far from assisting us, are neglecting this their supreme opportunity and are lending their arms to the German and the Turk, to the new despoiler and the old oppressor.

3. From Sharif Husayn, 9 September 1915....

In order to reassure your Excellency I can declare that the whole country, together with those who you say are submitting themselves to Turco-German orders, are all waiting the result of these negotiations, which are dependent only on your refusal or acceptance of the question of the limits and on your declaration of safeguarding their religion first and then the rest of rights from any harm or danger.

Whatever the illustrious Government of Great Britain finds conformable to its policy on this subject, communicate it to us and specify to us the course we should follow....

4. From Sir Henry McMahon, 24 October 1915...

[I]t is with great pleasure that I communicate to you ... the following statement, which I am confident you will receive with satisfaction:–

The two districts of Mersina and Alexandretta and portions of Syria lying to the west of the districts of Damascus, Homs, Hama and Aleppo cannot be said to be purely Arab, and should be excluded from the limits demanded.

With the above modification, and without prejudice to our existing treaties with Arab chiefs, we accept those limits.

As for those regions lying within those frontiers wherein Great Britain is free to act without detriment to the interests of her ally, France, I am empowered in the name of the Government of Great Britain to give the following assurances:–

(1) Subject to the above modifications, Great Britain is prepared to recognise and support the independence of the Arabs in all the regions within the limits demanded by the Sherif of Mecca.

(2) Great Britain will guarantee the Holy Places against all external aggression and will recognise their inviolability.

(3) When the situation admits, Great Britain will give to the Arabs her advice and will assist them to establish what may appear to be the most suitable forms of government in those various territories.

(4) On the other hand, it is understood that the Arabs have decided to seek the advice and guidance of Great Britain only, and that such European advisers and officials as may be required for the formation of a sound form of administration will be British.

(5) With regard to the *vilayets* of Bagdad and of Basra, the Arabs will recognise that the established position and interests of Great Britain necessitate special administrative arrangements in order to secure these territories from foreign aggression, to promote the welfare of the local populations and to safeguard our mutual economic interests. . . .

5. From Sharif Husayn, 5 November 1915. . . .

1. . . . [W]e renounce our insistence on the inclusion of the *vilayets* of Mersina and Adana in the Arab Kingdom. But the two *vilayets* of Aleppo and Beirut and their sea coasts are purely Arab *vilayets*, and there is no difference between a Moslem and a Christian Arab: they are both descendants of one forefather. . . .

5. When the Arabs know the Government of Great Britain is their ally who will not leave them to themselves at the conclusion of peace in the face of Turkey and Germany, and that she will support and will effectively defend them, then to enter the war at once will, no doubt, be in conformity with the general interest of the Arabs. . . .

7. . . . We know that our lot in this war will be either a success, which will guarantee to the Arabs a life becoming their past history, or destruction in the attempt to gain their objects. Had it not been for the determination which I see in the Arabs for the attainment of their objects, I would have preferred to seclude myself on one of the heights of a mountain, but they, the Arabs, have insisted that I should guide the movement to this end. . . .

Document 17
Ihsan Turjman's Diary, 1915–1916[18]

The Ottoman front in WWI has long been understood primarily through European sources and accounts. This excerpt, taken from the diary of an Arab recruit named Ihsan Turjman, provides a valuable glimpse into how Ottoman soldiers experienced the war.

For further discussion: *What were some reasons for the building resentment and frustration felt by Ottoman recruits as the war dragged on?*

Monday, March 29, 1915. People keep inquiring as to what I do and where I work. I tell them that I work at the Manzil [Commissariat of the Fourth Imperial Army] with Commander Ali Ruşen Bey. As to the first part of the question, I hesitate to answer since I am not sure what my job is exactly.... Most of the time I just sit there playing with my moustache. There are countless clerks in the Ottoman state who, like me, occupy office space, know nothing, and receive a salary at the end of each month. Such a state is bound to disappear.

More rumors today about the bombardment of Gaza by the English fleet. Another coastal village between Jaffa and Gaza was also hit.

Soldiers were seen stealing wood from our land in *Karm al A'raj*. Not satisfied with dead wood, they started tearing branches from our olive trees. Who can we complain to? The officers claim they cannot control their subordinates. Of course not. Officers are busy in the taverns getting drunk; then they go to the public places [brothels] to satisfy their base needs....

Heavy rain fell over Jerusalem today, which we needed badly. Locusts are attacking all over the country. The locust invasion started seven days ago and covered the sky. Today it took the locust clouds two hours to pass over the city. God protect us from the three plagues: war, locusts, and disease, for they are spreading through the country. Pity the poor....

---

18. From "The Diary of Ihsan Turjman," in Salim Tamari, *Year of the Locust: A Soldier's Diary and the Erasure of Palestine's Ottoman Past* (Berkeley: University of California Press, 2011), 92–94, 97–98, 105–7, 111–12, 118, 155.

Friday, April 9, 1915. Last week the flag of the Prophet was brought to Jerusalem [on its way from Istanbul to Mecca]. It was an occasion to hang public decorations and light the old city. Victory arches were raised on top of Damascus Gate underneath the slogan "Enter Egypt in Peace with the Will of God"!! The slogan was still hanging yesterday. But today the army decided to remove the banners as a result of public criticism.

Rumors abounded today indicating that our military command was to form a battalion made up mainly of Christian and Jewish citizens to clean the city. This morning while walking to my work at the Commissariat I came across several Jewish citizens, almost all above 40 years of age, holding brooms and cleaning the streets. I was horrified by this scene. Every few minutes a conscript would stand aside breathing from fatigue. How cruel can their commanders be? Wouldn't it be better if the military had hired a number of younger cleaners through the municipal services and solved the problem of these sods?

Wednesday, April 21, 1915 ... What are they saluting Cemal for? For his cowardice on the Egyptian front? I was told by one of his companions in the Suez campaign that when the battle was heated on the front, he went to the outlying trenches and started playing with his beard while trembling. ... I am not sure why people get worked up every time Cemal is mentioned. For his persistence in the Egyptian campaign? For his defeat at the front?

For a whole week we have ran out of *tutton* [tobacco] in Jerusalem. I had made some arrangements to buy a supply of Tetley Sirt, but it is all gone. I have only one day's smoke left. I am trying to get some smuggled *baladi* [local] tobacco, even though I have to get used to smoking it. ...

Thursday, April 22, 1915. An English plane threw leaflets over Ramleh this morning. I heard that one of our planes crashed between Hafeer and Ibin, but [I have] no concrete news. A small distance separates Hafeer and Ibin, yet the pilots manage to destroy their plane, while we rarely hear of English planes crashing. This can only be attributed to one of two reasons: badly trained pilots or badly maintained engines. Isn't it time for us Ottomans—or should I say "them Turks"—to leave this farce behind us and conclude a peace agreement? ...

Tuesday, April 27, 1915. Ahmad Cemal Pasha issued an order today, in celebration of the anniversary of Sultan Mehmet Rashad V's ascension

Document 17. Ihsan Turjman's Diary, 1915–1916

to the throne, to distribute mutton and sweets to members of the armed forces. He also ordered the illumination of public buildings. This was followed by another circular issued by Ruşen Bey canceling the very same order since not enough rice could be obtained from the depots. It seems that rice and meat can always be found for the officers. It is only we the soldiers who are bypassed every time. Another circular was issued today reducing by one-third the kerosene provisions for soldiers.

... In the meantime we heard that while Cemal Pasha's aide-de-camp [*yawir*] was on his way to Nablus, his car broke down near the village of Shu'fat. The vehicle was attacked by the peasants of Shu'fat, who stripped the car and robbed his *yawir*.

To celebrate the anniversary a number of notables and their ladies were invited to Notre Dame. An orchestra performed while liquor flowed. A number of Jerusalem prostitutes were also invited to entertain the officers. I was told that at least 50 well-known whores were among the invitees. Each officer enjoyed the company of one or two ladies in the garden compound.

While this was happening, our brothers were fighting in the Dardanelles....

Sunday, May 9, 1915. I write this with my mind totally preoccupied. I cannot think of anything except our present misfortune. When will we finish with the wretched war, and what will happen to us next?

Our lives are threatened from all sides: a European war and an Ottoman war, prices are skyrocketing, a financial crisis, and the locusts are attacking the country north and south. On top of all this, now infectious diseases are spreading throughout the Ottoman lands. May God protect us. I can hardly walk in the streets and talk to anybody for fear of facing these misfortunes. Usually I worry about the smallest matter that can happen to me, but now with disaster visiting everybody, I have stopped caring. Hasan told me today that the Dardanelles are about to fall.

Monday, July 10, 1916. Rebellion. Sherif Hussein Pasha declared rebellion against the state. There were demonstrations in Medina, and some of the Hijazi rail lines were destroyed. But the rebels' numbers were few, and they were dispersed.

Could this be the beginning? Every Arab should be pleased about this news.

How can we support this state after it killed our best youth? They were hanged in public squares like common criminals and gangsters. They were executed for demanding their rights and for questioning their fate in the general conscription. They died, and not one voice was raised in protest in this miserable Arab nation. Not one Palestinian or Syrian voice. May God bless our Hijazi leader and strengthen his hand.

Document 18
Leaflets Thrown from British Airplanes during the Arab Revolt[19]

Both the Ottomans and the British were eager to deploy modern propaganda methods and innovative new technologies to help secure the loyalty of Arabs, including but not limited to throwing leaflets, such as these below, out of airplanes. For their part, the British attempted to utilize their 1916 alliance with the sharif of Mecca to win over Arab sympathies, but most Arabs remained loyal to the Ottoman sultan.

For further discussion: *Compare this document with Sultan Mehmed V's call to* jihād *(Document 11). What other examples of the rapid and profound expansion of airpower over the course of the war can be found in this book?*

To all Arabs and other officers and men in the Ottoman Army.

We have with much regret heard that you are fighting against us who are working for the sake of preserving the edicts of the Holy Moslem Religion from being altered *and for liberating all Arabs from the Turkish rule.*

We believe that the real truth has not reached you. We have therefore sent you this proclamation sealed by Your seal to assure you that we are fighting for two noble aims—the preserving of the religion and the freedom of Arabs generally.

---

19. Great Britain, *Palestine Commission on the Disturbances of August, 1929, Volume 1. Evidence Heard During the 1st to 29th Sittings* (London: His Majesty's Stationery Office, 1930), 908.

We have sent strict orders to all the heads and men of our tribes that if our Army happen to capture any one of you they should treat you well and send you to my sons who will welcome and well treat you.

The Arab Kingdom has been for a long time in bondage to the Turks, who have killed your brethren, and crucified your men and deported your women and families and have altered your religion. How then can you stand this and bear the bitterness of continuing with them and agree to assist them?

Come and join us who are labouring for the sake of religion and the freedom of the Arabs so that the Arab Kingdom may again become what it was during the time of your fathers, if God wills. God is the leader to the right path.

(Sgd.) Sharif and Emir of Mecca and King of the Arab Countries, Hussein, son of Ali.

Document 19
George Antonius, *The Arab Awakening*, 1939[20]

George Antonius's (1891–1942) 1939 book The Arab Awakening *(1891–1942) is a seminal history of Arab nationalism. A Greek Orthodox Christian from Lebanon, Antonius was educated in Egypt and England before entering British colonial service. Disillusioned by Britain's imperial machinations, he believed in the fundamental legitimacy of a unified pan-Arab state. His book was published at a pivotal moment in the history of the Palestine mandate, and it divulged the long-suppressed terms of the Husayn-McMahon correspondence (Document 16).*

For further discussion: *Antonius is widely credited for developing the first comprehensive theory on the origins of Arab national identity. Why do you think historians continue to debate Antonius's framing of the Arab nationalist movement?*

---

20. George Antonius, *The Arab Awakening: The Story of the Arab National Movement* (Safety Harbor, FL: Simon Publications, 2001 [1939]), 276–78.

Document 19. George Antonius, *The Arab Awakening*, 1939

CHAPTER XIV: THE POST-WAR SETTLEMENT

The War was won, and for the first time in its history the Arab national movement stood abreast of its destiny. Victory had carried its standard as far north as it had been dreamed, to the very confines of its kingdom. Syria had been freed, from Sinai to the Taurus; so had Iraq, up to Mosul; while in the Peninsula itself all that remained of the Turkish power were a few helpless garrisons doomed to surrender. All the Arabic-speaking provinces of the Ottoman Empire in Asia were at last rid of the alien yoke that had lain on them for four stifling centuries. It seemed as though the war-god himself, in homage to the role of the language in the history of the Movement, had stayed the northward advance on the very watershed of speech, just where Arabic ceased and Turkish began. The area of the Turk's defeat was precisely the area of Arab aspirations, and its frontiers coincided exactly with those defined by the Sharif Husain as the natural limits of Arab independence.

It added to the exultation of the people and their leaders that the Revolt had signally helped the common victory. Save for Aden where their contribution had been indirect though by no means negligible, and Iraq where the expulsion of the Turks had been entirely accomplished by British arms, the forces of the Revolt had everywhere else played their assigned part—and more—in the enemy's defeat. They had not only fought the Turk, but also those of their own kin who had been actively siding with him. The leaders felt that they had amply fulfilled their share of the bargain concluded between Sir Henry McMahon and the Sharif Husain, and they confidently looked to Great Britain to fulfill hers.

But when it came to a reckoning at the Peace Conference, there was a wide divergence between what the Arabs claimed and what Great Britain was willing to recognise as her share of the bargain. . . .

As we shall see, Great Britain and France imposed upon the Arabs a 'settlement' which violated both the promises specifically made to them and the principles which the Allies had enunciated as the foundations of the future Peace. In face of what afterwards happened, it is tempting to speculate upon the course which events might have taken had Great Britain and France chosen, at the Peace deliberations, to live up to their pledges and principles. As a rule, such speculations are valid rather as mental exercises than as contributions to history. But in this case, it is beyond all doubt certain that the post-War handling of the Arab question led directly and inevitably to explosions which would not have happened but for that so-called settlement. Thousands of lives, millions of treasure and incalculable moral suffering and damage would have been avoided. The Iraq rising of 1920, the Syrian rebellion of 1925 and the repeated outbreaks in Palestine would not have occurred. For they were all the direct outcome of the various régimes which were wrongfully and forcibly imposed upon the Arabs in Iraq, Syria and Palestine in violation of the pledges which had brought them into the War. Whatever part subsidiary causes may have played, the underlying cause of all those upheavals, and of a good deal else that has clouded the natural friendliness of Arab to Englishman and Englishman to Arab, is to be sought in the bitterness and the revulsion of feeling which the post-War provisions engendered—and nowhere else. The Arabs felt that they had been betrayed, and betrayed by their best friend.

Document 20
1915 British Treaty with Ibn Saud[21]

This excerpt provides an important example of British treaty-making and diplomatic efforts in the Persian Gulf during WWI. In 1915, Ibn Saud (1876–1953), emir of Najd, was a young and ambitious local ruler with a power base centered around Riyadh. His loyalty, and that of his soldiers, was technically owed to the Ottoman sultan, but during the war Istanbul was poorly placed to give Ibn Saud what he really wanted, which was the opportunity to expand his domains at the expense of his tribal rivals.

For further discussion: *Compare the agreement Britain reached with Ibn Saud to that which Britain reached with his archrival Sharif Husayn.*

---

21. "British Treaty with Ibn Saud, 26 December 1915," in J. C. Hurewitz, ed., *The Middle East and North Africa in World Politics: A Documentary Record*, 2nd ed., Volume 2: *British-French Supremacy, 1914–1945* (New Haven, CT: Yale University Press, 1979), 57–58.

I. The British government do acknowledge and admit that Najd, Al Hassa, Qatif and Jubail, and their dependencies and territories, which will be discussed and determined hereafter, and their ports on the Persian Gulf are the countries of Bin Sa'ud and of his fathers before him, and do hereby recognise the said Bin Sa'ud as the Independent Ruler thereof and absolute Chief of their tribes, and after him his sons and descendants by inheritance; but the selection of the individual shall be in accordance with the nomination (i.e., by the living ruler) of his successor; but with the proviso that he shall not be a person antagonistic to the British Government in any respect....

II. In the event of aggression by any Foreign Power on the territories of the countries of the said Bin Sa'ud and his descendants ... the British government will aid Bin Sa'ud to such extent and in such a manner as the British Government after consulting Bin Sa'ud may consider most effective for protecting his interests in countries.

III. Bin Sa'ud hereby agrees and promises to refrain from entering into any correspondence, agreement, or treaty, with any Foreign Nation or Power, and further to give immediate notice to the Political authorities of the British Government of any attempt on the part of any other power to interfere with the above territories.

IV. Bin Sa'ud hereby undertakes that he will absolutely not cede, sell, mortgage, lease, or otherwise dispose of the above territories or any part of them, or grant concessions within those territories to any Foreign Power, or to the subjects of any Foreign Power, without the consent of the British Government.

And that he will follow her advice unreservedly provided that it be not damaging to his own interests.

V. Bin Sa'ud hereby undertakes to keep open within his territories, the roads leading to the Holy Places, and to protect pilgrims on their passage to and from the Holy Places.

VI. Bin Sa'ud undertakes, as his father did before him, to refrain from all aggression on, or interference with the territories of Kuwait, Bahrain, and of the Shaikhs of Qatar and the Oman Coast, who are under the protection of the British Government, and who have treaty relations with the said Government; and the limits of their territories shall be hereafter determined....

Document 21
1918 Anglo-French Declaration[22]

Shortly after the Mudros Armistice, France and Britain issued a joint declaration on November 7, 1918, promising to respect the rights and desires of local populations of former Ottoman territories. Such assurances would be directly contradicted by both the French and British colonial governments established in the following years.

For further discussion: *Why did the victorious Allied powers feel the need to justify their occupation of Middle Eastern lands by promising to respect the rights of locals? What was the legacy of such broken promises?*

The object aimed at by France and Great Britain in prosecuting in the East the War let loose by the ambition of Germany is the complete and definite emancipation of the peoples so long oppressed by the Turks and the establishment of national governments and administrations deriving their authority from the initiative and free choice of the indigenous populations.

In order to carry out these intentions France and Great Britain are at one in encouraging and assisting the establishment of indigenous Governments and administrations in Syria and Mesopotamia, now liberated by the Allies, and in the territories the liberation of which they are engaged in securing and recognising these as soon as they are actually established.

Far from wishing to impose on the populations of these regions any particular institutions they are only concerned to ensure by their support and by adequate assistance the regular working of Governments and administrations freely chosen by the populations themselves. To secure impartial and equal justice for all, to facilitate the economic development of the country by inspiring and encouraging local initiative, to favour the diffusion of education, to put an end to dissensions that have too long

---

22. "Anglo-French Declaration," November 7, 1918, https://en.wikipedia.org/wiki/Anglo-French_Declaration.

been taken advantage of by Turkish policy, such is the policy which the two Allied Governments uphold in the liberated territories.

Document 22
1921 Editorial from *The Times*[23]

After defeating the Ottomans in 1918, Britain set about building new colonial administrations in the Middle East. Back at home, however, where the British government struggled to demobilize and reintegrate millions of former soldiers, the public was not inclined to continue funding military occupations in faraway lands. This editorial from The Times *of London captures many of these domestic tensions.*

For further discussion: *Though British military forces appeared dominant on the ground in the wake of the Ottoman defeat, what factors hampered London's strategic position, forcing Britain into unforeseen compromises?*

Every child at school has heard of Babylon and its tragic fate; and the mounds of rubble which are all that now recall the vanished glories of the Babylonian empire may still serve to remind our rulers that every Power which has sought to control these dismal lands has met with ultimate disaster. To the British nation, however, the unhappy word Mesopotamia is ineffaceable. The people of this country cannot by a cheap play upon place-names erase from their minds the recollection of the region to which nearly a million men were diverted from the main theatre of war, which cost us more lives than any other single campaign in our history, and for the sake of which we are still being taxed beyond endurance. Mr. Churchill got to the root of the Mesopotamian issue when he said, on June 14, that our "obligation" there is "not unlimited," that a point might be reached when no more sacrifices could be demanded from British taxpayers, and that the time might come when "the conditions of our finance or our military resources were such that we could do no more"

---

23. "Mesopotamia," *The Times* (London), July 18, 1921, Issue 42775.

for Mesopotamia. In our view, the point defined by Mr. Churchill was reached long ago. The time when the condition of our finances forbade us to pour more money into Mesopotamia came when the Armistice was signed. It is reasonably certain that before the present year is out the Government will be unable to spare any funds at all for the further prosecution of Middle Eastern adventures.... Last Thursday SIR ALFRED MOND said that the Government could not provide more than £200,000 annually for the improvement of slum areas in Great Britain. On the same day the House of Commons again endorsed a policy which has involved an outlay of over £100,000,000 in Mesopotamia since the Armistice, which implies an additional expenditure of £27,000,000 this year . . . all for the sake of less than three million Arabs, many of whom have already risen in revolt against us. Our slum population alone unquestionably exceeds the number the whole of the inhabitants of Mesopotamia. What sort of greeting do the Government and the private members expect to receive from the electorate when the time comes for them to give an account of their stewardship, and when they have to confess that while they have spent nearly £150,000,000 since the Armistice upon semi-nomads in Mesopotamia, they can find only £200,000 a year for the regeneration of our slums, and have had to forbid all further expenditure under the Education Act of 1918?

Document 23
League of Nations Covenant, Article 22, including 1924 Amendments[24]

Founded in 1920, the League of Nations was the first worldwide intergovernmental organization dedicated to maintaining peace. Its principal goals were described in a document named a "Covenant" which sought to establish precedents and systems to prevent another major global conflict. Article 22 included some of the document's most controversial language. In notoriously patronizing terms, Article 22

---

24. "The Covenant of the League of Nations (including Amendments adopted to December, 1924), Article 22," Avalon Project, Yale Law School, https://avalon.law.yale.edu/20th_century/leagcov.asp.

Document 23. League of Nations Covenant, Article 22, including 1924 Amendments

established the "mandate" system by which "advanced nations" were to be entrusted to govern those parts of the world "not yet able to stand by themselves."

For further discussion: Often dismissed as a fig leaf for colonialism, how did the mandate system differ from pre-WWI extensions of imperial rule?

To those colonies and territories which as a consequence of the late war have ceased to be under the sovereignty of the States which formerly governed them and which are inhabited by peoples not yet able to stand by themselves under the strenuous conditions of the modern world, there should be applied the principle that the well-being and development of such peoples form a sacred trust of civilisation and that securities for the performance of this trust should be embodied in this Covenant.

The best method of giving practical effect to this principle is that the tutelage of such peoples should be entrusted to advanced nations who by reason of their resources, their experience or their geographical position can best undertake this responsibility, and who are willing to accept it, and that this tutelage should be exercised by them as Mandatories on behalf of the League.

The character of the mandate must differ according to the stage of the development of the people, the geographical situation of the territory, its economic conditions and other similar circumstances.

Certain communities formerly belonging to the Turkish Empire have reached a stage of development where their existence as independent nations can be provisionally recognized subject to the rendering of administrative advice and assistance by a Mandatory until such time as they are able to stand alone. The wishes of these communities must be a principal consideration in the selection of the Mandatory....

A permanent Commission shall be constituted to receive and examine the annual reports of the Mandatories and to advise the Council on all matters relating to the observance of the mandates.

Document 24
1919 King-Crane Commission[25]

The King-Crane Commission, a US commission of inquiry that traveled through Palestine, Syria, and Turkey in 1919, was co-chaired by Henry King (1858–1934) and Charles Crane (1858–1939), two important allies of President Wilson. It sought to establish what people living in former Ottoman lands actually wanted out of the peace process, including what government they would prefer and how they felt about Zionism.

For further discussion: *Reflect on the potential impact to the local population of seeing the final report of the King-Crane inquiry (the first, in the case of Palestine, in a long line of investigative commissions) remain shelved and undermined.*

The Commissioners have sought to make their survey of Syria, and the report upon Syria now submitted, in the spirit of the instructions given them by the Council of Four, and especially in harmony with the resolutions adopted on January 30, 1919, by the representatives of the United States, Great Britain, France, Italy and Japan, and with the Anglo-French declaration of November 9, 1918—both quoted at length in the Commission's instructions....

The resolutions and declaration invoked in the instructions given to our Commission thus form the basis of the whole policy of sending a Commission, and of ascertaining the desires of the people.

The sincerity of the professed aims of the Allies in the war, therefore, is particularly to be tested in the application of these aims in the treatment of the Arabic-speaking portions of the former Turkish Empire. For the promises here made were specific and unmistakable. It is worth consideration, too, that the whole policy of the mandataries under the League of Nations might here be worked out with special success, and success here would encourage the steady extension of the policy elsewhere, and

---

25. "Report of American Section of Inter-Allied Commission on Mandates in Turkey: An Official United States Government Report," *Editor & Publisher*, December 2, 1922, https://babel.hathitrust.org/cgi/pt?id=uiug.30112075996634&view=1up&seq=7.

do something so significant for world progress as to help to justify the immeasurable sacrifices of the war. There is also probably no region where the Allies are freer to decide their course in accordance with the principles they have professed.

The gravity of the Syrian problem is further to be seen in certain well-known facts. The fact that the Arabic-speaking portion of the Turkish Empire has been the birth place of the three great religions: Judaism, Christianity, and Islam, and that Palestine contains places sacred to all three, makes inevitably a center of interest and concern for the whole civilized world. No solution which is merely local or has any single people in mind can avail.

As a portion of the bridge-land uniting Europe, Asia, and Africa, too—where in a peculiar degree the East and the West meet—Syria has a place of such strategic importance, politically and commercially, and from the point of view of world civilization, as also to make it imperative that the settlement here brought about should be so just as to give promise of permanently good results for the whole cause of the development of a righteous civilization in the world. Every part of the former Turkish empire must be given a new life and opportunity under thoroughly changed political conditions.

The war and the consequent breaking up of the Turkish Empire, moreover, give a great opportunity . . . to build now in Syria a Near East State on the modern basis of full religious liberty, deliberately including various religious faiths, and especially guarding rights of minorities. It is a matter of justice to the Arabs, in the recognition of the Arab people and their desire for national expression, and of deep and lasting concern to the world, that an Arab state along modern political lines should be formed. While the elements are very various, the interests often divisive, and much of the population not yet fitted for self-government, the conditions are nevertheless as favorable as could be reasonably expected under the circumstances to make the trial now. The mixed and varied populations have lived together with a fair degree of unity under Turkish domination, and in spite of the divisive Turkish policy. They ought to do far better under a state on modern lines and with an enlightened mandatory. . . .

Any policy adopted . . . for Syria should look to the "establishment of a national government and administration deriving their authority from the initiative and free choice of the native populations," and should treat it as far as possible in harmony with its natural geographic and economic unity. This is the natural course to be taken, if at all feasible. It is directly in line with the expressed purpose of the Peace Conference. And it is the plain object of the desires and ambitions of a large majority of the population concerned....

We recommend, as most important of all, and in strict harmony with our Instructions, that whatever foreign administration (whether of one or more powers) is brought into Syria, should come in, not at all as a colonizing Power in the old sense of that term, but as a Mandatory under the League of Nations, with the clear consciousness that "the well-being and development" of the Syrian people form for it a "sacred trust."...

We recommend, in the second place that the unity of Syria be preserved, in accordance with the earnest petition of the great majority of the people of Syria....

In standing thus for the recognition of the unity of Syria, the natural desires of regions like the Lebanon, which have already had a measure of independence, should not be forgotten....

Lebanon has achieved a considerable degree of prosperity and autonomy within the Turkish Empire. She certainly should not find her legitimate aspirations less possible within a Syrian national State....

We recommend, in the third place, that Syria be placed under one Mandatory Power, as the natural way to secure real and efficient unity....

We recommend, in the fourth place, that Emir Feisal be made the head of the new united Syrian State....

This is expressly and unanimously called for by the representative Damascus Congress in the name of the Syrian people, and there seems to be no reason to doubt that the great majority of the population of Syria sincerely desire to have Emir Feisal as ruler....

We recommend, in the fifth place, serious modification of the extreme Zionist program for Palestine of unlimited immigration of Jews, looking finally to making Palestine distinctly a Jewish State....

The Commissioners began their study of Zionism with minds predisposed in its favor, but the actual facts in Palestine, coupled with the force of the general principles proclaimed by the Allies and accepted by the Syrians have driven them to the recommendation here made....

[I]t is to be remembered that the non-Jewish population of Palestine—nearly nine-tenths of the whole—are emphatically against the entire Zionist program....

From the point of view of the desires of the "people concerned," the Mandate should clearly go to America....

Document 25
Burning of Smyrna, 1922[26]

Sitting on Turkey's western Aegean coast, the city of Smyrna (today known as Izmir) was both landing site and final evacuation point for the Greek army during the Greco-Turkish War of 1919–1922. When Turkish forces retook Smyrna in September 1922, much of the city was destroyed in a fire. The event was an undisputed humanitarian catastrophe, rendering hundreds of thousands homeless and shocking international observers around the world. This particular account is offered by US diplomat George Horton (1859–1942).

For further discussion: *Given such a traumatic event unfolding within the Middle East at this time, does this eyewitness account reflect any presuppositions deeply rooted in the Western imagination?*

"What thou seest, write in a book, and send it unto the seven churches which are in Asia; unto Ephesus, and unto Smyrna, and unto Pergamos, and unto Thyatira, and unto Sardis, and unto Philadelphia, and unto Laodicea." Revelation, I:11....

As the conflagration spread and swept on down toward the quay where were the beautiful and well-built offices and warehouses of the great foreign merchants and the residences of the rich Levantines, Greeks and Armenians, the people poured in a rapidly increasing flood to the waterfront, old, young, women, children, sick and well. Those who were unable to walk were carried on stretchers, or on the shoulders of relatives.

The aged Doctor Arghyropolos, long and well-known figure on the streets of Smyrna, being ill, was brought down on a stretcher to the quay where he died.

The last Miltonic touch was now added to a scene of vast, unparalleled horror and human suffering. These thousands were crowded on a narrow street between the burning city and the deep waters of the bay....

---

26. George Horton, *The Blight of Asia: An Account of the Systematic Extermination of Christian Populations by Mohammedans and of the Culpability of Certain Great Powers, with the True Story of the Burning of Smyrna* (Indianapolis: Bobbs-Merrill, 1926), 144–54.

Document 25. Burning of Smyrna, 1922

Great clouds of smoke were by this time beginning to pour down upon the Consulate. The crowd in the street before this building, as well as that upon the quay, was now so dense that the commanding naval officer told me that in ten minutes more I should not be able to get through. The hour had struck for me to evacuate my colony, to find some refuge for it in a Christian country, and to find means for its temporary sustenance.

I was profoundly stirred by the plight of these people and was determined that they should get the kindest, most generous and patient treatment possible. I therefore loaded a few trunks into a waiting automobile, as well as a few bundles of my fine collection of rugs, which fortunately were lying packed up, waiting to be taken out of their casings for winter use, grabbed whatever was dearest to me that happened to be in sight, and with my wife and a Greek servant started for the quay and the waiting destroyer....

The last view of the ill-fated town by daylight was one of vast enveloping clouds rolling up to heaven, a narrow water-front covered with a great throng of people—an ever-increasing throng, with the fire behind and the sea before, and a powerful fleet of inter-allied battle-ships, among which were two American destroyers, moored a short distance from the quay and looking on.

As the destroyer moved away from the fearful scene and darkness descended, the flames, raging now over a vast area, grew brighter and brighter, presenting a scene of awful and sinister beauty. Historians and archeologists have declared that they know of but one event in the annals of the world which can equal in savagery, extent and all the elements of horror, cruelty and human suffering, the destruction of Smyrna and its Christian population by the Turks, and this was the demolition of Carthage by the Romans....

At the destruction of Smyrna there was one feature for which Carthage presents no parallel. There was no fleet of Christian battleships at Carthage looking on at a situation for which their governments were responsible. There was no American cruisers at Carthage.

The Turks were glutting freely their racial and religious lust for slaughter, rape and plunder within a stone's throw of the Allied and American battle-ships because they had been systematically led to believe that they would not be interfered with. A united order from the commanders or from any two of them—one harmless shell thrown across the Turkish quarter—would have brought the Turks to their senses.

And this, the presence of those battle-ships in Smyrna harbor, in the year of our Lord 1922, impotently watching the last great scene in the tragedy of the Christians of Turkey, was the saddest and most significant feature of the whole picture.

Document 26
Atatürk Declaration, 1927[27]

In this speech, given at the National Convention of the "People's Party of the Republic" held in Ankara in October 1927, Kemal explains his conduct in the years following 1918 and reaffirms his vision for a modern and secular Turkish state.

For further discussion: *How and why did secularism become such an important principle underlying Kemal's ideological approach to statecraft, now often referred to as "Kemalism"?*

... [During spring 1919] [t]he [Ottoman] Army existed merely in name. The commanders and other officers were still suffering from the exhaustion resulting from the war. Their hearts were bleeding on account of the threatened dismemberment of their country. Standing on the brink of the dark abyss which yawned before their eyes, they racked their brains to discover a way out of the danger. . . .

In these circumstances, one resolution alone was possible, namely, to create a New Turkish State, the sovereignty and independence of which would be unreservedly recognized by the whole world. . . .

The main point was that the Turkish nation should be free to lead a worthy and glorious existence. Such a condition could only be attained by complete independence. Vital as considerations of wealth and prosperity might be to a nation, if it is deprived of its independence it no longer deserves to be regarded otherwise than as a slave in the eyes of civilised humanity. . . .

---

27. Ghazi Mustapha Kemal, *A Speech Delivered by Ghazi Mustapha Kemal, President of the Turkish Republic, October 1927* (Leipzig: K. F. Koehler, 1929), 16–18, 378–79, 723–24.

Document 26. Atatürk Declaration, 1927

[T]he Turk is both dignified and proud; he is also capable and talented. Such a nation would prefer to perish rather than subject itself to the life of a slave. Therefore, Independence or Death! . . .

[T]o labour for the maintenance of the Ottoman dynasty and its sovereign would have been to inflict the greatest injustice upon the Turkish nation; for, if its independence could have been secured at the price of every possible sacrifice, it could not have been regarded as secure so long as the Sultanate existed. How could it be admitted that a crowd of madmen, united by neither a moral nor a spiritual bond to the country or the nation as a whole, could still be trusted to protect the independence and the dignity of the nation and the State?

As for the Caliphate, it could only have been a laughing-stock in the eyes of the really civilised and cultured people of the world. . . .

We were compelled to rebel against the Ottoman Government, against the Padishah, against the Caliph of all the Mohamedans, and we had to bring the whole nation and the army into a state of rebellion. . . .

There is nothing in history to show how the policy of Panislamism could have succeeded or how it could have found a basis for its realisation on this earth. . . .

The political system which we regard as clear and fully realisable is national policy. In view of the general conditions obtaining in the world at present and the truths which in the course of centuries have rooted themselves in the minds of and have formed the characters of mankind, no greater mistake could be made than that of being a utopian. This is borne out in history and is the expression of science, reason and common sense. . . .

In order that our nation should be able live a happy, strenuous and permanent life, it is necessary that the State should pursue an exclusively national policy and that this policy should be in perfect agreement with our internal organisation and be based on it. . . .

Another important question which I also brought before the Assembly related to the formation of the Government. You will admit that this question was at that time a very delicate one.

In reality, it was a question of acknowledging the collapse of the Ottoman State and the abolition of the Caliphate. It meant the creation of a new State standing on new foundations. . . .

Accordingly we made use of all circumstances only from one point of view which consisted therein: to raise the nation on to that step on which it is justified in standing in the civilised world, to stabilise the Turkish

Republic more and more on steadfast foundations . . . and in addition to destroy the spirit of despotism for ever. . . .

Gentlemen, I have taken trouble to show, in these accounts, how a great people, whose national course was considered as ended, reconquered its independence; how it created a national and modern State founded on the latest results of science.

The result we have attained to day is the fruit of teachings which arose from centuries of suffering, and the price of streams of blood which have drenched every foot of the ground of our beloved Fatherland.

This holy treasure I lay in the hands of the youth of Turkey.

Turkish Youth! your primary duty is every to preserve and defend the National independence, the Turkish Republic.

That is the only basis of your existence and your future. . . .

The strength that you will need for this is mighty in the noble blood which flows in your veins.

Document 27
Reza Shah Pahlavi Coronation, 1926[28]

In postwar Iran, a young army officer named Reza Khan (1878–1944) stepped into the precarious and fractured situation, crowning himself shah of Iran (and renaming himself Reza Shah Pahlavi, evoking pre-Islamic, Zoroastrian-infused, Persian imperial grandeur). While the following New York Times *account labels Pahlavi a dictator, it also describes him as an exotic and potentially attractive ally for the West. This tension would remain central in Western coverage on Iran until the 1979 Revolution ended the Pahlavi dynasty.*

For further discussion: *What kind of popular mandate and national legitimacy did Reza Shah achieve by ruling Iran through the institutions of the monarchy and the military? How does his modernizing mode of nation-state-building compare with Atatürk's?*

---

28. "Persian Dictator Puts on the Crown," Special cable to *The New York Times*, April 26, 1926, ProQuest Historical Newspapers.

Document 27. Reza Shah Pahlavi Coronation, 1926

LONDON, April 25.—Reza Shah Pahlevi, formerly known as Riza Khan, who twenty years ago was a trooper in the Persian Army, mounted the Persian throne today and crowned himself Shah. The ceremony took place in the great hall of the Palace of the Shahs, at Teheran, and was marked by scenes of Oriental splendor ...

Reza Shah Pahlevi today placed on his head with his own hands the new Pahlevi crown especially made for the coronation, and immediately afterward the first gun of a royal salute announced to Teheran and the world that the overthrow of the Kajars was complete and a new dynasty reigned in their stead.

The scene was dazzling in the extreme. The hall was crowded by a brilliant assemblage, which included the chiefs of the Army in blue and red, the entire Diplomatic Corps in full uniform and various tribal leaders wearing their picturesque native garb.

Soldiers carrying the flags of various regiments were ranged along the sides of the room, and the play of color and pattern was repeated over and over again in mirrors along the walls and at the back of the throne.

When all the spectators had taken their places in the hall, the eight-year-old prince, Shah Pur Mohammed Riza, very manly and entirely self-possessed, in a blue military uniform, advanced bowing and saluting, to take his place by the throne. He was followed by members of the Cabinet bearing crowns and swords and the imperial insignia.

It was interesting, says the correspondent, to contrast the new crown, all gold and flashing jewels, with the tall white crown of pearls worn by former Shahs.

A striking note of the coronation was that everything possible was done to emphasize the break with the former dynasty. The crown was new and the Shah did not use the famous peacock throne; but sat on the small throne of Nadir Shah, the great Persian conqueror, which had been placed in front of it.

The stage was all set when the Shah himself entered the hall wearing the diamond airgrette of Nadir Shah and a long gray cape heavily embroidered with pearls. The cape was Napoleonic in its lines and the Shah himself is said to have designed it....

The triumphant progress of the new monarch through the streets of Teheran between thousands of his cheering subjects, concluded the most picturesque ceremony that the Persian capital has seen in recent years.

Document 28
1919 Zaghlul Telegram[29]

In November 1918 an Egyptian delegation led by Saad Zaghlul (1859–1927) requested to present a plan for Egyptian self-determination at the Paris Peace Conferences. Not only did the British high commissioner reject Zaghlul, he had him deported to Malta. However, Britain's strategy backfired, triggering the Egyptian Revolution of 1919, which in turn forced London to strike an official commission headed by Colonial Secretary Alfred Milner to determine the future form of the British protectorate. In this telegram, sent months afterward in December 1919, Zaghul gives his account of these tumultuous months.

For further discussion: *Who was Saad Zaghlul and how does he articulate Egyptian nationalist opposition to British colonial rule?*

I have the honour to express to your Excellency the opinion of the Egyptian Delegation, which has been entrusted by the Egyptian nation with the task of working for its independence. I do hope, Sir, that our being described by the British Government as "extremists" will not prevent you from giving our judgement on these declarations the due consideration it deserves....

Your Excellency was to a great extent justified in declaring that, without the help of the Egyptians themselves, no form of a Constitution can be drawn up, and that, consequently, you have invited what you call "moderate people" to co-operate with Lord Milner and his colleagues. But this appeal of yours to the moderates will secure no response in Egypt, for the simple reason that a moderate section of the people, according to the British interpretation of it, or in other words, those who would tolerate foreign rule, are undoubtedly non-existent, unless the appeal, of course, is directed to those who are already in no need of it, namely, those five or six who have been duped to accept the role of Ministers against the interests of their country.... [I]f we put aside the new Ministers who have been recently appointed, and who, apparently, would help it, we can say with certainty that all the representatives of the nation in the Legislative Assembly and Municipal Councils have, without exception, declared, both publicly

---

29. Saad Zaghlul to Earl Curzon, telegram, December 9, 1919; received December 12, 1919, Archives Direct.

and privately, their grim determination to boycott the British Mission. Not only these but also all personages who have any influence in their spheres have given the same decision. In addition to this, the mass of people have expressed their opinion in the usual way by peaceful demonstrations, although these demonstrations have been continually dispersed by British machine-guns....

Having thus cleared the situation, it will be, no doubt, futile to speak of the people as two sections: Nationalists desiring complete independence; and Independent Liberals accepting the protectorate, and desirous to aid Lord Milner's Mission. The truth is, that the Egyptian people as one man are unanimous in their clamouring for "independence," and in refusing all solutions which do not coincide with this necessary independence. We are really puzzled how Lord Milner's Mission can possibly "consult all parties" when the whole people are averse to its coming (putting aside the new Ministers). All possible means of suppression—such as the arrest of the principal notables, of the intelligent and enlightened young men, the internment of the Ulemas of El Azhar University, together with the press censorship and the dispersion of national demonstration with British guns....

It may occur to some that this sort of protectorate is an innovation both in its nature and in the way it was proclaimed. But such international innovations must, as a matter of fact, take their origin from the spirit of the age in which they occur. This being so, it follows with crushing logic that in such an era as this, and after war waged for principles and ideals of right and justice, and, above all, when one of the chief principles fought for has been "that every people shall have the right to self-determination" and, that, to bring in the culminating point, under the protection of a League of Nations—we say it follows with crushing logic that it is highly inadvisable—nay, most objectionable, to maintain in the worst possible type the phantom of the once "Might is right."...

A protectorate of this nature, that runs counter to the international law and the principles which have been the basis of both the war and the armistice, and at the same time violates all the declarations and pledges made by England, cannot be made valid by mere words; that there are Egyptians who would accept it. And it is very difficult, if not impossible, to account for Lord Milner's Mission, except that it is a practical attempt at deluding the world that there are Egyptians who want the protectorate....

The British authorities have committed a great mistake in underrating the present movement for independence, just in the same way as their forefathers did in America in 1775, when American independence was in the balance. At that time, Earl Gower insisted that he "was well informed that the language held by Americans was the language of the rabble and a few fractious leaders; that the delegates at the Congress were far from expressing the true sense of the respectable part of their constituents." ...

The truth is that the present movement for independence is real, deep, spontaneous and real. Our people have awakened to the infamy and indignity of dependence, and have risen at last to be free or perish. The experiment which has been tried this year cannot but prove this fact; but the British in Egypt, through their naturally characteristic reserve and lack of contact with the people, and through their complete ignorance of the Egyptian tastes, habits and aspirations, are quite unaware and unconscious of the prevailing Egyptian national spirit. In this way, they often miscalculate and underrate matters of the first magnitude.

We are quite sure that, if the British Government could realize the depth and scope of the present national movement, they would not attempt the impossible by trying to subjugate a whole race by force. ...

The recent magnificent development in the outlook of mankind towards right, justice, "political independence and territorial integrity of great and small states alike" is now so overwhelming that such a thinly-veiled annexation bearing the name of "protectorate" can no longer deceive anybody; and the thick screen which the British Government have placed between us and the British public will soon be penetrated by our cries. We still believe that although the political firmament is now cloudy and charged with electrical possibilities, the great democracy of Great Britain is capable of doing justice to the Egyptian people. ...

Document 29
Hudá Sha'rāwi's Memoir of the 1919 Egyptian Revolution[30]

In the revolutionary change unleashed by WWI, many female activists and writers across the region took part in wider struggles for

---

30. Hudá Sha'rāwi, *Harem Years: The Memoirs of an Egyptian Feminist* (New York: Feminist Press, 1987), 112–14.

independence and dignity. One notable example is Hudá Sha'rāwi (1879–1947), an Egyptian nationalist and founder of the Egyptian Feminist Union. Sha'rāwi played a decisive role in the Egyptian Revolution of 1919.

For further discussion: Who was Hudá Sha'rāwi, and how does she frame her role in resisting the British colonial occupation?

We women held our first demonstration on 16 March to protest the repressive acts and intimidation practised by the British authority. In compliance with the orders of the authority we announced our plans to demonstrate in advance but were refused permission. We began to telephone this news to each other, only to read in *al-Muqattam* that the demonstration had received official sanction. We got on the telephone again, telling as many women as possible that we would proceed according to schedule the following morning. Had we been able to contact more than a limited number of women, virtually all the women of Cairo would have taken part in the demonstration.

On the morning of 16 March, I sent placards to the house of the wife of Ahmad Bey Abu Usbaa, bearing slogans in Arabic and French painted in white on a background of black—the colour of mourning. Some of the slogans read, 'Long Live the Supporters of Justice and Freedom', others said 'Down with Oppressors and Tyrants' and 'Down with Occupation'.

We assembled according to plan at the Garden City Park, where we left our carriages. Having agreed upon our route and carefully instructed the young women assigned to carry the flags and placards in front, we set out in columns towards the legation of the United States and intended to proceed from there to the legations of Italy and France. However, when we reached Qasr al-Aini Street, I observed that the young women in front were deviating from the original plan and had begun to head in the direction of *Bait al-Umma* (The House of the Nation), as Saad Zaghlul's house was called. I asked my friend Wagida Khulusi to find out why we were going toward Saad Pasha's house and she returned saying that the women had decided it was a better route. According to our first plan we were to have ended our demonstration there. Reluctantly I went along with this change. No sooner were we approaching Zaghlul's house than British troops surrounded us. They blocked the streets with machine guns, forcing us to stop along with the students who had formed columns on both sides of us.

I was determined the demonstration should resume. When I advanced, a British soldier stepped toward me pointing his gun, but I made my way past him. As one of the women tried to pull me back, I shouted in a loud voice, 'Let me die so Egypt shall have an Edith Cavell' (an English nurse shot and killed by the Germans during the First World War, who became an instant martyr). Continuing in the direction of the soldiers, I called upon the women to follow. A pair of arms grabbed me and the voice of Regina Khayyat rang in my ears. 'This is madness. Do you want to risk the lives of the students? It will happen if the British raise a hand against you.' At the thought of our unarmed sons doing battle against the weaponry of British troops, and of the Egyptian losses sure to occur, I came to my senses and stopped still. We stood still for three hours while the sun blazed down on us. The students meanwhile continued to encourage us, saying that the heat of the day would soon abate. Some of the students departed for the legations of the United States, France, and Italy, announcing that the British had surrounded the women in front of Saad Pasha's house. I did not care if I suffered sunstroke—the blame would fall upon the tyrannical British authority—but we stood up to the heat and suffered no harm. The British also brought out Egyptian soldiers armed with sticks.

Document 30
1922 Churchill White Paper[31]

Following British occupation, Palestine experienced a steady escalation in tensions and violence. The British, who were responsible for initially setting up these ethno-national divisions, soon found themselves unable to arbitrate, torn between contradictory promises they had made to both communities. But in 1922, Britain's putative belief in a "spirit of cooperation" was officially outlined in a document known as the Churchill White Paper.

For further discussion: *Explain Churchill's interpretation of what is (and what is not) meant by the development of a Jewish National Home in Palestine.*

---

31. "Statement of British Policy (Churchill Memorandum) on Palestine, 1 July 1922," in J. C. Hurewitz, ed., *The Middle East and North Africa in World Politics: A Documentary Record*, 2nd ed., Volume 2: *British-French Supremacy, 1914–1945* (New Haven, CT: Yale University Press, 1979), 301–5.

Document 30. 1922 Churchill White Paper 193

The tension which has prevailed from time to time in Palestine is mainly due to apprehensions, which are entertained both by sections of the Arab and by sections of the Jewish population. These apprehensions, so far as the Arabs are concerned, are partly based upon exaggerated interpretations of the meaning of the Declaration favouring the establishment of a Jewish National Home in Palestine, made on behalf of His Majesty's Government on 2nd November, 1917. Unauthorized statements have been made to the effect that the purpose in view is to create a wholly Jewish Palestine. Phrases have been used such as that Palestine is to become "as Jewish as England is English." His Majesty's Government regard any such expectation as impracticable and have no such aim in view. Nor have they at any time contemplated, as appears to be feared by the Arab Delegation, the disappearance or the subordination of the Arabic population, language or culture in Palestine. They would draw attention to the fact that the terms of the Declaration referred to do not contemplate that Palestine as a whole should be converted into a Jewish National Home, but that such a Home should be founded *in Palestine*. In this connection it has been observed with satisfaction that at the meeting of the Zionist Congress, the supreme governing body of the Zionist Organisation, held at Carlsbad in September, 1921, a resolution was passed expressing as the official statement of Zionist aims "the determination of the Jewish people to live with the Arab people on terms of unity and mutual respect, and together with them to make the common home into a flourishing community, the upbuilding of which may assure to each of its peoples an undisturbed national development."...

[I]t is contemplated that the status of all citizens of Palestine in the eyes of the law shall be Palestinian, and it has never been intended that they, or any section of them, should possess any other juridical status.

So far as the Jewish population of Palestine are concerned it appears that some among them are apprehensive that His Majesty's Government may depart from the policy embodied in the Declaration of 1917. It is necessary, therefore, once more to affirm that these fears are unfounded, and that that Declaration, re-affirmed by the Conference of the Principal Allied Powers at San Remo and again in the Treaty of Sèvres, is not susceptible of change.

During the last two or three generations the Jews have recreated in Palestine a community now numbering 80,000, of whom about one-fourth are farmers or workers upon the land. This community has its own political organs; an elected assembly for the direction of its domestic concerns; elected councils in the towns; and an organization for the control of its schools. It has its elected Chief Rabbinate and Rabbinical Council for the direction of its religious affairs. Its business is conducted in Hebrew as a vernacular language, and a Hebrew press serves its needs. It has its distinctive intellectual life and displays considerable economic activity. This community, then, with its town and country population, its political, religious and social organizations, its own language, its own customs, its own life, has in fact "national" characteristics. When it is asked what is meant by the development of the Jewish National Home in Palestine, it may be answered that it is not the imposition of a Jewish nationality upon the inhabitants of Palestine as a whole, but the further development of the existing Jewish community, with the assistance of Jews in other parts of the world, in order that it may become a centre in which the Jewish people as a whole may take, on grounds of religion and race, an interest and a pride. But in order that this community should have the best prospect of free development and provide full opportunity for the Jewish people to display its capacities, it is essential that it should know that it is in Palestine as of right and not on sufferance. That is the reason why it is necessary that the existence of a Jewish National Home in Palestine should be internationally guaranteed, and that it should be formally recognised to rest upon ancient historic connection....

For the fulfillment of this policy it is necessary that the Jewish community in Palestine should be able to increase its numbers by immigration. This immigration cannot be so great in volume as to exceed whatever may be the economic capacity of the country at the time to absorb new arrivals. It is essential to ensure that the immigrants should not be a burden upon the people of Palestine as a whole, and that they should not deprive any section of the present population of their employment. Hitherto the immigration has fulfilled these conditions. The number of immigrants since the British occupation has been about 25,000....

With reference to the Constitution which it is now intended to establish in Palestine, the draft of which has already been published, it is desirable to make certain points clear. In the first place, it is not the case, as has been represented by the Arab Delegation, that during the war His Majesty's Government gave an undertaking that an independent national government should be at once established in Palestine. This representation mainly rests upon a letter dated the 24th October, 1915, from Sir Henry McMahon, then His Majesty's High Commissioner in Egypt, to the Sharif of Mecca, now King Hussein of the Kingdom of the Hejaz.

That letter is quoted as conveying the promise to the Sherif of Mecca to recognise and support the independence of the Arabs within the territories proposed by him. But this promise was given subject to a reservation made in the same letter, which excluded from its scope, among other territories, the portions of Syria lying to the west of the district of Damascus. This reservation has always been regarded by His Majesty's Government as covering the vilayet of Beirut and the independent Sanjak of Jerusalem. The whole of Palestine west of the Jordan was thus excluded from Sir Henry McMahon's pledge.

Nevertheless, it is the intention of His Majesty's Government to foster the establishment of a full measure of self-government in Palestine. But they are of the opinion that, in the special circumstances of that country, this should be accomplished by gradual stages and not suddenly....

The Secretary of State would point out that already the present administration has transferred to a Supreme Council elected by the Moslem community of Palestine the entire control of Moslem religious endowments (Wakfs), and of the Moslem religious Courts. To this Council the Administration has also voluntarily restored considerable revenues derived from ancient endowments which have been sequestrated by the Turkish Government....

The Secretary of State believes that a policy upon these lines, coupled with the maintenance of the fullest religious liberty in Palestine and with scrupulous regard for the rights of each community with reference to its Holy Places, cannot but commend itself to the various sections of the population, and that upon this basis may be built up that a spirit of cooperation upon which the future progress and prosperity of the Holy Land must largely depend.

Document 31
1922 Mandate for Palestine[32]

At San Remo, Italy, in 1920, British and French negotiators finally agreed upon their allotment of mandates over the former Arab territories of the

---

32. "The Mandate for Palestine, 24 July 1922," in J. C. Hurewitz, ed., *The Middle East and North Africa in World Politics: A Documentary Record*, 2nd ed., *Volume 2: British-French Supremacy, 1914–1945* (New Haven, CT: Yale University Press, 1979), 305–9.

Ottoman Empire. *The administrative framework and legal status of the mandate was then codified in a 1922 document entitled the "Mandate for Palestine." Employing the language of Article 22 of the Covenant of the League of Nations, and thereby the colonial logic presupposing the best interests of the local population, the document also incorporated the full text of the 1917 Balfour Declaration. In the language of the time, Britain assumed a "dual mandate."*

For further discussion: *Consider the role of the mandate in transforming the Balfour Declaration from a wartime letter into an international obligation subject to the oversight of the League of Nations. What constraints might this have imposed on British colonial rule in Palestine?*

Whereas the Principal Allied Powers have agreed, for the purpose of giving effect to the provisions of Article 22 of the Covenant of the League of Nations, to entrust to a Mandatory selected by the said Powers the administration of the territory of Palestine, which formerly belonged to the Turkish Empire, within such boundaries as may be fixed by them; and

Whereas the Principal Allied Powers have also agreed that the Mandatory should be responsible for putting into effect the declaration originally made on November 2nd, 1917, by the Government of His Britannic Majesty, and adopted by the said Powers, in favour of the establishment in Palestine of a national home for the Jewish people, it being clearly understood that nothing should be done which might prejudice the civil and religious rights of existing non-Jewish communities in Palestine, or the rights and political status enjoyed by Jews in any other country; and

Whereas recognition has thereby been given to the historical connection of the Jewish people with Palestine and to the grounds for reconstituting their national home in that country; and

Whereas the Principal Allied Powers have selected His Britannic Majesty as the Mandatory for Palestine....

Confirming the said mandate, defines its terms as follows:

ART. 1. The Mandatory shall have full powers of legislation and of administration, save as they may be limited by the terms of this mandate.

ART. 2. The Mandatory shall be responsible for placing the country under such political, administrative and economic conditions as will secure the establishment of the Jewish national home, as laid down in the preamble, and the development of self-governing institutions, and also for safeguarding the civil and religious rights of all the inhabitants of Palestine, irrespective of race and religion.

ART. 3. The Mandatory shall, so far as circumstances permit, encourage local autonomy.

ART. 4. An appropriate Jewish agency shall be recognised as a public body for the purpose of advising and co-operating with the Administration of Palestine in such economic, social and other matters as may affect the establishment of the Jewish national home and the interests of the Jewish population in Palestine, and, subject always to the control of the Administration, to assist and take part in the development of the country.

The Zionist Organisation, so long as its organisation and constitution are in the opinion of the Mandatory appropriate, shall be recognised as such agency. It shall take steps in consultation with His Britannic Majesty's Government to secure the co-operation of all Jews who are willing to assist in the establishment of the Jewish national home. ...

ART. 6. The Administration of Palestine, while ensuring that the rights and position of other sections of the population are not prejudiced, shall facilitate Jewish immigration under suitable conditions and shall encourage, in co-operation with the Jewish agency referred to in Article 4, close settlement by Jews on the land, including State lands and waste lands not required for public purposes.

ART. 7. The Administration of Palestine shall be responsible for enacting a nationality law. There shall be included in this law provisions framed so as to facilitate the acquisition of Palestinian citizenship by Jews who take up their permanent residence in Palestine. ...

ART. 9. The Mandatory shall be responsible for seeing that the judicial system established in Palestine shall assure to foreigners, as well as to natives, a complete guarantee of their rights.

Respect for the personal status of the various peoples and communities and for their religious interests shall be fully guaranteed. In particular, the control and administration of Wakfs shall be exercised in accordance with religious law and the dispositions of the founders. ...

ART. 11. The Administration of Palestine shall take all necessary measures to safeguard the interests of the community in connection with the development of the country, and, subject to any international obligations accepted by the Mandatory, shall have full power to provide for public ownership or control of any of the natural resources of the country or of the public works, services and utilities established or to be established therein. It shall introduce a land system appropriate to the needs of the country, having regard, among other things, to the desirability of promoting the close settlement and intensive cultivation of the land.

The Administration may arrange with the Jewish agency mentioned in Article 4 to construct or operate, upon fair and equitable terms, any public works, services and utilities, and to develop any of the natural resources of the country. . . .

ART. 12. The Mandatory shall be entrusted with the control of the foreign relations of Palestine. . . .

ART. 13. All responsibility in connection with the Holy Places and religious buildings or sites in Palestine, including that of preserving existing rights and of securing free access to the Holy Places, religious buildings and sites and the free exercise of worship, while ensuring the requirements of public order and decorum, is assumed by the Mandatory. . . .

ART. 15. The Mandatory shall see that complete freedom of conscience and the free exercise of all forms of worship, subject only to the maintenance of public order and morals, are ensured to all. No discrimination of any kind shall be made between the inhabitants of Palestine on the ground of race, religion or language. No person shall be excluded from Palestine on the sole ground of his religious belief.

The right of each community to maintain its own schools for the education of its own members in its own language, while conforming to such educational requirements of a general nature as the Administration may impose, shall not be denied or impaired. . . .

ART. 22. English, Arabic and Hebrew shall be the official languages of Palestine. Any statement or inscription in Arabic on stamps or money in Palestine shall be repeated in Hebrew and any statement or inscription in Hebrew shall be repeated in Arabic.

ART. 25. In the territories lying between the Jordan and the eastern boundary of Palestine as ultimately determined, the Mandatory shall be entitled, with the consent of the Council of the League of Nations, to postpone or withhold application of such provisions of this mandate as he may consider inapplicable to the existing local conditions, and to make such provision for the administration of the territories as he may consider suitable to those conditions. . . .

Document 32
Sāti' al-Husrī on the 1920 Battle of Maysalūn[33]

In the independent Arab kingdom briefly established by Emir Faysal in Damascus from 1918 to 1920, Sāti' al-Husrī (1880–1968) served as minister of education. He became a trusted friend of Faysal and was totally engaged in the fraught day-to-day politics of the time. These excerpts are taken from a book published by al-Husrī in 1966 giving his account of the last days of the independent Syrian kingdom. Specifically, he recounts the events before and after the Battle of Maysalūn on July 24, 1920, when the French forcibly imposed their mandate in regions over which Arabs had been promised independence.

For further discussion: *Explain the significance and legacy of the four-hour Battle of Maysalūn.*

The beginning of July 24th was the time set for the expiration of the truce concluded with General Gouraud. It was expected that the French would first attack in the foothills at dawn. Details of the battle, which started at the predicted time, began to trickle back. Although I couldn't entertain any hopes of victory in view of what I knew about our army and the equipment of the French, I kept wishing that the outcome would remain in doubt as long as possible for the sake of our military honor. By 10 o'clock, however, we received word that the army had been defeated and the front shattered. Yūsuf al-'Azmah was reported to have been killed. I said no—he committed suicide at Maysalūn, a true martyr!

Neither the soldiers and the weapons we collected nor the fortifications we managed to improvise proved able to withstand for more than a few hours the violent assault of a French army in possession of every conceivable weapon of destruction—heavy artillery, tanks, and airplanes....

It was decided that the cabinet should move to al-Kiswah by train and the King by automobile. I suggested that we first explain to the people that the government was leaving in order to continue the struggle for the rights and independence of the country. My colleagues agreed and we wrote

---

33. Abū Khaldūn Sāti'al-Husrī, *The Day of Maysalūn: A Page from the Modern History of the Arabs*, trans. Sidney Glazer (Washington, DC: Middle East Institute, 1966), 79–82, 84, https://www.mei.edu/book/11523.

the text of a statement which we submitted to the royal cabinet for final drafting and the release over the signature of the Prime Minister Hāshim al-Atāsī. We arranged for everyone to be in Hejaz Station at 1:00 p.m.

I went home and packed some clothing and a few papers. When I got to the station I found it crowded with nationalists who considered it prudent to leave Damascus before the arrival of the French. Most of them were in a state of panic, their ears attuned to gossip, their minds inclined to believe and exaggerate everything. In such an electric atmosphere there were naturally many baseless reports.... We tried hard to dispel the rumors and soothe frayed nerves. Above all, we wanted the train to leave only at the scheduled hour....

The train was about to pull out of the station when I thought of asking Hāshim al-Atāsī what he had done with the statement. He exploded with anger. "The statement! The statement! Why do you keep harping on it," he shouted at the top of his lungs.

Realizing his nerves were on edge owing to the tenseness of the atmosphere, I said gently: "Because I believe that we will fail in our work if we go without releasing it. We aren't running from our obligations; on the contrary, we are trying to discharge them in the best way possible."

Some of the refugees became extremely agitated and demanded we leave without delay. Hāshim al-Atāsī was clearly affected by the excitement, so I had to reassure him. "We have no right to leave until the statement is released. We mustn't fail now after having had the responsibility for governing up to this point."...

Upon our arrival in al-Kiswah, we converted the railroad cars into offices and sleeping quarters. One of them was specially fitted out for King Faisal who drove up with his retinue towards sunset. He seemed quite different to his usual self. Both his hesitant movements and reticence indicated that he was upset. I thought he was trying to conceal something from us. I said to myself "Perhaps he is still hoping for a mutual understanding with the French and expecting word to this effect." I was right, for, as I soon found out, he has sent Nūrī al-Saʿīd to meet the French and deferred all decisions until he heard from him. In his anxiety for news he virtually refused to talk or express an opinion on any subject.

What the King was waiting for came in this telegram from Nūrī: "To the Prime Minister: The agreement is temporary. The government may remain provided that it regard past acts as having been committed against its peaceful desires and publish a communique along these lines. The French will stay in al-Mazzah for the time being and will not interfere in anything unless the original terms are not carried out. Regular troops may remain in Qadam, the police and security forces in the city. In order to maintain security, regular army units may be converted into police. Your Majesty must come to Damascus. I await written authorization for diplomatic negotiations. Curfew is 8:00 p.m. The city is all quiet. Don't worry...."

The telegram didn't convince me at all. I had no doubt that "its author was wholly uninformed regarding the true intentions of the French" and "incapable of appreciating the degree to which they would persist in deception and trickery." But the King, who was searching for a ray of hope in this dark hour, was comforted by his message. The next day many oral reports similar to the tone of the telegram reinforced his optimism and induced him to make an important decision, i.e., to ask 'Alā' al-Dīn al-Durūbī to form a new government....

Recent events indicated unmistakably that 'Alā' al-Dīn al-Durūbī had already reached an accord with the French and his dissociating himself from us in Damascus when we were about to depart for al-Kiswah was one of the consequences of it. King Faisal therefore thought that al-Durūbī could form a cabinet capable of working out an accommodation with the French.

I clearly realised that King Faisal's cheerfulness was completely unfounded and that this sacrifice would be futile. Events soon proved the correctness of my view....

[T]he French once again revealed their designs. Chief Chamberlain Ihsān al-Jabiri met Italian consul General de Paterno in Damascus and was told the French had resolved to proclaim the end of the Faisal regime and to bolster their decision by a "legal ruling," prepared by their myrmidons, which would say that the "investiture of King Faisal was null and void inasmuch as he fled from the capital." The Marquis hinted that it would be a wise move if the King returned to Damascus where he could neutralize the French intrigues and strengthen his position in European diplomatic matters.

King Faisal adopted the suggestion and decided to anticipate events by going back. All of us left for Damascus by train....

Developments swiftly followed one another. General Goybet, commander of the forces occupying Damascus, assembled the members of the new government and read to them a long statement in which he said: "Emir Faisal dragged the country within an inch of destruction and his responsibility for the bloody disturbances in Syria during the past few months is so clear and so great that it is utterly impossible for him to remain in the country."

King Faisal immediately sent a telegram to General Gouraud: "I protest the statements made yesterday to my government by the commander of your expeditionary forces. I reject the responsibility you have sought to place upon me. I consider any communication or instructions that you may send to my government directly and not through me as null and illegal before the League of Nations."...

Shortly afterwards Colonel Toulat delivered an official note ordering the King to leave the country: "I have the honor to inform Your Royal Highness that the Government of the Republic of France has decided to request you together with your family and retinue leave Damascus as soon as possible by the Hejaz Railroad. A special train departing from Hejaz Station tomorrow July 28 at 5:00 a.m. will be at the disposal of Your Highness and party."...

Thus did King Faisal leave the country over which he had reigned for almost two and a half years. Thereafter circumstances evolved in such a way as gradually to distance the great leader from Syria and bring him to Iraq less than a year from the Day of Maysalūn. Here, as ruler chosen by the people to found a stable new kingdom, he was to have ample scope for the display of his natural talents, knowledge, administrative and diplomatic experience acquired before and after the Day of Maysalūn in Syria and Europe.

Document 33
1920 Muhammad Habib al-'Ubaydi Poem[34]

Crucial to Iraq's struggle for self-determination in the interwar period was the task of crafting new concepts of national identity. The process was complicated by both the religious and ethnic diversity of the country and constant efforts by British colonial officials to maintain influence in Iraq through divide-and-rule tactics (as Britain also did in other locales). Nonetheless, as elaborated by modern theorists of nationalism such as Benedict Anderson (1936–2015), the formation of a national identity was based both in state initiatives, such as employment, education, and conscription, as well as on the expansion of cultural fields operating in a common language.

---

34. Muhammad Habib al-'Ubaydi, in Yitzhak Nakash, *The Shi'is of Iraq*, 2nd ed. (Princeton, NJ: Princeton University Press, 2003), 69.

For further discussion: What role did innovative forms of cultural expression such as poetry play in mobilizing nationalist resistance to British rule?

Set the fire O you noble Iraqis
and wash the shame with flowing blood
O you the people of Iraq, you are not slaves
to adorn your necks with collars
O you the people of Iraq, you are not prisoners
to submit your shoulders to the chains
O you the people of Iraq, you are not women
whose weapon is the tears that flow from the depth of the eye
O you the people of Iraq, you are not orphans
to seek guardianship [a mandate] for Iraq
You shall no longer enjoy the water of the Tigris
if you are content with humiliation and oppression

Document 34
Gertrude Bell, "[W]e've Got Our King Crowned," 1921[35]

A renowned British writer, archeologist, and Arabist, Gertrude Bell (1868–1926) was appointed a political officer in Mesopotamia during the war. Based in Baghdad, she tried to assist with the governing efforts of Iraq's new King Faysal I, serving as his confidant and utilizing her wide network of friends and acquaintances. Her letters (in this instance, to her father, Sir Hugh Bell) and extensive writings illustrate the internal political dynamics of Iraq during the early days of British rule.

For further discussion: What can the memoirs of political administrators (too often referred to in a gendered manner as "men on the spot") tell us about the capricious and individualistic nature of the imperial decision-making process?

---

35. Gertrude Bell to Sir Hugh Bell, August 28, 1921, https://gertrudebell.ncl.ac.uk/l/gb-1-1-2-1-17-29.

Document 34. Gertrude Bell, "[W]e've Got Our King Crowned," 1921

Baghdad Aug 28. Darling Father. . . . Well, we've had a terrific week, but we've got our king crowned and Sir Percy and I agree that we are now half seas over. The remaining half is the Congress and the Organic Law. By the way (secret) I told you the impossible problem which HMG had presented to us at the last moment and the rejoinder of Faisal and Sir Percy. H.M.G. climbed down at once, I may say grovelled. It was all a mistake and far from their intentions to interfere and God bless us all. Thereat we went gaily forward.

On Monday night I dined en famille with Ja'far and Nuri and their wives, and Ja'far's young brother Tahsin, inspector of police at Samarra, a very good and capable young man. It was a happy evening. Ja'far and Nuri were brimming over with joy and I not less. The enthronement took place at 6 a.m. on Tuesday, admirably managed. A dais about 2 ft 6 high was set up in the middle of the big Sarai courtyard; behind it are the Quarters Faisal is occupying, the big Government reception rooms; in front we were seated in blocks, English, Arab officials, townsmen, ministries, local deputations, to the number of 1500. We came in by ticket through the Sarai gateway and after the function had begun the Arab police let no one in, whereby a good many magnates who strolled along late were, to their pained surprise, excluded. It was all Arab organization and it was quite right. . . . Exactly at 6 we saw Faisal in uniform, Sir Percy in white diplomatic uniform with all his ribbons and stars. . . . Faisal looked very dignified but much strung up—it was an agitating moment. He looked along the front row and caught my eye and I gave him a tiny salute. Then Saiyid Husain stood up and read Sir Percy's proclamation in which he announced that Faisal had been elected king by 96% of the people in Mesopotamia, long live the King! with that we stood up and saluted him, the national flag was broken on the flagstaff by his side and the band played God Save the King—they have no national anthem yet. There followed a salute of 21 guns, during which, Saiyid Mahmud, very inappropriately, read a prayer of thanksgiving to God and ended by doing homage to Faisal on behalf of the Council. . . . King Faisal I then addressed his people. . . . It was . . . very fine and simple and heartfelt. With that they walked away as they had come and we remained seated for a bit till Sir Percy and the General passed out in their cars whereat we all began to go away talking and exchanging greetings and compliments and congratulations. It was an amazing thing to see all 'Iraq, from north to south gathered together. It is the first time it has happened, in history. So I went back to the office, breakfasted with the Coxes and received

Document 34. Gertrude Bell, "[W]e've Got Our King Crowned," 1921

masses of people who came in for a little excited gossip.... I heard from others that the great excitement among shaikhs from remote places who hadn't met Sir Percy before, was to see him. It's a good thing that he is such a figure when you do see him; with his gaunt height and eagle's beak he was very striking. He looks so benevolent as well as so strong....

I had spent two hours with Faisal the day before. He asked me to tea; I brought him photographs of our picnics (one of which I send to you) and a map of Syria taken from the Times showing the way the French have cut up Syria into separate provinces. He loved the photographs and swore over the map. "By God, it's forbidden" he said and we proceeded to talk shocking heresy about Syria. Soon after Ja'far, Nuri and Rustam (he's a Syrian) dropped in. I told them that except for Rustam I thought I knew Syria better than any of them and loved it more—village by village, mountain by mountain, river by river. And I believed there was only one hope for Syria, that we should sit quiet here, say no word, and do our own job. When we had made Mesopotamia a model Arab state, not an Arab of Syria and Palestine that wouldn't want to be part of it, and before I died I looked to see Faisal ruling from the Persian frontier to the Mediterranean. But if we stirred here in the matter, lifted a finger or raised a voice, it would be ruin to Syria and 'Iraq alike....

We then spent a happy hour discussing (a) our desert frontier to south and west and (b) the national flag and Faisal's personal flag. For the latter we arranged provisionally this [sketch] i.e. the Hijaz flag with a gold crown on the red triangle. The red I must tell you is the colour of his house so he bears his own nom on it. Father, do for Heaven's sake tell me whether the Hijaz flag is heraldically right. You might telegraph. It's a very good flag and we could differentiate it for the Iraq by putting a gold star on the black stripe or on the red triangle. The Congress will settle it directly it meets—do let me know in time. Also whether you have a better suggestion for Faisal's standard....

There's no doubt that this is the most absorbing job that I've ever taken a hand in.

FURTHER READING

Akçam, Taner. *The Young Turks' Crime against Humanity: The Armenian Genocide and Ethnic Cleansing in the Ottoman Empire*. Princeton, NJ: Princeton University Press, 2012.

Akin, Yiğit. *When the War Came Home: The Ottomans' Great War and the Devastation of an Empire*. Stanford, CA: Stanford University Press, 2018.

Aksakal, Mustafa. *The Ottoman Road to War in 1914: The Ottoman Empire and the First World War*. Cambridge: Cambridge University Press, 2008.

Allawi, Ali. *Faisal I of Iraq*. New Haven, CT: Yale University Press, 2014.

Amanat, Abbas. *Iran: A Modern History*. New Haven, CT: Yale University Press, 2017.

Anderson, Benedict. *Imagined Communities: Reflections on the Origin and Spread of Nationalism*. Rev. ed. London: Verso, 2006.

Anderson, Scott. *Lawrence in Arabia: War, Deceit, Imperial Folly and the Making of the Modern Middle East*. New York: Doubleday, 2013.

Antonius, George. *The Arab Awakening: The Story of the Arab National Movement*. Safety Harbor, FL: Simon Publications, 2001 [1939].

Baer, Marc. *The Ottomans: Khans, Caesars, and Caliphs*. New York: Basic Books, 2021.

Barr, James. *A Line in the Sand: Britain, France and the Struggle That Shaped the Middle East*. London: Simon & Schuster, 2011.

Bonine, Michael E., Abbas Amanat, and Michael Ezekiel Gasper, eds. *Is There a Middle East?: The Evolution of a Geopolitical Concept*. Stanford, CA: Stanford University Press, 2012.

Campos, Michelle U. *Ottoman Brothers: Muslims, Christians, and Jews in Early Twentieth-Century Palestine*. Stanford, CA: Stanford University Press, 2011.

Clancy-Smith, Julia, and Charles Smith, eds. *The Modern Middle East and North Africa: A History in Documents*. Oxford: Oxford University Press, 2013.

Clark, Christopher. *The Sleepwalkers: How Europe Went to War in 1914*. New York: HarperCollins, 2013.

Cleveland, William, and Martin Bunton. *A History of the Modern Middle East*. Boulder, CO: Westview Press, 2016.

Darke, Diana. *The Ottomans: A Cultural Legacy*. London: Thames & Hudson, 2022.

de Bellaigue, Christopher. *The Islamic Enlightenment: The Struggle Between Faith and Reason, 1798 to Modern Times*. New York: Liveright, 2018.

Fawaz, Leila Tarazi. *A Land of Aching Hearts: The Middle East in the Great War*. Cambridge, MA: Harvard University Press, 2014.

Fieldhouse, D. K. *Western Imperialism in the Middle East, 1914–1958*. Oxford: Oxford University Press, 2006.

Finkel, Caroline. *Osman's Dream: The History of the Ottoman Empire*. New York: Basic Books, 2007.

Fromkin, David. *A Peace to End All Peace: The Fall of the Ottoman Empire and the Creation of the Modern Middle East*. New York: Henry Holt, 2009 [1989].

Gelvin, James. *The Modern Middle East: A History*. 5th ed. Oxford: Oxford University Press, 2020.

Gerwarth, Robert. *The Vanquished: Why the First World War Failed to End*. New York: Farrar, Straus and Giroux, 2016.

Howard, Douglas. *A History of the Ottoman Empire*. Cambridge: Cambridge University Press, 2017.

Johnson, Rob. *The Great War and the Middle East*. Oxford: Oxford University Press, 2016.

Kessler, Oren. *Palestine 1936: The Great Revolt and the Roots of the Middle East Conflict*. Lanham, MD: Rowman & Littlefield, 2023.

Khalidi, Rashid. *Resurrecting Empire: Western Footprints and America's Perilous Path in the Middle East*. Boston: Beacon Press, 2005.

Leonhard, Jörn. *Pandora's Box: A History of the First World War*. Translated by Patrick Camiller. Cambridge, MA: Harvard University Press, 2018.

Lockman, Zachary. *Contending Visions of the Middle East: The History and Politics of Orientalism*. Cambridge: Cambridge University Press, 2010.

MacMillan, Margaret. *Paris 1919: Six Months That Changed the World*. New York: Random House, 2003.

Makdisi, Ussama. *Age of Coexistence: The Ecumenical Frame and the Making of the Modern Arab World*. Oakland: University of California Press, 2019.

———. *The Culture of Sectarianism: Community, History, and Violence in Nineteenth-Century Ottoman Lebanon*. Berkeley: University of California Press, 2000.

McMeekin, Sean. *The Berlin-Baghdad Express: The Ottoman Empire and Germany's Bid for World Power*. London: Penguin, 2011.

———. *The Ottoman Endgame: War, Revolution, and the Making of the Modern Middle East, 1908–1923*. New York: Penguin, 2016.

McMillan, M. E. *From the First World War to the Arab Spring: What's Really Going On in the Middle East?* New York: Palgrave Macmillan, 2016.

Mishra, Pankaj. *From the Ruins of Empire: The Intellectuals Who Remade Asia*. New York: Farrar, Straus and Giroux, 2012.

Morris, Benny, and Dror Ze'evi. *The Thirty-Year Genocide: Turkey's Destruction of Its Christian Minorities, 1894–1924*. Cambridge, MA: Harvard University Press, 2019.

Owen, Roger. *State, Power, and Politics in the Making of the Modern Middle East*. London: Routledge, 2000.

Polk, William. *Crusade and Jihad: The Thousand-Year War between the Muslim World and the Global North*. New Haven, CT: Yale University Press, 2018.

Provence, Michael. *The Last Ottoman Generation and the Making of the Modern Middle East*. Cambridge: Cambridge University Press, 2017.

Rogan, Eugene. *The Fall of the Ottomans: The Great War in the Middle East*. New York: Basic Books, 2015.

Rutledge, Ian. *Enemy on the Euphrates: The Battle for Iraq, 1914–1921*. London: Saqi, 2014.

———. *Sea of Troubles: The European Conquest of the Islamic Mediterranean and the Origins of the First World War, 1750–1918*. London: Saqi, 2023.

Schneer, Jonathan. *Balfour Declaration: The Origins of the Arab-Israeli Conflict*. London: Bloomsbury, 2010.

Sharkey, Heather. *A History of Muslims, Christians, and Jews in the Middle East*. Cambridge: Cambridge University Press, 2017.

Suny, Ronald Grigor. *"They Can Live in the Desert but Nowhere Else": A History of the Armenian Genocide*. Princeton, NJ: Princeton University Press, 2015.

Tamari, Salim. *Year of the Locust: A Soldier's Diary and the Erasure of Palestine's Ottoman Past*. Berkeley: University of California Press, 2011.

Thompson, Elizabeth. *How the West Stole Democracy from the Arabs: The Syrian Arab Congress of 1920 and the Destruction of Its Historic Liberal-Islamic Alliance*. New York: Atlantic Monthly Press, 2020.

Tripp, Charles. *A History of Iraq.* 3rd ed. Cambridge: Cambridge University Press, 2007.
Ulrichsen, Kristian Coates. *The First World War in the Middle East.* London: Hurst, 2014.
Wyrtzen, Jonathan. *Worldmaking in the Long Great War: How Local and Colonial Struggles Shaped the Modern Middle East.* New York: Columbia University Press, 2022.
Yapp, Malcolm. *The Making of the Modern Near East, 1792–1923.* London: Longman, 1987.

INDEX

Abbas I (Safavid Shah), 21
'Abduh, Muhammad, 38, 41
Abdülhamid II, Sultan, xi; and constitution, 27; legacy, 45–46; overthrow, xxii, 13, 48–49; pan-Islamism, 38–39; relations with Germany, xiv; rise to power, 15, 27; rule, xvii, 15, 28, 33–35, 42
Abdullah bin al-Husayn, xi, xiii, xviii, 114, 118–19
Abdülmecid, Sultan, xi, xviii, 19–20
Afghānī, Jamāl ad-Dīn al-, xi, 39, 41
Afghanistan, 5, 8, 10, 12, 19, 123, 124, 125; and Amanullah Khan, 19, 123
airplanes, 49, 80, 106, 111, 124
'Alawis, 112
Alexandretta peninsula, xv, 99, 112, 117
aliyah, 44
Allenby, Lord Edmund, xi, xix, 37, 63–64, 77, 82–83, 109, 118
Anglo-Afghan Wars, xv, xvii, 5, 14, 19
Anglo-French Declaration (1918), xv, 84
Anglo-Iraqi Treaty (1930), xv
Anglo-Kuwaiti Agreement (1899), 60

Anglo-Ottoman Convention (1838), xv, xxi, 13, 18
Anglo-Persian Oil Company, 32
Anglo-Russian agreement (1907), 9–10, 33
Antonius, George, 41–42, 78, 114, 123
ANZAC forces, xv, 6, 62, 72–73
Arab kingdom (1918–1920), xv, 42, 109, 111, 118
Arab revolt (1916), xiii, xv, xix, 42, 75–77, 82, 109
Arabism, 40–42
Arab-Syrian Congress of Paris (1913), 51
Armenian genocide, xv, 3, 59, 68–70, 95–96
Atatürk, Mustafa Kemal, xi, xxv, 27; as leader of nationalist resistance, 96–97, 98–99; as Ottoman officer, 49, 73, 82, 88; as president of Turkey, 43, 73, 99–100
'Ayn, Qurrat al- (Fatemeh Baraghani), xii, 22–23

Babi movement, xii, xvi, 21–22; and Baha'i faith, xii, xvi, 22, 94n16
Balfour Declaration, xiv, xvi, 64–67, 105, 123
Balkan Wars, xvi, xxi, xxvi, 14, 46, 50–51, 55–56, 69, 121
Banna, Hassan al-, xii, xix, 102–3

Index

battles: Maysalūn, 111; Megiddo, 82; Pyramids, 15; Sakarya, 98; Sarikamis, 68
Bell, Gertrude, 114
Ben-Gurion, David, 44, 65, 106
Berlin Conference (1884), xvi, 30
Berlin to Baghdad railway, 35, 79
Bonaparte, Napoleon, 11–12, 16, 28
Bosporus, xvi, 14, 48, 50, 55, 89
Buchan, John, 59
Bulgaria, xvi, 34, 50–51, 71, 73
Bulgarian Horrors, 25–26

Cairo Conference (1921), xii, 114, 119
Caliphate, xvi, xxvi, 34, 42, 97, 119, 127
Capitulations, 18, 31, 57
Caucasus campaign, 58–59, 60, 67–69, 73, 82
Cemal Pasha, Ahmed, xxi, 52, 55, 56, 61–62, 76, 95–96, 109
Central powers, xvi, 37, 54, 57, 59, 73
Chanak Crisis, xvi, 99
Churchill, Winston, xii, 32, 57, 71, 113
Churchill White Paper (1922), 105
"civilizing mission," 23
Clemenceau, Georges, xii, 90–91
Cold War, 100, 125
Committee of Union and Progress (CUP), xvii, xxii, 42–43, 47–49, 52, 58, 82, 95, 97
Congress of Berlin (1878), 34
Congress of Vienna (1815), xvii, xxv
Constantinople Agreement (1915), 74
Constantinople Conference (1876), 27
constitutions, xx, 12, 27–28, 32–33, 48, 102, 111
Cossack Brigade, xvii, 31, 100
Crimean War, xvii, 3–4, 14, 23, 34
Curzon, Lord, 8–9

D'Arcy Concession, xvii, 32
Dardanelles strait, xvii, 6, 14, 50, 5–58, 71–74, 89, 99–100
de Lesseps, Ferdinand, 28–29
dhimmi principle, xxvii, 20; and *jizya* tax, xviii, xxvii, 20
"divide and rule," xiii, xx, 2, 16, 25, 42, 93, 105, 106, 112, 114, 123
Dreyfus, Alfred, 43
Druze, xvii, 104, 112

Eastern Question, xvii, xxv, xxvii, 8, 10, 14, 23, 30, 35
Edib, Halide, 48
Edirne (Adrianople), xxi, 50–52, 67, 94
Egypt, 28; and British occupation, 15, 30–31; Cemal's campaign, 61–63; Dinshaway incident (1906), 31; Egyptian Expeditionary Force (EEF), xi, 64, 82; Egyptian Labour Corps, 63; Evelyn Baring (Lord Cromer), xii, 31; Gamal Abdel Nasser, 102, 125; Ismail, 29–30; Muhammad Ali, xiii, 16–18;

Egypt (*Continued*)
Napoleon's campaign, xiii, 11–12, 13, 15–16; 1922 Unilateral Declaration of Independence, 102; postwar, 101–3; establishment of protectorate, 17, 63; self-determination, xiv; Tawfiq, 30; 'Urabi revolt, xxii, 30
Enver Pasha, xxi, 50–52, 55, 57, 67–68, 95–96
Erzurum, 48

Faysal, xii, xviii, 76; and Arab Kingdom of Syria, 83, 91, 109–11, 118; Arab revolt, 77, 82; king of Iraq, 114–17

Gallipoli campaign, 6, 63, 69, 71–74, 78, 80, 88
Goeben and *Breslau*, 57–58
Goethe, Johann Wolfgang von, 8, 37
Gökalp, Mehmed Ziya, xii, 43
Gouraud, Henri, 104, 111–12
Great Game, xvii, 14, 18, 21, 33, 81
Great Revolt (Palestine), xvii, 108
Great Revolt (Syria), xvii, 112
Greco-Turkish War, xvii, 98; and Eleftherios Venizelos, 98; Megali Idea, 98
Gülhane Edict (1839), xviii, xxi, 20

Hamas, 2, 127
Hamidiye regiments, 35–36
Hatt-ı Hümayan (Reform Edict) (1856), xviii, xxi, 20
Hejaz railway, xviii, 35, 37, 118
Herzl, Theodor, 43–44, 46
Husayn, Sharif, xiii, xviii, 60, 75–76, 78, 81, 88, 119, 120
Husayn-McMahon correspondence, xiii, xv, xix, 64, 77, 91, 118
Husrī, Sāti' al-, 123

Ibn Khaldun, 7
India, 8–9, 11, 13–15, 18–19, 30, 33, 58–59; and Indian Expeditionary Force, 79
Iran, 4–5, 13, 21–23, 31–33, 79, 88, 100–101, 116, 121, 123; and Constitutional Revolution, xix, 12–13, 32–33, 46. *See also* Anglo-Persian Oil Company; Qajar dynasty
Iraq, 8, 12, 21, 60, 77, 93, 99, 110, 113–17; and oil, 116–17; uprising (1920), 112–14. *See also* Anglo-Iraqi Treaty; Faysal (king of Iraq)
Islamic State (ISIS), 126–27
Israel, 2, 106, 119, 127
Istanbul, xxvii, 24, 34, 48–51, 61, 69, 71, 73, 80, 82, 95–96, 99
Italo-Turkish War, xviii, 3, 49–50, 57

Jabartī, Abd al-Rahman al-, xiii, 16
Jerusalem, 23, 44, 46, 59, 74, 106–7, 119; and Allied occupation, xi, 63–64, 83;

Kaiser Wilhelm's entrance, 36–37
jihād, xviii, 59; and Sultan's call for, 37, 58–61, 75, 79, 81, 119–20
Kemal, Mustafa. *See* Atatürk, Mustafa Kemal
Kemal, Namık, 26
King-Crane Commission, xviii, 92–93, 105
Kurds, 35–36, 70, 99–100, 115–16; and Kurdish nationalism, 3, 10, 97–98, 99
Kut al-Amara, siege of, xiv, xx, 80–81
Kuwait, 52, 60, 79, 117–18

Lausanne conference (1922–1923), 94, 99
Lawrence, T. E., xiii, 76, 110, 114
League of Nations, xviii, xix, 87–88, 93, 98, 116, 124; and Covenant of, 91–92, 105
Lebanon, xix, 2, 8, 16, 23, 25, 93, 102–4
Libya, 3, 79, 124, 127
Lloyd George, David, xiii, 63, 90, 98–99

Mahan, Alfred T., 7-9
mandate system, xix, 91–94; and Permanent Mandates Commission, 105
Maronites, xix, 2, 23, 103–4
Maude, General Stanley, 81
McMahon, Sir Henry, xiii, 63, 77–78, 118

Mecca, xiii, 17, 37, 60, 75, 77, 118, 120
Mehmed V, Sultan, xxvii, 58
Mehmet VI Vahdeddin, Sultan, 96
Mesopotamian campaign, 60, 78–85
Middle East, idea of, 2, 7–10, 28, 122; and Middle East and North Africa (MENA), 8
Midhat Pasha, 26–27
modernity, 121–2
Mohammad 'Ali Shah, 33
Mozaffar ad-Dīn Shah, 32
Mudanya, Armistice of (1922), 99
Mudros Armistice (1918), xix, 64, 82, 89, 94, 116
Muhammad Ali, xiii, 16–18, 28–29, 102
Muslim Brotherhood, xii, xix, 40, 102–3

Nahda, xix, 41
Nāsir ad-Dīn Shah, 22, 31–32, 39
Nicholas I, Tsar, 18, 23

Occupied Enemy Territory Administration (OETA), xix, 82–83, 109, 118
Orientalism, xix, 11–12, 17, 122
Ottoman Empire: constitution (1876), xx, 27–28; debt, 15, 29–30; decline thesis and Ottomans as sick man of Europe, xxv–xxix, 5–6, 14–15, 122; extinguishing of, 97, 119, 122; Islam, xi, xiv, xxvii, 20–21, 24–26,

Ottoman Empire (*Continued*)
34–40, 42–43, 52; millets,
xix; navy, 49–50, 56–58;
seferberlik, xx, 55, 123;
war-crimes trials, 95–96
Ottomanism, xxviii, 13, 20, 24,
40, 42, 47, 51

Pahlavi dynasty, 5, 100–101;
and Reza Khan, xiii, 31, 88,
100–101, 123; Mohammad
Reza, 101
Palestine, 41, 82–83, 90, 92–93,
105–8, 124; and Palestine
campaign, 63–67, 82–85;
Peel Commission, xx, 108;
White Paper (1939), xvii,
xxii, 108
pan-Islamism, 38–40, 62–63
Paris Peace Conferences, xx,
88–89, 101
Persian Gulf, 8–9, 18, 33, 52, 79,
118, 120
"presentism," 125

Qajar dynasty, xvi, xvii, xx, 4–5,
12, 21–23, 31–33, 88

Rida, Rashid, 38–39, 41, 111
Russia: 1905 Revolution, 13;
1917 Bolshevik Revolution,
14, 68, 82–84; 1918–1921
Civil War, 14, 81; 2022–
present Russia-Ukraine
War, 3; Soviet Union, 19,
95–97, 101, 120, 125;
WW I aftermath, 89
Russo-Ottoman War, xx, 14,
34, 67

Salonica, xxv–xxix, 48–49, 127
San Remo Conference (1920),
xx, 93–94
Saudi Arabia, 119–20; and 'Abd
al-'Aziz ibn al Sa'ud, 52, 79;
Muhammad al-Saud, 17;
ikhwan, 52, 79
sectarianism, xx, 25, 45–46, 93,
95, 104, 112
self-determination, 91–92
Sha'rāwi, Hudá, 102
"Sharifian solution," 114
Sinai Peninsula, 62–63; and
railway, 35
Smyrna (Izmir), 51, 98–99
"spirit of the age," 83, 86, 124
Sudan, xi, 31, 102; and condominium, 62; Fashoda
Incident, 31; Mahdi,
xi–xii, 22
Suez Canal, xx, 14–15, 28–30,
55, 58, 61–62, 106
Sykes, Sir Mark, xiii, 67, 85, 91
Sykes-Picot Agreement (1916),
xxi, 64, 74-75, 81, 84, 90,
105, 118, 127
Syria, 2–3, 74, 77, 82–83, 86,
91–94, 98–99, 109–13,
116–19, 124, 127; and
National Bloc, 113
Syrian National Congress, 105

Tahtawi, Rifa'a Rafi' al-, xiv,
17, 21
Talat Pasha, Mehmed, xxi, 52,
55, 95–96
Tanzimat, xviii, xx–xxi, xxvii, 13,
15, 19–21, 24–29, 39, 41,
44–46, 104, 123

"three lost provinces," xxi, 34, 57, 67
Tolstoy, Leo, 4, 23
Townshend, Charles, xiv, 80
Transjordan, xii, 94, 111, 114, 118–19
Treaties: Balta Limanı (1838) (*see* Anglo-Ottoman Convention); Brest-Litovsk (1918), 82; Constantinople (1913), xxi; Lausanne (1923), xxi, 93, 99, 127; London (1913), 50; Paris (1856), 23–24; San Stefano (1878), 34; Sèvres (1920), xxi, 89, 94–97; Versailles (1919), xii, 93
Triple Alliance, 49, 52
Triple Entente, xxi, 33, 49, 56–57, 60
Trucial States, 18, 52
Turkey, 95; and Cold War, 100; formation of, xi, 94–100, 122, 127; Grand National Assembly, 97, 99; nationalism, xii, 40, 42–43; National Pact, 97; neo-Ottoman policies, 2–3; refusal to recognize Armenian genocide, 70; "Societies for the Defence of National Rights," 97

'Urabi, Ahmad, xxii, 30; and Battle of Tell al-Kabir, 30

Wafd Party, xxii, 102
Wahhabi(sm), xxii, 17, 21, 52
Weizmann, Chaim, xiv, 65
Wilhelm II, xiv, 35–37, 55, 58, 64; and *weltpolitik*, xiv, 36
Wilson, Woodrow, xiv, xviii, 83, 88, 91–93, 124
World War I: defeat of Ottomans, xi, xxi, xxv, 1–2, 42, 82–94, 122; historiography, 1–6, 54–55, 121–27; Ottomans' entry into the conflict, 54–58
World War II, xv, 46, 99, 120

Young Ottomans, 26–27
Young Turk Revolution, xxii, 13, 28, 42, 46–49, 121

Zaghlul, Saad, xiv, xxii, 101–2
Zaghlul, Safiyya, 102
Zionism, xvi, xviii, xxii, 2, 40–41, 43–46, 59–60, 64–67, 92–93, 105–8, 120; and Ashkenazim, 44; Jewish Agency, 106; Mizrahim, 44; Sephardim, xxvi, 44, 46; Vladimir (Ze'ev) Jabotinsky, xviii, 106–7, 119